A SMART APPROACH

TO

PORTFOLIO MANAGEMENT

A SMART APPROACH TO PORTFOLIO MANAGEMENT

The year 2008 was a watershed year for pension fund management. Dramatic market movements exposed the flaws in its theory and practice. Solvency declined dramatically, hedge funds did not deliver, rebalancing policies detracted value, and liquidity dried up, tainting the allure of "alternative" investments. Static policies for dynamic markets are undoubtedly flawed and have to be changed with the support of appropriate liquid, transparent, and low-cost benchmarks; implicit bets have to be made explicit and managed; naïve performance measures must be improved; and the CAPM needs to be revamped dramatically. This process can start only when investors take the time to understand how various market factors influence assets or managers and then develop a set of rules, enabling the optimal portfolio to evolve simultaneously with market factors. This book presents a new design for pension fund management that helps CIOs to be smart about managing assets relative to liabilities and, at the same time, allows them to access alpha flexibly (and compensate managers only when they demonstrate skill), thereby improving solvency. SMART (Systematic Management of Assets using a Rules-based Technique) management of assets and liabilities results in improved solvency and lowering of ALM risk. SMART introduces good process – that is, only measured and monitored risks can be managed.

Arun Muralidhar has experience in and has written extensively on pension reform, asset allocation, and currency management. Arun is Chairman of **M^{cube} Investment Technologies, LLC,** and Chairman and Chief Investment Officer of **AlphaEngine Global Investment Solutions, LLC**. Both firms assist funds in asset allocation, currency management, and external manager oversight through customized advice and the award-winning AlphaEngine® technology. Arun has served as Managing Director at FX Concepts Inc (2001-2008), Managing Director/Head of Currency Research at J.P. Morgan Fleming Asset Management (1999-2001), and Head of Research and member of the Investment Management Committee at The World Bank (1992-99). He is the author of *Innovations in Pension Fund Management, Stanford University Press, 2001,* and co-author with the late Nobel laureate Prof. Franco Modigliani of *Rethinking Pension Reform, Cambridge University Press, 2004,* on reforming Social Security. He contributed to and edited *European Pension Reform, Luxembourg Institute of International Studies, 2007.* He holds a Ph.D. in Managerial Economics from the MIT Sloan School of Management, and a B.S. from Wabash College.

A SMART Approach to Portfolio Management

ARUN MURALIDHAR
Founder and Chairman of M^{cube} Investment Technologies, LLC
Founder and Chairman of AlphaEngine Global Investment Solutions, LLC

Copyright © 2009

ROYAL FERN PUBLISHING, LLC
Great Falls, VA 22066, USA
ISBN 978-0-615-38651-7

First published 2011
Library of Congress Cataloging in Publication Data (TXu 1-652003)

Printed at PRINTMATIC, Bangalore - INDIA

CONTENTS

PREFACE

"Not only it's not right, it's not even wrong." Wolfgang Ernst Pauli [1]

My friend Joe Azelby has a great story about how, on a deep-sea fishing trip, you want a captain who is missing one eye, a few fingers, possibly an ear, among other infirmities. You know your crew is going to make mistakes, so you prefer someone who has already made the full quota of mistakes on prior trips!

After making a few 'mistakes' at the World Bank, J.P. Morgan Investment Management, FX Concepts, and my own companies, I have arrived at a positive, time-tested approach to managing assets – a veritable documentary on how to be a "SMART" investor! My previous book (Muralidhar 2001) boldly proclaimed an offer of innovative approaches to plan sponsors; on further introspection, while many of the concepts presented have proved useful, a number of prescriptions fell short. Fortunately, I stopped writing about how to manage assets and, instead, turned my attention to practicing what I preached by helping plan sponsors make effective decisions to measure, monitor, and manage their risks.

This book is a timely response to some current issues – (i) the investment strategic asset allocations (SAAs) and naïve rebalancing; (ii) the literature on liability driven investing (LDI) industry has fixated too long on **static** prescriptions, and portable alpha is biased by asset managers trying to sell products rather than solve sponsors' problems; (iii) performance measures that do not incorporate risks or skill are problematic, as are the compensation schemes that serve the asset manager more than the pension plan; and (iv) most important, the anchor of financial theory – the capital asset pricing model (CAPM) – has ignored the entire class of pension fund (or institutional) investors who delegated decisions to others as also the impact of their behavior on markets. In short, static policies for dynamic markets are undoubtedly flawed; naïve performance measures have to be improved; and the CAPM needs to be re-examined.

In an attempt to dis-intermediate asset managers, as far back as 2002, my firm developed software to allow investors to independently re-create the same state-of-the-art investment procedures they sought from their asset managers. Case studies developed in 2004-2005 showed clients how rebalancing could be improved from an asset-only perspective, how dynamic LDI strategies are superior to simple duration extension, and how manager allocation management is preferable to focusing solely on manager selection. These ideas were published extensively in trade journals, and creative pension funds that were resource-constrained forced

---

[1] www.wikipedia.com

us to put our money where our mouth is and made us work on a largely performance fee basis…then came 2008!

Bogle (2009) highlights the dramatic impact of market movements on the U.S. pension fund industry, which can be applied to other markets as well. "Assets of corporate pension plans have declined from $2.1 trillion as far back as 1999 to an estimated $1.9 trillion as 2009 began…pension plan assets to cover future payments to retirees have tumbled from a *surplus* of some $270 billion in 1999 to a *deficit* of $376 billion at the end of 2008. Largely because of the stock market's sharp decline, assets of state and local plans also tumbled, from a high of $3.3 trillion early in 2007 to an estimated $2.5 trillion last year."[2] There has been a severe impact on defined contribution (DC) plans also, as "[t]he growth in DC plans has been remarkable. Assets totaled $500 billion in 1985; $1 trillion in 1991; and $4.5 trillion in 2007. With the market crash, assets are now estimated at $3.5 trillion…IRA assets presently total about $3.2 trillion, down from $4.7 trillion in 2007."[3]

Whether by luck or skill (an equation in Chapter 2 helps to judge this), our models - applied by pension plan clients and ourselves - have delivered positive performance relative to all other naïve rebalancing approaches; they have improved solvency (had they been implemented) relative to other approaches, and lowered *absolute* risk or drawdowns, whether measured on an asset-liability or an asset-only basis. Many academics and practitioners have made the case for dynamic strategies[4] since the 1980s. This book presents a simple route for plan sponsors in defined benefit (DB) plans and participants in DC plans to achieve their goals without paying excessive manager fees.

This book is organized as follows: Chapter 1 provides a different perspective on the role of the Chief Investment Officer (CIO), partly reflecting the frustration of a CIO as being more an auditor than an investor. Chapter 2 discusses a new approach to CAPM, emphasizing the need for a new **dynamic finance theory** that incorporates the actions of CIOs and their interactions with the Board and asset managers. Chapter 3 argues for a clearer articulation of investment goals (focused on solvency rather than strictly asset performance), the need to adjust performance based on skill and risk, and ideas for ensuring the creation of simple, effective, and easy-to-implement liability and asset benchmarks. This chapter is critical, as earlier benchmarks have been costly and inefficient to replicate, thereby unnecessarily detracting from performance and the ability to be nimble. Chapter 4 is the lynchpin of this book – it provides the case for the SMART (Systematic Management of

---

[2] Page 4.

[3] Page 5.

[4] Barrett (2006); Brock (2005); Hodgson (2006); Mulvey (1988); Mulvey (1994); Arikawa et al (2005); Muralidhar (2007); and Muralidhar and Muralidhar (2009).

Assets using a Rules-based Technique) approach and is an exposé of some of the more voluble, if misguided, institutional investors. Chapter 5 moves on to actual portfolio management, demonstrating the failure of typical SAA policies, and argues for SMART View-Neutral SAAs – earlier advocated in Muralidhar (2001). Chapter 6 takes it up a notch and demonstrates how SMART View -based portfolio management is essential – especially given the assumption on correlations in primary asset allocation studies. Chapter 7 studies the implication of emphasizing skill in manager analyses and discusses its importance in risk budgeting – demonstrating that two tracking errors of 3 percent are not the same from a confidence-in-skill perspective – and, more important, proposes a totally new compensation method for asset managers which underscores risk and skill adjustment. Chapter 8 brings the discussion full circle, showing how dynamic management of alpha (i.e., external managers), beta, and liabilities can improve solvency. Chapter 9 is a mild digression exploring DC investing, as findings show the current offering of Target Date Funds (TDFs) to be a potentially deceptive manipulation of the investing public – sadly, maneuvered in part by the U.S.Department of Labor's (DoL) unintended regulation.

In summary, the book develops an enduring case study approach, using the vast experience of clients and colleagues in North America, Europe (mainly the Netherlands), and Japan. It demonstrates how the same principles can be applied in many different situations. This approach is likely to be attacked, given the belief that "market timing" is untenable. But the fact is, the minute a decision is made on a portfolio – even in setting up an SAA – it involves market timing, and the most meaningful market timers are the asset-liability management (ALM) consultants (who often do not help pension funds understand and manage these long-term bets). So rather than attach labels to what the industry does, the goal is to get CIOs to adopt good processes that ensure the effective delivery of pensions promised to their members, well within the risks permitted and at the lowest possible cost.

Hopefully, the techniques explained here will be used by CIOs without depending on asset managers and consultants, thereby saving significant costs and further improving solvency and governance.

DISCLAIMER
All views expressed in this book are the author's personal opinions. No former or current organization he has been affiliated with bears any responsibility for these opinions.

ACKNOWLEDGMENTS

"I stand by all the misstatements." Dan Quayle[5]

I have been blessed with mentors such as the late Prof. Franco Modigliani whose constant expectations of the best professional work and an exacting social conscience have shaped my life, thinking, and my writing. His spirit lives on in the work of his students. I have also been fortunate in being able to lean on friends like Lester Siegel, who took a call from me at an ungodly hour one morning in 1997 when I jumped out of the shower to tell him why the CAPM was wrong (Chapter 2); Patrick Groenendijk, for seeing the potential in our idea of dynamic management even before we crystallized it; Eric Busay, who started as a client and has become a dear friend; Charlie Ruffel, who took pity on a lost soul and offered sage advice and some hope; Roland van den Brink, for being the first one to jump on board, for sharing his vision of a CIO dashboard, and for his brilliant ideas written on numerous napkins and table covers; Karin Brodbeck, for giving us our first break to manage assets on this basis, her attention to detail and willingness to innovate; Roger Paschke, for always being willing to push the envelope – our overlay on an overlay using options required vision and innovation beyond the ordinary; Harish Neelakandan, for his humor and smarts in creating the overlay on the overlay using options – brilliant but, sadly, under-appreciated; Ken Lay, for showing me very early in my career how to fight for what is right; Hideo Kondo, for teaching me how to run a plan with one staff and still be phenomenally innovative; Khaled Balama, for believing in what we were doing in a difficult environment and for his friendship; Kirit Patel, for being who he is – a wise man with a small ego; Mark Schmid, for giving me the time when he had more important things to worry about; Andrew T. Ward for his constant support; Masataka Hama, Koichi Shijima, and Masayuki Azuma, for getting the point of the software and the need for SMART rebalancing when few others in Japan saw the potential; Bradley Leak and Tim Barrett, for showing me that rebalancing ranges are counter-productive when you are smart; Donald Pierce, for taking our work to a new level and his good restaurant selection; James Perry, for his happy outlook on life and wisdom; Pieter de Vries Robbe', for fighting all odds to give us a chance; Hein Brans, for persevering with us even when he did not have the resources; Joseph Silveira, for spending weekends trying to help us improve our work; David Deutsch, for his sustained support and innovative idea about a Beta Engine; Lisa Needle, for urging us to up our game and backing us against all odds; K.C. Howell, for paying us even when his team could

---

[5] Petras (2001), page 25. Then vice-presidential candidate, Dan Quayle, defending himself against criticism for making verbal gaffes.

not add the value I promised; Larry Kochard, for his comment about disintermediating the asset management business; Paul Fahey, for taking pains to show how this worked in Canada; Tom Zuchosky, for being the first fund-of-funds manager to be convinced of SMART Allocation; Skip Halpern, for his discerning wisdom about good governance; Thomas Fiske, for the engaging conversations on doing the right things for pension plans; Audrey Kent, for bearing with us in working out a mutually beneficial arrangement; Zhuoying Xu, for all her hard work and persistent drive to extract information from data; Roshani Thakur and Omid Rezania, for challenging me every time I want to take it easy; Guus Boender, for being Guus; Cees Dert, for his brilliant thesis on ALM; Geraldine Leegwater, for her contribution to Chapter 5; Tai Tee Chia, who despite being one of the smartest guys around continues to be my friend; Atsuhiro Yoshitsugu, Shinya Miyazaki, and Hiroya Ikuta for being three of the smartest investors I have met in Japan; and Allan Martin and Paul Harte, for being the first consultants to see what we were doing and then throwing their weight and reputation behind our work. In an industry where everyone wants to be "first to be second," these are rare professionals and I am blessed our paths crossed early in our lifecycle. Thanks also to Frank Pfeffer for his help and sartorial advice.

I am also fortunate to have my brother Sanjay as my foil – maybe someday he will forgive me for all the hell I created in bringing these ideas to reality. I am grateful to all my current colleagues (Sriram Narayanan, Brian Baker, Masakazu Arikawa, Judy Humza, Bhaskar Balan, Sapna Thomas, and the rest of the M-cube Bangalore crew); former colleagues at M-cube (Margaret Towle, Benne Bette, Rahul Rauniyar, Ronald Kneppers, and Mathe van Heeswijk); the consultants at ORTEC (especially Ton van Welie), colleagues at FX Concepts (especially Cristina Scherer, Dan Szor, John Taylor, and Philip Simotas), J.P. Morgan Asset Management (especially Brian Strange), and the World Bank; folks like Theodore Economou, Nancy Calkins, Annette St. Urbain, Linda Herman, Srini Pulavarti, Ken Miranda, Arun Mantri, Jeff States, Christopher Gonzales, Jan Willem van Stuivenberg, Coen van de Laar, Jeroen Gondrie, Barbra Byington, Christiaan Ticheler, Barbara Bleijenbergh, Alfred Slager, Boris Wessely, Yegin Chen, John Osborn, Kurtay Ogunc, Masayuki Azuma, Yasuchika Asaoka, Marie Pillai, Cecil Hemingway, Leah Modigliani, Barry Burr, Maha Khan Philips, Ronald van der Wouden, Fennell Betson, T. Andy Smith, Prof. Takao Kobayashi, Prof. Kazuhiko Ohashi, Prof. Toshiki Honda, Masaharu Usuki, Taka Yabuuchi, Matt Smith, Nevin Adams, Alix Hughes, Carol Popkins, Foster Wright, Jacques Lussier, Dan Lancellotti, John Fell, Tim Thonis, Walther Brand, Sung Hwan Shin, Vince Brown, Donald Kendig, Sarah Bernstein, John Mogg, John Adams, Sarah Bever, Stuart Potter, Kelda Caldwell, Eli Martinez, Harvey Leiderman, Scott Delaney, Scott Whalen, Kip McDaniel, Lisa Haag, Jonathan O'Donnell, Jim

Morrissey and the team at Investor Force, the consultants at Ennis Knupp and Rocaton, and the entire team at The Clifton Group.

I thank my buddy Rohan for showing me that even an 18-year-old can grasp the nuances of this industry in just a month! Many thanks to my wife Shaila and my sons Sidharth and Sachin for allowing me the time to write this book. Shaila is slowly learning that Serena Modigliani was not kidding when she told her that, if her own experience with Franco was anything to go by, then living with me would only get worse with time... and still Shaila sticks by me. Finally, thanks to Jeanette Fernandes for an amazing job of editing the manuscript at short notice and to Royal Fern Publishing for all the hard work in turning around this book expeditiously.

June 2009

I dedicate this book to Mrs. Turner and Mrs. Rhatigan of Maurice Hawk Elementary School in West Windsor, NJ, for teaching my first and third graders to write books at this tender age (including how to write an index and glossary!), and to my mom (Minakshi) and Shaila's mom (Jeanette) for encouraging their kids, too, to write.

In memory of Kirit Patel ... a dear friend and a smart investor!

1

New Paradigm for CIOs – Doing More with Less

Mohammed Ali boarded a plane one day and, just before take-off, was requested by a stewardess, "Sir, please fasten your seat-belt." The youthful, exuberant Mohammed Ali is believed to have remarked, "Superman does not need a seat-belt...." to which the smart young lady replied, "And Superman does not need a plane either!"

Role of the Chief Investment Officer

The volatility of the markets in 2008 created turbulence in finance portfolios not envisaged by even the most astute investors. Only those who had fastened their seat-belts emerged from the debacle relatively unscathed. However, this unanticipated crisis can be put to good use as a lesson for the institutional investment management industry. It exposes the failings of previous research, regulation, and advice on the investment of institutional assets.

Bearing in mind the counsel of Rahm Emanuel, President Obama's Chief of Staff, "Never let a crisis go to waste," this book uses the lessons of the 2008 reality-check to help CIOs do much more with less, especially since budgets have been drastically cut. Equally important, this book reveals the drawbacks in the current practice of managing assets and rewarding asset managers. CalPERS, one of the leaders in investor activism, has proclaimed that fees of hedge fund managers need to be reviewed, and it is likely that other pension funds will join this chorus. Fortunately (and unfortunately), the recent market turmoil has also exposed the impact of corrupt middlemen on fees and manager selection.

It is therefore pertinent to focus on an entirely new paradigm for managing assets – one focused on dynamism of decisions, vital in an environment driven by dynamic market performance. In so doing, this book expunges the old paradigm, professed by asset managers and many consultants, that hiring an external manager with all the fee issues it entails to perform a given task (e.g., manage portable alpha or LDI) was a silver bullet requiring no further action.

Sadly, the CIO's role during the tension of 2008 has been one of firefighter – often having to bear bad news of failed hedge funds, securities lending, or even illiquid cash investments. Then, CIOs had to make frantic attempts to raise cash to meet outstanding obligations, as the failure of alternative investments and seemingly safe assets exposed chinks in the armor of even the Ivy League endowments. Moreover, many CIOs have paid the price for choosing to be innovative: in response to a cry for blood, Boards have had to fire CIOs when funds lost 20-30 percent of their value in a single year. Many times, the call to dismiss a CIO came from a misinformed local press or public that picked on a single bad decision and a supposedly outsized pay package. Such distress could have been easily averted had the task been set up efficiently, expectations discerned and fulfilled with care, and performance and risk-adjusted performance adequately monitored.

Roland van den Brink, CIO of Bedrijfstakpensioenfonds Metalektro in the Netherlands (PME) and currently Executive Director of Mn Services, ran one of the most effective pension funds in the world. He entrusted only three key investment staffers with management of assets in excess of € 20 billion, and liberally outsourced activities best performed on a larger scale. This clear division of labor controlled costs and minimized staff management time. More importantly, he likened himself to the pilot of a plane and monitored his plan accordingly. He organized his plan data in a simple, succinct Pension Dashboard, which kept him constantly updated on where his fund was headed relative to liabilities, risks being taken, and the direction needed to proceed to ensure continued solvency. His motivation stemmed from the belief that "once you manage risks, you can then focus on returns." Philip Menco of de Eendragt (and one-time colleague of Roland), who shares this philosophy, turned in positive performance for the economically-floundering year of 2008 through effective, high-level investment strategies.

The CIO role in the new millennium faces new challenges, including declining solvency, budget cuts, and increasing complexity of managing assets, with less transparency, less liquidity, and less bargaining power on the part of investors. However, it is incumbent on the CIO in this environment to re-establish the Board's objectives and risk tolerance, as well as its investment horizon. The CIO must re-structure the entire investment paradigm to evaluate investments that best achieve the objectives of efficacy, liquidity, transparency, and low cost. The Chinese proverb that states, "One cannot be a genius in one's own village" applies most often to CIOs at public institutions, because the general presumption is that outside managers are smarter than internal staff. However, once the appropriate governance and monitoring structure is set up, the Board would be better served if they rely more on their own CIOs and less on external advisors.

Effective real estate decisions are driven by "Location, Location, Location." Similarly, the SMART (Systematic Management of Assets using a Rules-based

Technique) paradigm is based on "Allocation, Allocation, Allocation." The three key areas where these allocation decisions will be emphasized are: (i) Allocation to a Liability Hedge; (ii) Allocation to Beta Assets; and (iii) Allocation to Alpha Opportunities. The SMART process attempts to bring best practices (adopted by asset managers) into the suite of capabilities of pension assets, because the potential benefit from adding a few basis points to the total portfolio is likely to be more valuable than finding the best managers. SMART also has the advantage of better decision-making (not subject to emotion), transparency, consistency, governance, and risk management.

THE NEW SMART LDI APPROACH – LIABILITIES, BETA, ASSETS, AND COSTS

The recent financial market meltdown has imperiled the financial status of pension funds (and other investors) worldwide. There have been dramatic declines in solvency or size of portfolios even in the Netherlands, where the focus on ALM is both extensive and impressive, and the regulation of pension funds by the Dutch Central Bank (DnB) is based on funding rather than asset performance. In many cases, solvency dropped from 140 percent to 90 percent, and even the DnB's own pension fund had fallen below 100 percent solvency.[6] Regulators in the Netherlands, the UK, and the United States are being pressured into adopting conciliatory measures, including avoiding onerous recovery plans, relaxing mark-to-market accounting, allowing flexible asset smoothing, and extending recovery periods.[7] For example, in the Netherlands, current regulations require pension funds to return to 105 percent solvency in three years (regulators are being pressured to raise the term to five years), which would entail a drastic cut in pensions,[8] an increase in contributions, or more risk-taking – all unpleasant measures in the current environment.[9] Though this book focuses on pension funds, many of the same principles are also applicable to endowments/foundations, sovereign wealth funds (SWFs), social security (SS) funds, insurance companies, and retiree health care plans.

[6] "DnB's own pension plan must submit recovery plan," *www.ipe.com*, March 25, 2009.
[7] *Investments and Pensions Europe*– on-line version (February 16, 2009). http://www.ipe.com/news Trade_bodies_warn_against_hard_hitting_measures__30830.php http://www.pionline.com/apps/pbcs.dll/article?AID=/20090318/DAILYREG/903189974 on measures by the U.S. Internal Revenue Service to relax restrictions on asset smoothing.
[8] http://www.ipe.com/news/PME_mulls_pensions_cut_in_2010_31010.php?type=news&id=31010
[9] Thanks to Patrick Groenendijk of Vervoer Pension Fund for this insight.

Amidst the slew of innovations in the management of pension funds and other assets, two major trends have emerged in recent months. First, the "LDI" trend, with a clearer recognition of the need to tie assets to liabilities, is gaining attention after 2008. The adoption rate has been slow due to changing regulation. The goal of the standard approach is strictly to increase the correlation between assets and liabilities; but this is just one part of the equation – the returns also have to be matched. The second is a separation of two different sets of contributors to returns and their management – called "Separating Alpha and Beta."[10] This book demonstrates that these two trends are not separate, but rather can be implemented effectively in one superior approach, especially if clients use SMART. In short, CIOs can improve performance and solvency by being smart about regular cash flow and rebalancing decisions that they make on alpha and beta assets. This is different from the current approach where the spotlight is on manager selection (or static alpha) and a naïve extension in duration, as opposed to managing beta and manager allocations against an effective and easily tracked liability benchmark.[11]

For simplicity, this book separates the portfolio management discussion into three segments – (i) Liabilities, (ii) the Beta Engine, and (iii) the Alpha Engine – and briefly contrasts current practice with a more innovative approach.[12] A recent MetLife (2009) study of 153 U.S. pension plans, of which 43 percent had assets under management in excess of $1 billion, highlights that "Asset Allocation" was selected 54 percent of the time as the risk factor to which plan sponsors pay most attention;[13] "Underfunding of Liabilities" was selected 47 percent of the time;[14] and "Asset and Liability Mismatch" was selected 43 percent of the time.[15] This warrants focus on liabilities, beta management, and good process, since over 57 percent of respondents agreed that, in their experience, there is evidence of limited or no holistic risk management.

---

[10] Callin (20008) is a good example of bad advice by asset managers seeking to sell products rather than help investors make effective decisions. Their arguments are invalidated, helping investors get a clearer understanding of the true risks and how to manage them. Another bad recommendation is to pitch 20-year bonds as a long-term substitute to equities based on point-of-time statistics - Robert Arnott (2009).

[11] For example, the DIC Pension Fund in Japan thinks very creatively about hedging liability risk and private equity beta risk. This book borrows ideas from innovative CIOs such as Mr. Hideo Kondo, but it advocates a much broader perspective than only generating return on hedging.

[12] We thank David Deutsch and Lisa Needle, former CIO and Acting CIO, respectively, of the San Diego County Employees Retirement Association, for permitting the use of these terms, which they have utilized in the effective implementation of their fund.

[13] The response was: We use disciplined rebalancing to implement a documented strategic asset allocation policy.

[14] The response was: The design and execution of our investment strategies have proven effective in comfortably managing our funding contribution level.

[15] The response was: We carry out regular studies that have proven accurate and effective in managing mismatches between the duration of plan assets and liabilities.

Regrettably, costs were neglected in the last few years as investment vehicles became increasingly complex. Cost reduction directly results in improvement in performance, and Chapter 9 shows how this dramatically helps individual investors. CIOs can set up their overall SAA at extremely low cost, and ensure that staff and managers are paid commensurate to not only the risk taken but also to the skill displayed.

This is not a proposal to jump on the government bandwagon to restrict executive pay. On the contrary, the most talented investors warrant hefty bonuses, with the caveat that their performance is based on appropriate risk management and a clear demonstration of skill. Chapters 7 and 9 turn a common argument made by asset managers on its head – namely, that CIOs and Boards were accused of being too short-term in their evaluation of products. This argument is reversed to compel asset managers to be long-term as well, and to defer payment for the performance component of fees to later in the product cycle, once skill is established.

As an aside, nowhere is such an approach as essential as in the DC space where retail investors have to sacrifice today for the promise of a rosy future, with products such as "Target Date Funds." Pogue and Modigliani (1973, 1975) argued for the reform of mutual fund fees that appropriately adjusted for risk, but the lack of progress in this direction demonstrates the clout of the product provider and less than optimal federal regulation. To avert a pension crisis in the retail investment space, such a re-evaluation in compensation to mutual fund managers may have to be mandated by regulation, as individual investors lack the bargaining power of pension fund CIOs – the likely audience of this book.

CHALLENGES – CASH FLOWS/REBALANCING, DYNAMIC DECISION-MAKING

In the late 1990s, one of the more sophisticated global pension funds - the World Bank's pension fund – was managed by a talented staff, under the leadership of Afsaneh Beschloss, but the bulk of the work befitted an auditor rather than an investor. The approach, though innovative at the time, was not that of hard-core investors – too much time was spent on ALM studies and meeting managers, and too little time on being effective investment managers. In contrast, in the asset management space, the process for making all investment decisions was very clearly articulated. Equally important to large asset managers was that, while performance was variable and questionable at best, process allowed for a consistent approach, immunity against staff departures, and the ability for global information sharing.

Every morning, a one-pager specified the day's recommended transactions. Based on data released the night before (economic, price, sentiment, value, etc.), for every portfolio under management, it would highlight:

(i)   **What** actions had to be taken – buy/sell/do nothing;

(ii)   **How much** was to be taken – 1 percent, 0.5 percent;

(iii)   **When** it had to be done – at the open of London markets though some managers had strict time-based recommendations; and

(iv)   **Why** these actions made sense – focusing on the specific change in momentum or economic data that caused a re-evaluation of the recommendations.

The most critical aspect of this approach was the explicit recognition that not doing anything was also a bet – something most pension funds have not realized, though investment policies suggested by consultants, and implemented by pension funds, routinely follow this passive approach. The practice at J.P. Morgan was to reflect on the systematic recommendations of the models, give portfolio managers the discretion to add to or subtract from the positions – based on their views about the market (e.g., politics, etc.) that may not have been factored in the systematic process – and then implement the final recommendation, tracking in detail the ensuing performance and risks.

In the simplest terms, to become an effective Pension Pilot, every implicit decision in a pension fund needs to be made explicit – after all, only what gets "M"easured and "M"onitored gets "M"anaged: the "M³ of Investing." A pension fund CIO has the exact same job of managing assets as do the external managers they hire – only the asset labels are different. Therefore, SMART pension fund CIOs should put themselves through the same RFP questions they ask of their external managers, namely:

1.   What are the key areas on which to focus daily decision-making?

     a. Beta Allocation, Liability Hedge, Manager Allocations (typical elements of a pension fund)

2.   What is the decision on these identified areas today?

3.   What is the basis of this decision?

     a. Qualitative judgment (perfectly acceptable) or a systematic process;

     b. If systematic, what factors are used to make the daily recommendation?

4.   Which staff member is responsible for which decision?

     a. CIO for liability hedge and rebalancing/currency management;

     b. Staff for external manager allocations

5.   How is consistency in decision-making ensured, and what is the process for reviewing whether these decisions have been effective and for changing them if they have not?

Danny Ozark, manager of the Philadelphia Phillies sports team, is credited with the amusing observation, "Half this game is 90 percent mental."[16] Similarly, this book argues that half the time, good investing is 95 percent process and 5 percent good ideas. At the end of the day, investing is not rocket science but the effective application of economic intuition to a set of decisions.

FORGET ALTERNATIVES – FOCUS ON LIQUID ASSETS/TRANSPARENCY

Many old-style investors were shocked with the dramatic and sudden move to alternatives, including private equity, hedge funds, and more exotic investments. In large part, this embodied a drift to the "endowment" model, the mantra of Ivy League CIOs who were elevated to Buddha-like status. Their every move was emulated without anyone pausing to ask the basic question: "Is it worth taking such a costly, illiquid bet?" (In other words, "What is the cost of illiquidity and lock-ups, and when will it hurt me the most?"). The balance of power shifted so dramatically towards asset managers that even CIOs of the largest funds had little input in the terms and restrictions of these alternative investments.

In 1995, the World Bank was asked by a consultant to review a private equity deal (the consultant was paid on commitments rather than disbursed amounts). Surprisingly, the list of co-Limited Partners (LPs) was the same as those on previous deals – an enviable Who's Who list for asset managers. However, the document was designed by the General Partner (GP), with terms most favorable to the GP, with little recourse to the most sophisticated global pension funds. So why didn't the LPs band together and dictate terms to the GP, rather than willingly submit to self-flagellation, that too for an investment where the ability to gauge future success was as meager as "Trust Me"? Years later, this approach was being perpetuated by "hedge funds" and fund-of-funds (FoFs) to the detriment of the investor.

It's time to return to basics and ask whether the goals of managing a pension fund can be met through effective, low-cost, transparent, liquid, dynamic management of beta and liabilities. If so, forget about alternatives or, at the most, play with them at the margin to extract any 'alpha' from illiquidity, but recognize that gates, lock-ups, provisions on selling partnership interests in secondary markets, and restrictions on revealing the nature of the investment (especially in private equity) are effectively an increase in the investment cost, and hence a lower after-fee performance.[17, 18]

The simple prescription is for CIOs to follow the low-cost, high value-added KISS principle: "Keep it SMART and Simple."

---

[16] The two simplest implicit bets in investment policy are (i) the choice of strategic currency hedge, as that is a bet on the local currency; and (ii) the rebalancing policy, which suggests doing nothing when the portfolio drifts between the ranges or rebalancing periods.

[17] Muralidhar and van der Wouden (1999).

[18] It surprises us that consultants and FoFs did not price out the various options that pension clients sold for "free" to asset managers, and that these options were exercised at the worst possible time for the investor.

RISK MEASUREMENT IS NOT EQUAL TO RISK MANAGEMENT

Risk Management is lamentably a misnomer in the asset management industry today. A major U.S. pension plan spent millions purchasing an expensive risk system, and additional millions to pay consultants to implement the system, only to have their senior investment officers ignore the risk report – so much so that when the frequency of distribution of the report dropped from daily, to weekly, and then monthly, there was no protest from the staff members it was supposed to serve.

People often confuse Risk Measurement with Risk Management. The latter is the responsibility of the CIO and investment staff, and is accomplished by making effective decisions on every allocation or selection decision in the fund. Risk Measurement, on the other hand, is what outside vendors offer at high cost, most often for little value! The Pension Dashboard discussed earlier focuses on daily risk measurement (i.e., value-at-risk, black swan risk), but the CIO using it focused on Risk Management. To illustrate, in 1997, the Treasurer of the World Bank, Gary Perlin, posed the question: how much would the fund lose if emerging markets collapsed? Since the World Bank had already implemented what was probably the first LDI-based pension risk system at the time, it was relatively simple to run the numbers and give him an estimate. When markets did collapse the following year, the models were within a tad of the 1997 estimate. Gary's soft and extremely polite reaction was, "If you were so damn smart, why didn't you make me money?" Never again did I confuse Risk Management with Risk Measurement.

STAFFING AND COMPENSATION

Another interesting aspect of institutional asset management is the willingness of pension fund Boards to pay external managers many times more than what they paid internal staff for equivalent, if not better, decisions and greater control. Yet, it is common to have many CIOs pilloried in the press for high salaries, only to have the Fund hire an external asset manager for higher multiples.

Paying Wall Street high salaries is not the fault of Wall Street, but of Main Street. The industry has no pre-qualifying certification for becoming an investor. More important, every investor at an asset management firm has learned their craft at the expense of the end client; so it is time for pension fund Boards and CFOs to see the fund as a potential profit center and allocate resources appropriately. For example, on a $1 billion fund, a 2 bps enhancement by improving rebalancing is equivalent to $200,000 – something worth paying for.

Every organization has to decide where they have the greatest competitive edge, and hire staff accordingly. One may argue, as manager research is a generic activity with publicly available data, an effective small-sized pension fund may want to have a CIO focus on Liabilities and Beta Management, delegating the job of selection and the management of allocation to alpha managers to one or two staff member/s. The actual data collection and due diligence are outsourced to an industry (of consultants) that has grown for this purpose and where this data has become a commodity – hence the low cost for smaller funds. If the Dutch had adopted this model in their drive to improve governance and solvency and to lower costs, they may not have ended up allocating assets to foreign fund managers with little-to-no background in managing Dutch pension assets, and firing many well-qualified CIOs. Some of the blame for this trend lies at the door of the DnB, which decided to apply onerous reporting/model restrictions and then worried about the outsourcing of Dutch assets to foreign, potentially poorly qualified (regardless of brand name) asset managers.

There has to be a better relationship between Boards and staff, based on appropriate, long-term compensation structures, eliminating the need for "Advisory Boards," which had earlier been erroneously suggested to help CIOs garner support for their innovative ideas. Smart Boards should entrust their staff with clear mandates and allow them to innovate, instead of wasting time and effort building consensus. Moreover, while it was suggested that a group of quantitative analysts should carry out performance attribution and risk assessment, these tasks are easily outsourced at low cost to custodians or consultants who collect the requisite data – though CIOs would have to be specific about exactly what is needed, instead of the custodian determining what should be presented.

The SMART paradigm requires no more than a CIO and a deputy-CIO to focus solely on liability, beta, and currency management (and manage the Board and internal staff), and the appropriate number of staff to oversee external managers, holding the CIO ultimately accountable for pulling together all the operations and ensuring that risks and returns are appropriately diversified. It is no surprise that the case studies presented here are from clients who have run a meaningful size of assets with limited staff and have yet managed to raise the bar in pension investing.

THE PENSION DASHBOARD

Each client is different, but some basic information at the start of every business day is a prerequisite for an effective pilot/CIO. A disciplined pilot needs to (i) ensure that all systems are in good working order; (ii) be clear about where their final destination is; and, (iii) based on factors such as weather and traffic, whether it is expedient to travel in a straight line or make appropriate deviations to arrive at the destination safely and on schedule.

The Pension Dashboard displays, on a quantitative and qualitative basis, the following information in a single table:

1. Performance on an absolute, relative, and risk-adjusted basis year-to-date and since inception, given the previous night's data. Such information on the current situation of the fund helps to determine whether to increase/decrease risk going forward.
2. Key decisions responsible for performance.
3. Current liability hedge, and the action needed to change it.
4. Current asset allocation including currency, and whether it is the correct one for the prevailing market environment.
5. Asset classes impacted, and if changes are suggested, the magnitude of the change, and why the change is relevant.

Figures 1.2-1.4 provide examples of the content of the Dashboard, but each client would customize their own structure according to their individual objectives, organization set-up, and decision-making process. Let us consider a U.S. Pension Fund with a portfolio structure as in Figure 1.1 and a strict asset focus. (More generic European and Japanese structures are provided in Chapters 5 and 8 – the Dutch are more ALM-focused.)

First developed by the Shell Netherlands Pension Plan, and coined the "Investment Decision Process" (IDP), this structure clearly lays out the hierarchy of decisions. Once the structure is articulated, the CIO can delegate decisions and hold the staff responsible for performance, though the CIO is primarily responsible for ensuring that all risks are diversified and risk-adjusted return goals are achieved at the total fund level.

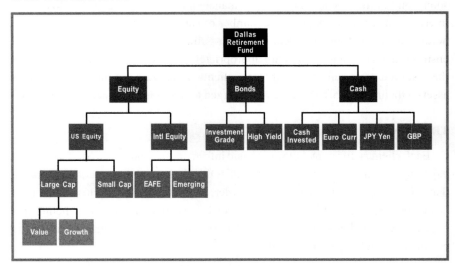

Figure 1.1. A typical U.S. pension fund investment decision process.

More important, the IDP shows that decisions relating to the daily mix of Equity, Bonds, and Cash account for 100 percent of the Assets Under Management (AUM) and hence require maximum attention. The liability, while not shown explicitly, is the benchmark for the top box and must similarly be managed as a top priority. Manager selection is at the lowest point in the portfolio tree and therefore of lower significance. Hence, it is much more efficient to spend more time managing beta than identifying the next exotic hedge fund manager to whom to allocate 2 percent of the fund.

Figure 1.2 serves as a "Rear View Mirror and Speedometer" for the CIO. They can perform better than their liabilities or strategic asset allocations (SAAs) in three major ways, as shown in the right-hand chart of Figure 1.2:

(i)   Manager contribution

(ii)   "Benchmark misfit" – created by (a) assigning managers benchmark indices different from the SAA benchmark indices and/or (b) weighting sub-components of SAA indices across managers so the aggregation is different from the SAA benchmark index[19]; and

(iii) "Strategy contribution" – the value created by being dynamic/ SMART in managing alpha and beta decisions.

The left side of Figure 1.2 provides high-level summary information about the fund, year-to-date and since inception. The focus is on excess return generated (relative to liabilities or an SAA); relative risk taken to achieve this result; relative return-risk ratio (or the Information Ratio), which indicates the reward per unit of risk; M^2 excess – which is a performance measure presented in Modigliani-Modigliani (1997), highlighting the need to present excess returns after normalizing for absolute volatility and removing any leverage that might have been created in portfolio construction; maximum drawdown (my favorite statistic and what I call "Yield to Fire", i.e., how much and for how long the fund can underperform before the Board loses patience and fires the manager); ratio of excess good risk to excess bad risk – again, trying to break up naïve risk statistics into an indication of good versus bad risk (with preference for ratios above 1; confidence in skill, which indicates the expertise of the CIO in outperforming the benchmark (explored further in Chapters 2 and 3); and, finally, the success ratio or percentage of days that the performance was greater than the benchmark (a batting average of sorts, and more relevant for public institutions, where being right more than 50 percent of the time may appeal more to the press than being right a few times and doing extremely well).

---

[19] Muralidhar (2001), Chapter 9, describes this attribution in greater detail.

A smart pension fund can easily set up a process to produce a similar report for its investment staff, especially for each respective branch of the tree, thereby improving overall control. For some CIOs, a daily report is too demanding, but the focus is more on process than frequency. CIOs must realize that lack of information during the month only means that *investment decisions are left unmanaged and being made by the market, not by the CIO, but the CIO is held accountable for the end result.*

Dallas Retirement Fund
Evaluation Period: 01/01/2000-08/18/2010

Aggregated Performance		
	Year t to Date	Total Period
Excess Annualized Return	0.83%	2.42%
Tracking Error	1.18%	1.98%
Information Ratio	0.7	1.23%
M2 Excess Return	0.78%	2.57%
Maximum Excess Drawdown	4.00%	-6.70%
Ratio of Excess Good Risk to Bad Risk	0.68	1.24%
Benchmark Annualized Return	4.37%	7.80%
Portfolio Annualized Return	5.20%	10.22%
Confidence in Skill	74.82%	100%
Success Ratio	38.46%	55.97%

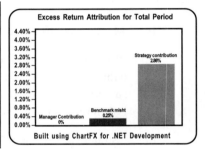

Figure 1.2. The "Rear View Mirror and Speedometer" of the pension fund.

The next part of the Dashboard helps CIOs position the portfolio to outperform in the future (à la a Global Positioning System or GPS). The purely hypothetical data tabulated in Figure 1.3 provides all the investment recommendations in one concise report, enabling the investment officers to see the recommended investment tilts. These recommendations can be derived entirely from a naïve rebalancing program, which brings all the decisions back to the SAA at a pre-determined date; they can be derived from a more intelligent quantitative process (the SMART approach proposed in Chapters 5 and 7); or they can be the result of input from the investment officers on a purely qualitative basis. Again, though the bias is for systematic processes, ultimately the process only formalizes effective qualitative analysis; hence, the goal is to give more structure to qualitative processes to help integrate them into the fund management operation. One may note that the sum of all recommendations at the top asset class level of all Stocks, Bonds, and Cash is zero (i.e., there is no leverage unless permitted by the Board), but the sub-asset class level decisions add to the recommended asset class tilt. For example, the equity overweight of 5.25 percent comes from U.S. equity overweight of 6.95 percent and International equity underweight of -1.7 percent, and the same equity overweight is funded from a bond (-4.5 percent) and cash (-0.75 percent) underweight. This cash underweight is financed entirely in USD, and no currency positions are recommended.

Current Allocation Monitor		
		Allocation Tilt (Percentage of Portfolio)
EQUITY	↑	5.25
US Equity	↑	6.95
Large Cap	↑	11.16
Value	↑	12.46
Growth	↓	-1.31
Small Cap	↓	-4.21
International Equity	↓	-1.70
EAFE	↓	-1.02
Emerging	↓	-0.68
BONDS	↓	-4.50
Investment Grade	↓	-2.61
High Yield	↓	-1.89
CASH	↓	-0.75
Cash Invested	↓	-0.75
Euro Currency	←→	0
Japanese Yen	←→	0
GBP	←→	0

Figure 1.3. The GPS – Where should the fund be allocated today?

Given the bias towards recommendations driven by systematic factors, Figure 1.4 highlights the rules affiliated with this portfolio that triggered in the last three months, and tracks the date on which they triggered. Equally important, for the CIO, is the bottom part of the table which specifies the economic parameter that moved, and by how much, to trigger a recommendation. For example, the portfolio tilt between equity and fixed income was adjusted on August 15, 2010, due to a change in the 200-day momentum indicator of the Russell 3000 U.S. equity index.

It is mind-boggling to think of the potential complexity of managing even a simple four-asset class pension fund (typical in Japan), where it is assumed that 20 economic factors affect the basic asset classes. It is humanly impossible for a CIO to keep track of all these data variables in his/her head; hence, a systematic process must be established to highlight when economic or financial data have crossed a certain threshold. Figure 1.4 shows that while the price of oil dropped from the preceding week, the momentum of stocks was positive and the risk indicator of

Decision Drivers

Active Rules in the past 3 months (from Portfolio evaluation end date 08/18/2010)	Date of Action	
Eq vs FI: 200 day Momentum	08/16/2010	* Instill Discipline by
Eq vs. FI: Oil Momentum	08/16/2010	Translating Economic
HY vs. Inv. Grade: VIX and Equity	08/16/2010	Ideas into Simple Rules
EAFE vs. EMG: Bond Performance	08/09/2010	
EAFE vs. EMG : 200 Day Momentum	08/02/2010	
LC vs. SC: Mean Reversion 2	07/30/2010	
EAFE vs EMG: Yield Curve	06/30/2010	
LC vs SC : Mean Reversion 2	07/30/2010	* Rules Driven by
EAFE vs. EMG; Yield Curve	06/30/2010	Economic Data
Value vs. Growth; Growth Momentum	06/28/2010	
Eq vs. Cash : Slope of Yield Curve	06/14/2010	
Eq vs. FI: Halloween Effect	06/01/2010	
HY vs. Inv Grade: Halloween Effect	06/01/2010	
USEQ vs. INTEQ: Sentiment	05/31/2010	

Signal Tracker

Signal Series	Latest (last date & value of Signal)		Week Ago	Month Ago	Month Ago
Russell 3000 Index Close	08/18/2010	753.02	730.79	722.81	703.54
World, Energy, Oil, Brent dated, FOB Sullom Voe, Close, USD	08/19/2010	71.36	75.39	72.63	62
CBOE, Volatility Index (VIX), Close	08/20/2010	0.12	0.14	0.16	0.13
Russell 2000 Growth Index Close	08/21/2010	357.39	338.43	343.35	334.68
J.P.Morgan Emerging Markets Bond Indes (EMBI) Total Return, Close	08/22/2010	366.08	363.08	354.75	333.85
MSCI, Emerging Market Free USD Index, Close	08/23/2010	777.22	768.48	734.99	608.15
R1000 1 YR% Change	08/24/2010	12%	8 %	6 %	15%

Figure 1.4. Knowing why these decisions have to be made.

U.S. equities (VIX) declined. The SMART approach makes it easier to formalize one's basic economic intuition into a few, powerful rules across many asset pairs, and let a computer track them, rather than mentally attempting to work out the optimal allocations in a multi-tier portfolio. Chapter 4 explores this in more detail. The four-panel Dashboard presented (Figures 1.2-1.4) should, at a minimum, be made available daily to a CIO, with the ability to drill down further into any asset class or manager allocation, as desired. As indicated earlier, *only what is measured and monitored is actually managed.*

Applicability to Endowments/Foundations/ Social Security Systems/ SWFs

Nothing so far precludes these same principles being applied by other institutional investors, including endowments, foundations, Social Security systems, SWFs, insurance companies, and even individual investors. For investors who focus on the illiquid bet, at a minimum, these principles should be applied to the liquid portion of the portfolio. At a more sophisticated level, a CIO in charge of a fund invested heavily in illiquid assets should spend time understanding the liquid beta replication component of the illiquid asset, so that when the beta of the illiquid asset is likely to decline in performance, the Dashboard helps to effectively manage these bets. In short, illiquid investments should be less in SAAs and seen more as a tactical bet made to capture the illiquidity premium (Chapter 3 develops this recommendation further); but until such time as effective measures exist to capture volatility and illiquidity, it is realistic to expect that good governance would entail a more beta-oriented approach to managing funds. Alternatively, where governance prevents CIOs from taking a career risk in tactically allocating to illiquid assets (as it is often a bet better taken by a Board), the two portfolios should be carved out separately, and managed with similar Dashboards for each.

SUMMARY

This chapter has defined the CIO's key responsibilities and how Boards can help fulfill them. Though the focus is on pension fund CIOs, the findings are relevant to any CIO, especially as attention is drawn to cases where the **objectives or liabilities differ, but investment operations are identical.** Typically, a CIO is in a unique position between the Board and the external manager, and spends a lot of time preparing Board presentations, attending external manager meetings, reviewing performance reports, making cash flow decisions, etc. However, once the objectives are clearly articulated, the major tasks of managing assets can be outsourced, allowing the CIO to focus on the highest value-added activities: managing liabilities and beta (instead of hiring hedge fund managers). In other words, if CIOs follow the KISS principle - Keep it Simple and SMART - it would clear the deck to concentrate focus on the pension fund structure and goal-specific Dashboard. However, such an exercise requires adequate staffing, effective risk management, and appropriate compensation. The following chapters address the last two issues in greater detail.

2

Delegated Decisions and the Capital Relative Asset Pricing Model

"The reports of my death are greatly exaggerated!" Mark Twain

BACKGROUND

Mark Twain, on reading his own obituary, is popularly known to have made the above remark.[20] It is tempting to make a similar case for CAPM, the "indisputable" foundation of modern investment theory. Ever since its introduction more than 50 years ago, researchers have attempted to test the theory with market data, and have found several ways to denounce it or alternative ways to resuscitate it. Even *The Economist* published a series of articles in 1999-2000 on how the real options theory, or research on the flow of funds, threatened CAPM's validity. Yet, the model continues to be the backbone of finance theory as it evolves into the new millennium.

The 2008 market downturn, however, and a renewed focus on new paradigms for fund management and manager compensation, prompts a review of CAPM and poses a perfect opportunity to propose a new paradigm. This is particularly relevant for CIOs of pension funds, as they have either been using CAPM to value assets or have hired managers who use CAPM as the basis of their decision-making.

This chapter exposes the flaws in the current CAPM, and suggests that CIOs would do well to reassess consultants and asset managers who anchor their decision-making process to it. After a brief review of the theory, highlighting its appeal, the chapter presents a simple reason for the inaccuracy of many previous tests of CAPM's validity – namely, that CAPM's beguiling allure is its very simplicity, but its applicability pertains to only a limited class of investors who constitute a small fraction of the market. However, changes in the behavior of individuals, and in pension systems (including large social security systems) and other institutional investors, could impact this trend. The chapter concludes by

---

[20] *http://www.cs.cmu.edu/~ralf/quotes.html*

charting some fresh directions likely to form the basis of a new paradigm for asset pricing. The research presented here has implications for objective setting (Chapter 3), risk budgeting and compensation (Chapter 7), and investment decision-making (Chapters 5, 6, and 8).

TRADITIONAL CAPM

Traditional CAPM, associated with Markowitz, Sharpe, Littner, etc., makes the assumption that the representative investor desires greater wealth and is averse to volatility of wealth (called mean-variance preferences).

A typical utility function would be:

$$\text{Maximize } E[r] - \pi * \sigma^2, \tag{2.1}$$

where $E[*]$ is the expectations operator, r the return of the portfolio, π denotes a measure of the investor's risk aversion, and σ the portfolio's volatility.

By this definition and a few simple assumptions on asset returns, it is possible to determine an asset's equilibrium price independent of individual preferences. The expected risk premium of a risky asset (defined as the expected return minus a risk-free rate) is the product of the asset's beta (defined as the co-variance with the market portfolio dividend by the variance of the market portfolio) and the market risk premium (defined as the expected return of a market portfolio minus a risk-free rate). The beta may be expressed as:

$$\beta_a = (\sigma_a * \rho_{a,m}) / \sigma_m, \tag{2.2}$$

where β_a is the beta of asset a, σ_a is the volatility of the asset, σ_m is the volatility of the market portfolio (or the benchmark portfolio), and $\rho_{a,m}$ is the correlation between portfolio a and the market portfolio.

In CAPM theory, the market portfolio is the value weighted aggregate portfolio composed of all the risky assets. Therefore, with known historical beta[21] of an asset (or a portfolio of assets), expected return of a portfolio broadly representative of the market, and expected return of a risk-free asset (such as a Treasury note or Treasury bond, but theoretically with zero volatility), it is possible to determine the expected return and, thus, the price of the risky asset. Since the market portfolio is not readily observed, it is assumed that market benchmarks (e.g., the Wilshire 5000 or the S&P 500), which represent a broad aggregate of risky assets, are reasonable proxies to apply this theory.[22]

---

[21] As it is difficult to know the true beta of an asset, investors assume that the historical beta measured relative to the "market" is an accurate representation of the future. More important, a true risk-free asset does not exist.

[22] In theory, the market portfolio should represent risky equities and bonds in both domestic and international markets. However, it has been difficult to identify a true market portfolio in practice; hence the use of proxies.

Simply put, beta is the product of the correlation of the asset (or portfolio) vis-à-vis the market portfolio and the standard deviation of the asset (portfolio) divided by the standard deviation of the market portfolio (equation 2.2). Since beta is a measure of an asset's co-variance[23] with the market portfolio, a beta higher (lower) than 1 implies that the asset would have a return higher (lower) than the market portfolio. An asset with zero beta is a risk-free asset, and the most risky assets have positive betas greater than unity.

In addition, it has been demonstrated that every investor would hold their assets in some proportion of the risky market portfolio and the risk-free asset, commonly known as the Two-Fund Separation Theorem. Individual preferences enter the picture only in proportion to these two broad asset classes, as risk-averse investors would hold more of the risk-free asset whereas investors with a tolerance for risk would be more heavily invested in the infamous "market portfolio".

More complicated versions of CAPM exist; however, the theory's essence is preserved, as researchers sought to extend its framework to a situation where markets are reviewed over multiple periods (Intertemporal CAPM[24]) or over different national boundaries (International CAPM[25]). By virtue of its simplicity of excluding individual preferences and reliance on the simple data series,[26] CAPM lent itself to widespread appeal and a battery of tests, which were split between extolling its virtues and faulting it for not bearing out well under tests of this rather simple relationship. However, the simplicity of CAPM lies in the assumptions it makes about the representative investor, and therein lies the problem, as also the pathway to a new paradigm for asset pricing.

The foregoing analysis may lead even the most naïve modern investor without any training in finance to conclude that the one element conspicuous by its absence from early expressions of the theory is the time dimension, as it is a foregone conclusion that time is integral to the investment decision-making process. After all, CAPM suggests that the representative investor is willing to accept returns on a portfolio over the long term if it meets the asset-pricing rule, regardless of the path achieved over time vis-à-vis the market portfolio. The Intertemporal CAPM assumes that the market is always in equilibrium and captures time in its analysis, but not enough to satisfy the average investment policy-maker. The classic investment policy-maker is **not** indifferent to a portfolio's return path, even if he is assured that the final outcome will reach the CAPM-predicted return. This is because he could get fired for underperformance (which suggests lack of skill) even before achieving

---

[23]   We use the words "asset" and "portfolio" (of assets) interchangeably, as a "portfolio" is a collection of many "assets".

[24]   Merton (1973).

[25]   Solnik (1974).

[26]   Some experts have pointed out that testing for expected return theories by using realized returns is incorrect, making it necessary to qualify these studies.

the long-term return. Interestingly, the correlation coefficient captures the path of the portfolio relative to the market portfolio, and Chapters 3 and 7 show that an investor must not be indifferent to two identical betas.

PENSION FUND STRUCTURE – PRINCIPALS AND AGENTS

"I suppose you think that on our board half the directors do the work and the other half do nothing. As a matter of fact, gentlemen, the reverse is the case."[27]

Let us digress briefly to identify two constituent classes of investors in the market – principals (those who own the funds and may/may not invest on their own behalf) and agents (those who make investment decisions on behalf of the principals).[28] This distinction is important, as major developments in the asset management industry over the last 40 years required incorporation of the time dimension and a clearer understanding of relative risk in any asset pricing theory.

Assets controlled by principals (pension funds) have grown dramatically, leading to a similar growth in institutional fund management. This is because a significant portion of these assets is externally managed, with discretion delegated within specific investment guidelines. In addition, agents (the mutual fund industry and asset managers) have experienced similar asset growth, also with delegated decision-making (Swensen 2005, page 210). Clearly, the use of agents has increased over time, as has their share of the total market. Two other phenomena in capital markets today are noteworthy: (i) more individuals are taking control of asset decisions through either DC funds or day trading; and (ii) there is a marked leaning towards indexation or passive management, as investors tend to believe they have overpaid managers. This reversal of trends suggests that more principals are making (or taking control of) their own investment decisions. This begs the question, how does CAPM apply to these investors, and how does the shift in delegation of authority affect asset pricing?

CIOs are at a crossroads in this theoretical framework of principals and agents: they have to play on both sides of the fence (Figure 2.1). In pension funds, the CIO serves as the agent, reporting to the principals (a Board composed of employer and employee representatives). However, once CIOs select external managers (agents), they function as principals. In general, the relationship between principals and agents is complex in three fundamental areas: (i) the average horizon of a pension fund (a principal) is long term (30-40 years), whereas the average performance measurement period of those hired to manage the funds (agents) is short term

[27] Petras (2001), page 18.
[28] Brennan (1993) makes a similar distinction between individuals and agents. More recently, Cornell and Roll (2004) have extended this analysis. We will return to this classification later.

(annual and, in some extreme cases, even monthly); (ii) agents are measured relative to a benchmark and expected to outperform at least on an after-fees, risk-adjusted basis (not paid for free leverage and beta); and (iii) a nagging suspicion lurks that outperformance of agents results from luck rather than skill, and by the time this is realized it far exceeds the measurement horizon. In other words, the issue of luck versus skill suggests that principals pay the agents' salaries or fees, but lack the confidence, based on the available short return data series, that the agent's outperformance vis-à-vis the benchmark is based on skilled judgment, and, in turn, the fee is well deserved. This is largely because, unlike the sciences in which engineers and doctors are rigorously trained and tested before they qualify for major responsibility, no clear standard is available to distinguish *ex-ante* who would make a good asset manager.

From the agent's point of view, marked underperformance in any period is a strong disincentive, as they need to protect not only returns but also (by corollary) their own reputation. This explains, in part, the growth of passive index funds with their residual implications, as also the rise of the carry trade in currency markets, which makes it easier to lock in a positive carry and hope that currency appreciation is less than the interest rate differential. Covered interest rate parity suggests

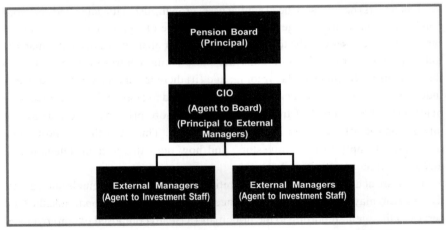

Figure 2.1. The multi-tiered principal-agent problem in institutional funds.

that the currency with the higher interest rate would depreciate to offset the interest rate differential, but it has been shown repeatedly that the simple carry trade across multiple currencies is profitable.[29] These issues are important, as they can distort market performance away from standard economic theory, which is the crux of this chapter.

---

[29] See Strange (1988), and Baz, Breedon, Naik, and Peress (1996).

Take the carry trade example again: it takes minimal conviction for an agent to implement a positive carry trade, but it takes enormous conviction and deep pockets for an agent to implement a negative carry trade. If enough agents with low conviction, "out for a quick buck", buy high-interest-rate currencies, the high-interest currency *will appreciate* because of disproportionate demand (low-interest-rate currencies will be under pressure to depreciate, thereby defying standard economic theory, at least for a reasonable period of time). However, if every agent is on a single side of a trade when they are risk-seeking, the trade looks attractive until risk aversion sets in (and this can be caused by exogenous or endogenous factors). Then, low-interest-rate currencies appreciate dramatically as money rushes home to countries with high savings rates that exported capital when they were in the risk-seeking mode. This was seen most clearly when Russia defaulted on its debt and the Japanese yen appreciated dramatically in a single day. Since then, many banks created carry trades conditioned by risk aversion indices, but the theory has never been explained in terms of principals and agents.[30]

The current theory on Luck versus Skill states: (i) the greater the confidence required to make this distinction, (ii) the higher the volatility of assets, and (iii) the lower the correlation between portfolio and benchmark, the greater the number of years required to separate luck from skill.[31] Since it takes a considerable length of time to determine the Luck versus Skill of an agent after he is hired, it is important to see how this affects the behavior of principals and agents. There is comprehensive literature on the generic problems of principal-agent relationships, and academics are now trying to establish whether performance-based fees will align interests more closely in the fund management industry. However, this does not appear to solve the Luck versus Skill problem completely, or what academic literature calls "incentive compatibility"; and these academic proposals do not adjust for risk in performance-based fees. Surely, no principal would hire an agent who has generated returns based purely on luck, and clearly would not want to compensate them. This problem manifested itself on Wall Street over a long period of time but became obvious only recently in 2008, when bonuses paid at the consummation of a transaction were revealed to be for trades that did not have *any* long-term value!

While investment policy-makers (and asset management firms) are concerned about fees in any period, a more critical concern is *job risk* – as the termination of a

---

[30] Muralidhar (2001b).

[31] For example, to achieve even 84 percent accuracy for a portfolio that outperformed by an annualized 300 bps, where the annualized standard deviation of the benchmark is 15 percent, the annualized standard deviation of the portfolio is 25 percent, and the correlation is 0.9, one would need 175 years of data! See Ambarish and Siegel (1996) and Muralidhar (1999) for application to fund managers, and Muralidhar and U (1997) for application to pension fund peer evaluations.

job or mandate after weak relative performance (either to the benchmark or the competition) cuts off future revenue and has implications for reputation. Finally, no investment policy-maker would want to be guilty of firing a "good" manager based on a short period of underperformance.

In brief, principals and agents cannot be indifferent to performance of the benchmark and of peers, and the path of a portfolio over time vis-à-vis a benchmark. It would take a courageous fund manager to choose a portfolio independent of, or with a weak correlation to, the benchmark, as this would imply high tracking error (defined as the standard deviation of the benchmark's excess returns) and large drawdowns.[32] Principals, acting on their own, do not harbor such suspicions, as they know the basis for their decisions, do not have to pay any fees, and can therefore make investment decisions independent of these factors.

This is the focal point of this chapter: *The principal, as the true representative investor in traditional CAPM, may value assets as such, whereas an agent has a more complex trade-off to make among such valuations and the performance of the benchmark and its competitors.*

Thus, for an agent, factors beyond those embedded in the naïve CAPM affect the valuation of portfolios, eventually influencing buy/sell decisions which, in turn, impact security prices. Therefore, earlier tests of CAPM that did not take into account market structure and factors driving demand for assets by different types of investors are incorrect. *Tests of traditional CAPM that rejected it reject only the fact that not all investors are principals!*[33] By ignoring market structure and behavioral issues, these tests have the correct answer, but probably the wrong hypothesis.

As already indicated, the concentration of assets in pension funds is increasing, and the growth of mutual funds represents a fundamental change in the nature of asset markets and the investment environment. To the extent that agents' activities cause inaccurate pricing of securities, at least in the minds of CAPM purists, either the current form of CAPM is no longer valid (unless the trend of using agents is completely reversed) and a new paradigm needs to be developed, or prices are at risk of undergoing a significant correction. The problem encountered is: what preferences are implied by these complex relationships (individually and in aggregate), and what proportion of the market do they constitute?

---

[32]   Tracking error is a function of volatility of the benchmark and the portfolio, and correlation of the portfolio to the benchmark. A low correlation is equal to high tracking error. High tracking error implies not only a significant amount of relative risk, but also a long time period to separate luck from skill.

[33]   The beta that one would test for, using the theoretical paradigm, is unobservable, as the historical beta is polluted by the actions of agents. Therefore, historical betas need to be deconstructed into a pure component and an agent-biased component.

The answer to the first question indicates how prices and returns should be evaluated by the respective investor classes; and the answer to the second indicates the impact these prices and returns have on determining price levels in equilibrium. The use of external asset managers has increased (Swensen 2005 and Bogle 2009) and, based on available statistics, this suggests that agency risk issues impact a large section of the market.

NEW APPROACHES FALL SHORT

The traditional CAPM is an absolute theory of asset pricing and relies on the valuation of assets based on an ephemeral market portfolio, whereas the market-place is replete with benchmarks such as the S&P, Russell equity indices, and JP Morgan bond indices for U.S. clients; TOPIX or Nikkei for Japanese clients; etc. Moreover, the original CAPM pre-dates the need for benchmarks, as it was introduced when the market was dominated by principals. What is needed now is a complementary relative theory of asset pricing of which the current CAPM is a very special case (i.e., a relative theory of asset pricing as the base for all finance theory). It has already become a practice for participants in the asset management industry to use relative risk measures to evaluate the risk inherent in their decisions, and therefore a relative theory of asset value is a logical extension.

For example, pension funds often consider the tracking error (defined here as the volatility of excess returns) of their investment managers as a part of both an evaluation of prospective managers and a review of current managers. Some early research suggests that agents who receive "pure" performance fees will price assets based on two factors: the market and benchmark portfolios, as opposed to the standard CAPM which depended on only a risk-free asset and the market portfolio. *In this new paradigm, the "risk-free asset" becomes the benchmark by which the agent is evaluated!* Specifically, portfolios that have a higher correlation with the benchmark will be bid up and have a lower expected return.[34] This is a critical step in the direction of a relative theory; but, by his own admission, Brennan (1993) states that this simple analysis of a single period incorporates neither the analysis of Luck versus Skill nor whether such an arrangement is optimal for the pension fund or the asset manager. Cornell and Roll (2005) extend Brennan's theory, but again seem to overlook the practical nuances in the industry – namely, they attempt to model the asset manager's penchant for higher revenue (with less risk), but do not attempt to establish the optimal contract between principal and agents, given the principal's desire to find skillful, high-performing asset managers (on a risk-adjusted basis).[35]

---

[34] Brennan (1993).
[35] See Muralidhar (2001), Chapter 9, for discussions on Luck versus Skill and the correct method for risk-adjusted performance. Muralidhar (2009) and Chapter 8 demonstrate how the compensation of asset managers needs to be modified to adjust for risk and skill.

The empirical tests of this theory seem to shed light on the possibility that this theory would work, but the wrong assumption on the growth of passive indexed funds, managed through mutual funds, clouded some of the results.

In fact, the reason for Brennan (1993) arriving at this conclusion is in the definition of the types of investors. If an increase in passive management is viewed as individuals/principals taking more control of their assets (i.e., delegating only execution and not discretion to their fund managers), rather than increasing the agents' proportion of the market, then the empirical results of Brennan (1993) tend to ratify this concept of a relative theory. In other words, if Brennan had adjusted the data set for a mischaracterization of principal/passive behavior, his tests may have validated the theory.

Academic research has scanned the structure of mutual fund fees to ascertain if asset selection has been influenced by these contracts. They seem to conclude that the fulcrum-type fee arrangements distort portfolio allocations in a way that results in a positive effect on equilibrium prices of stocks in benchmark portfolios, a significant negative effect on their Sharpe ratios, and a marginally positive effect on their volatility. Clearly, the price action on stocks in the case of Deutsche Telekom, or even country indices as in the case of Malaysia, when they are included in the benchmarks, seem to bear out the conclusion, if not the hypothesis. The issue that arises from starting with the assumption that fund managers try to maximize fees is its failure to recognize that fund managers are more likely to worry about risk-adjusted outperformance vis-à-vis the benchmark and competitors, and convincing their current and prospective clients that they are the most capable of adding such returns, than they are concerned about optimal fee contracts. Hence, the need for appropriate risk-adjusted and skill-based fee contracts (Muralidhar 2009a and Chapter 7). Further, in my 14 years of involvement in the asset management business, I have yet to come by either a pension fund or a fund manager who used fee negotiations as a way to determine a capable manager – instead, the signaling is done through performance data.

The following section presents a methodology by which the signaling can be done through performance, especially risk-adjusted performance, which achieves many of the above-mentioned goals (including optimal fee arrangements) and provides the general framework for the new paradigm.

THE NEW PARADIGM – THE CAPITAL RELATIVE ASSET PRICING MODEL

In addition to Brennan (1993) and Roll and Cornell (2005), two relevantly recent pieces of research have sought to answer the questions raised above – namely, (i) how does one compare a manager's returns relative to a benchmark on a risk-adjusted basis, as well as the performance relative to peers?[36] and (ii) how does one distinguish between a manager's luck and skill measured relative to a benchmark, and how detailed a report card will demonstrate the asset manager's skill with any degree of confidence? [37]

To resolve the first, Modigliani and Modigliani (1997) show that in order to compare a portfolio to a benchmark in terms of basis points of risk-adjusted performance, one must ensure that both have the same standard deviation. Therefore, it has been proposed that the portfolio be leveraged or deleveraged, using the risk-free asset. This transformation is demonstrated in Figure 2.2. It creates a new portfolio, called the risk-adjusted portfolio (RAP), whose return (M^2 or M-square) would be equal to the leverage factor multiplied by the original return plus one, minus the leverage factor multiplied by the risk-free rate. Chapter 3 explains this in detail. It should be apparent to the intuitive reader that this is a form of the Two-Fund Separation. Now, it is possible for the RAP to outperform the benchmark by taking into account only the tracking error (or having a correlation less than one).[38] The adjustment allows for an "apples-to-apples" comparison, namely, returns from both the benchmark and the RAP have the same volatility. The authors show that peer rankings can be reversed with this adjustment. The astute reader will see that if a manager is told to outperform a benchmark on an absolute basis, the simplest way to do so is to borrow money and use the funds to invest in the benchmark – thereby gaming the mandate!

A counter-intuitive result of this approach, not envisioned by the Modiglianis, is that if the RAP outperforms the benchmark (with the same standard deviation as the benchmark) and has a correlation less than one, then if the benchmark was the market portfolio, one has created a portfolio with a beta less than one outperforming the benchmark.[39] In effect, *managers of RAPs can only outperform by being skillful in taking correlation risk!* Therefore, in the relative paradigm, beta appears to be less important than the volatility of the benchmark and the correlation of the portfolio to the benchmark. In effect, finance theory must move into a three-dimensional paradigm (without even adding time)

[36]   Modigliani and Modigliani (1999), and Muralidhar and U (1997).
[37]   Ambarish and Siegel (1996), and Muralidhar (1999).
[38]   If the portfolio's volatility is set equal to the benchmark, then the tracking error or risk relative to the benchmark can be generated only by maintaining a correlation less than one.
[39]   Roll (1992) had posed such a problem but could not explain the outcome. Also, the correlation of the original portfolio to the benchmark will be identical to the correlation of the RAP to the benchmark, as "leverage or deleverage" using the risk-free rate does not change the correlation characteristics. However, a CAPM purist will conclude that such a result is obtained, as the benchmark is not the market portfolio and hence makes no comment on market efficiency. Also, the recent work by Jorion (2003) has shown that the best way to optimize tracking error is to ensure that the standard deviation of the benchmark is equal to that of the manager. However, Jorion (2003) surprisingly does not reference or acknowledge Modigliani and Modigliani (1996).

of return, correlation, and volatility, as opposed to the standard risk-return paradigm. *More important, two portfolios with identical betas may not be equally desired by a principal who cares about the fund manager's skill, as demonstrated later in this chapter and in Chapter 7.*

The M² measure and its unique insights are shown in Figure 2.2, which highlights four key regions:

I.   Portfolio outperformance on an absolute and risk-adjusted basis.

II. Portfolio outperformance on an absolute basis and *underperformance on a risk-adjusted basis.*

III. Portfolio underperformance on an absolute and risk-adjusted basis.

IV. Portfolio underperformance on an absolute basis and *outperformance on a risk-adjusted basis.*

This paradigm has been extended by Muralidhar (2000) (refer to Chapter 3). It shows that the performance of asset managers can be normalized for differences in correlations to the benchmark as well. The revised paradigm (M³ or M-cube) creates correlation-adjusted portfolios (CAPs): these combine the optimal mix of active managers, the market benchmark, and risk-free assets (Three-Fund Separation) to ensure that not only is the standard deviation of CAP equal to the standard deviation of the benchmark, but also the correlation of CAP is equal to some target (which is uniquely selected, based on the relative risk budget). The second condition is needed to ensure that all CAPs have the same target tracking error (or relative risk), derived with identical standard deviations and correlations. A shortcoming of these measures is that they do not take the length of track record into consideration, i.e., they ignore the time factor.

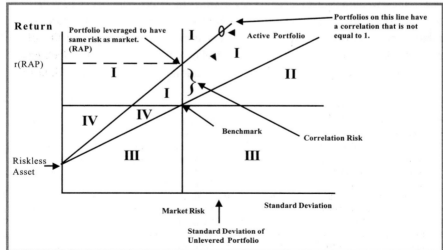

Figure 2.2. The Modigliani-Modigliani risk adjustment.

To resolve the Luck versus Skill question, time and the degree of confidence are critical factors, as are the returns, standard deviations of the portfolios and the benchmark, and the degree of correlation between the two. The problem is that performance data can contain considerable noise, and the more volatile the portfolio and a manager's excess return series, the greater the noise, and hence the more the time needed to resolve this issue. Ambarish and Siegel (1996) suggest that even a 300-basis point outperformance may require 175 years of data to claim, with 84 percent confidence, that the manager is skillful. The Ambarish and Siegel (1996) approach is specified in greater detail in Appendix 2.1. However, a noteworthy result is that when the portfolio's standard deviation is set equal to the benchmark's standard deviation, as in the RAP, for a given standard deviation of the benchmark and degree of confidence, the time required becomes a simple function of the correlation parameter – the lower the correlation, the more the time required. Moreover, as shown in Muralidhar (2000), once the correlation adjustment is made, the rankings based on the M^3 are identical to those made on the basis of skill for an equivalent length of track record. Hence, Muralidhar (2002) – summarized in Chapter 3 – extends this paradigm to show how agents with different lengths of track record can be compared to one another by incorporating their full track record, thereby bringing time into the equation. However, the potential flaw in Muralidhar (2002) is that it assumes a unique (and conceptually unspecified) objective function, thereby making it less than perfect for a general result.

However, these propositions pose a conundrum: the Modigliani adjustment suggests that managers can get more risk-adjusted outperformance by lowering the correlation; the Luck versus Skill measure says that those actions will either lower the confidence in the manager's skill or extend the time period under evaluation. However, it is critical that the correlation measure is an important part of the portfolio selection process and not a parameter that is blindly folded into a beta measure. Hence, the confidence in skill for two portfolios with identical betas but very different correlations is not the same. Chapter 7 demonstrates the implications of this result for optimal risk budgeting.

Let us illustrate this with a simple example: Interestingly, for a given relative risk, many portfolios can be created with different betas, the portfolio with the highest beta being the one that inspired the most confidence in skill (assuming identical length of track record and excess returns). Conversely, even for the same beta, a principal is not indifferent when faced with the choice of two identical betas. Consider two portfolios with identical betas: (i) correlation of 1, portfolio volatility of 12 percent, and benchmark volatility of 10 percent gives a beta of 1.20; and (ii) correlation of 0.985294, portfolio volatility of 8.5 percent, and benchmark volatility of 7 percent also gives a beta of 1.20. Both have identical tracking errors (2 percent), excess returns and length of track records (2 years), but confidence in skill in the first case (88.81 percent) is higher than in the second case (87.35 percent).[40] Clearly, a principal with a limited time frame to evaluate these two portfolios would prefer the first portfolio, even though the excess returns and betas are identical, whereas a principal with a very long time horizon or managing assets themselves might be indifferent to one portfolio versus the other. This analysis would seem to be a violation of the CAPM, but from a relative perspective, it appears quite reasonable. For a CAPM purist, the risk-free rate is a Treasury security; for a relative theory believer and practitioner, the risk-free rate is the benchmark, whether it is the S&P 500 or the JP Morgan Bond Index. Therefore, from a theoretical point of view, some measure of correlation will have to be included in the "optimal fee contract", as it becomes a gauge of the fund manager's skill (see also Chapter 7). The M^3 measure of Muralidhar (2000) starts to align these issues more accurately by normalizing for correlations and obtaining rankings that are identical to those based on confidence in skill, but stops short of asking the more fundamental question: what is the implication for asset pricing when agents start to behave in this way?

THE PARTIAL SOLUTION – ISO-CONFIDENCE CURVES (IGNORING TIME)

To keep the analysis simple, the time factor is ignored (even though this is incorrect) which adds a fourth dimension without necessarily helping to clarify how assets are valued and optimal portfolios selected in the Three-Fund Separation Theorem. As indicated above, the formulae for confidence in skill can be used to create iso-confidence curves – i.e., combinations of returns of a portfolio relative to a benchmark, volatility of a portfolio relative to a benchmark, and correlations that give the same confidence in skill, as specified in Ambarish and Siegel (1996) and enhanced in Muralidhar and U (1997) and Muralidhar (2001).

The relative return objective function is repeated here:

$$\text{Maximize } E[r_a - r_b] - \pi * \sigma_{(a-b)}^2, \tag{2.3}$$

where $E[*]$ is the expectations operator, r_a is the return of the portfolio and r_b is the return of the benchmark, π denotes a measure of the investor's risk aversion, and $\sigma_{(a-b)}$, the portfolio's tracking error.

The three-dimensional iso-confidence curves are plotted in Figure 2.3 for a hypothetical market portfolio with an expected standard deviation of 10 percent. For simplicity, the iso-confidence curve is plotted in decrements of 5 percent, starting with 95 percent and assuming that the excess annualized return is 1.5 percent, and

---

[40]   Muralidhar (2009b). Note that it is not possible to have the same beta for the same benchmark volatility.

even then the chart is not pretty. As with typical economic theory, this iso-confidence curve can be seen as the budget constraint for agents. If we now superimpose the principal's objective function, as in equation (2.3), but with the caveat that they do not want their relative risk to exceed 3 percent, as every good principal should budget risk optimally (Chapter 7), a utility curve can be drawn in 3-D space of excess return, volatility of the portfolio, and correlation (or four-dimensional space with the addition of time). If the principal adds the additional condition à la M^2 that the portfolio cannot have volatility different from that of the benchmark, then a unique portfolio is selected.

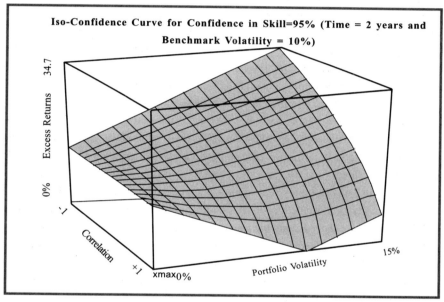

Figure 2.3. The Capital Relative Asset Pricing Model – Iso-confidence curves.

CHALLENGES FOR ACADEMIA – DEVELOP NEW PARADIGM

Investors have typically proceeded on the faith that a market portfolio exists. Academia will need to help isolate such market portfolios with a more general equilibrium theory of asset pricing. However, assuming that the principal-selected benchmark is the market portfolio, then – given different objective functions and absolute risk aversions (i.e., different π) and different target risk budgets composed for choice of confidence in skill – the optimal mixes of the risk-free asset and benchmark will be chosen by different investors (and hence a three-dimensional Relative Capital Market Line).

SUMMARY

One of the most common assumptions of investment benchmark studies (also known as asset-liability studies) is that the CAPM framework drives the returns of asset classes. In essence, institutions make investment policy decisions at a strategic and tactical level, assuming that the returns on asset class benchmarks are determined independent of their actions. Individually, this may be true but, in aggregate, asset markets are clearly affected. For example, the increasing selection of a particular benchmark will potentially lower benchmark returns; and further, the relative risk permitted by principals will have an impact on returns on assets over time, subject to how they co-vary with these benchmarks. This is important, as it has the potential to skew the price of assets that people choose and also those that are excluded from such benchmarks. The issue of benchmark selection is addressed in Chapter 3, which examines benchmarks from the perspective of efficiency, ease of implementation, market completeness, and cost.

However, academic theory and empirical results increasingly seem to lean towards assuming that returns are affected by the behavior of principals and agents; and the challenge will be to determine a comprehensive asset pricing theory that captures the inter-relatedness of action and valuation of assets (and potentially, the optimal contracts between principals and agents – specified in Chapter 7). It would be interesting to see if, as in the physical sciences, a relative theory can be determined, where the absolute theory along the lines of Markowitz (1959) is just a stylized case of the relative theory. This would lead to different valuation measures, based on the nature of aggregate principal-agent relationships. *What this clearly shows is that earlier studies of SAA, Optimal Portfolios, etc. are flawed, as proved by the economic meltdown of 2008.*

The trick will be to establish what constitutes a risk-free asset as well as include a dimension of the correlation of assets/portfolios to investment benchmarks to capture not only risk adjustment but also an element of measuring skill. Therefore, the correlation term will gain more importance than is currently assigned to it by the pure CAPM framework (as a subordinated element of the beta), and it will be the focus of more attention in any new relative asset valuation paradigm. This is developed in greater detail in Chapter 4 where the lack of correlation between two assets is shown to have implications for the dynamic management of assets. The above discussion suggests that the new paradigm is on the cusp of being developed, as the individual pieces have already been devised, and the challenge now is to assemble it all in a consolidated framework. Though this may not signal the death of CAPM, it would certainly be a reincarnation in a different frame of reference, sending out a call to CIOs to be careful how they manage assets and possibly move to a less predictive approach to asset allocation and a more dynamic factor-based approach to relative allocation (see Chapters 5, 6, and 8).

APPENDIX 2.1   The Luck versus Skill Formulation

Outperformance over a benchmark unfortunately does not tell the investor whether the external manager or the mutual fund manager is skillful. Nor does it provide the investor with a measure of confidence that they can have the alpha generated by skill-based processes. Critical factors involved in answering the Luck versus Skill question include time, the desired degree of confidence, the investment returns of the portfolio and the benchmark, the standard deviation of the portfolio and the benchmark, and the degree of correlation between the two. The problem is that considerable noise is inherent in performance data, and the more volatile the portfolio and a manager's excess return series, the greater the noise, and hence the more the time needed to resolve the issue. Ambarish and Siegel (1996) demonstrate that the minimum number of data points, or time horizon *H*, should be large enough for skill to emerge from the noise or, equivalently,

$$H > \frac{S^2(\sigma_1^2 - 2\rho\sigma_1\sigma_B + \sigma_B^2)}{\left[\left(r(1) - \frac{\sigma_1^2}{2}\right) - \left(r(B) - \frac{\sigma_B^2}{2}\right)\right]^2}, \tag{A.2.1}$$

where 1 is the manager, *B* the benchmark, *r* the return, σ denotes the standard deviation, $\rho_{1,B}$ the correlation of returns between the manager and the benchmark, and *S* is the number of standard deviations for a given confidence level. Their resolution appears theoretically more appropriate and simpler than statistical process control alternatives such as Philips and Yashchin (1999).[41]

If the tracking error *TE* of portfolio 1 versus the benchmark is defined as the standard deviation of excess returns, it is trivial to define *TE*(1) as follows:

$$TE(1) = \sqrt{(\sigma_1^2 - 2\rho\sigma_1\sigma_B + \sigma_B^2)}. \tag{A.2.2}$$

Note: The second term in the numerator of the confidence-in-skill calculation, or equation (A.2.1), is the same as the square of the *TE* of portfolio 1 versus the benchmark.

Equation (A.2.1) suggests that even a 300-basis point outperformance may require 175 years of data to claim, with 84 percent confidence, that the manager is

---

[41]   One of the problems of Philips and Yashchin (1999) is that the user is required to specify an Information Ratio above which funds would be rated good. The technique employed here requires no such classification.

skillful.[42] Muralidhar and U (1997) and Muralidhar (1999) recognize that H is often given by performance history, and therefore solve for the degree of confidence S instead.

Equation (A.2.1) makes it clear that the confidence-in-skill calculation is intricately linked to the Information Ratio (IR). The annualized IR is equal to the annualized excess return divided by the annualized TE or:

$$IR(1) = [r(1) - r(B)]/TE(1). \tag{A.2.3}$$

As a result, and using (A.2.2) and (A.2.3), equation (A.2.1) can be rewritten in terms of S, where S is a function of IR:

$$S < \sqrt{H}\left[IR(1) - \left(\frac{\sigma^2_1 - \sigma^2_B}{2TE(1)} \right) \right]. \tag{A.2.4}$$

The confidence in skill is derived from converting S to percentage terms for a normal distribution or the cumulative probability of a unit normal with a standard deviation of S ($C(S_1)$), and this will be the measure of the confidence in skill. This measure will lie between 0 percent and 100 percent, and hence acts as a probability measure. For example, when S is equal to 1, then $C(S) = 84$ percent. Also, when the

second term in equation (A.2.4), i.e., $\left[\left(\dfrac{\sigma_1 - \sigma_B}{2TE(1)} \right) \right]$ is generally small or

insignificant, the IR and the length of data history will largely determine the confidence in skill. This is the case when the tracking error is substantial and driven largely by a low correlation between the portfolio and the benchmark (i.e., $\sigma_i \cong \sigma_b$). As a result, two portfolios with identical variances, information ratios, and tracking errors but different in lengths of history will have a different confidence in skill - longer the history, greater the confidence.

---

[42] This result is from outperformance engendered through 13.2 percent basis points of tracking error, where the benchmark standard deviation is 15 percent, the actual standard deviation is 25 percent, and the correlation between the two is 0.9.

3

New Approach to Passive Management and Risk-adjusted Performance

"We had to add a third dimension: the time dimension...If you don't add time, you'll find nothing." Zhichun Jing, Chinese archaeologist[43]

BACKGROUND

The fund management industry has underscored the importance of asset returns to the extent of exalting CIOs who generate the highest returns in peer rankings, and dismissing those who bring up the rear. This emphasis is wrong on many levels.

1.   For a typical CIO, assuming a liability needs to be serviced or some asset return goal has to be achieved, the true measure is not absolute asset returns, but rather return relative to liability. Therefore, best asset performance, where liability returns may be twice as high, should not have a high ranking. The best absolute performance may be small consolation, but the media typically overlooks such discomfiting data.

2.   All costs must be subtracted from returns, as the industry mistakenly tends to assume that the benchmark can be reproduced free of cost. In fact, a true assessment of a CIO's skill should be calculated after deducting cost. (Appropriate benchmarks are discussed later.)

3.   Since risk affects returns, it is critical to ensure whether the risk measure is absolute or relative, and adjustment is made for risk.

4.   Current evaluations neglect illiquidity in investments; and, ideally, cost- and risk-adjusted relative returns must be further adjusted for illiquidity. This was most evident in 2008, when the stars of the previous decade were struck by the unforeseen lack of liquidity, sending CIOs into panic and desperately liquidating assets to generate requisite cash.[44]

---

[43]   *National Geographic*, July 2003.

[44]   The traditional growth of continuously compounded asset returns $g = \mu - \frac{\sigma}{2}$ (where μ is the asset's expected rate of return and σ is the standard deviation of returns. Note that funds that are infrequently marked-to-market (private equity, hedge funds, etc.) may appear to have high growth, but also have high risk of collapse because of illiquidity. Hence, a more appropriate formula must read $g = \mu - \frac{\sigma}{2} - [L(t)]^n$, or an exponential adjustment from when an illiquid investment last blew up – the greater the time, the greater the likelihood and size of collapse, unless it is miraculously converted into a liquid asset.

5.   Time is of the essence - one period's good performance is rendered
     insignificant, given the noise in performance data. Hence, a realistic ranking
     of CIOs should consider the entire history of performance (and
     commensurate risk), and an analysis of skill.

Most peer comparisons are inconsequential, as most often they compare apples
to oranges (two large funds are compared, based on similar AUM without regard to
liabilities and objectives). Moreover, the information content (with regard to
outperformance due to skill) is questionable. Muralidhar and U (1997) substantiate
the conclusion that peer rankings using short data histories have minimal information
content and are probably just noise.

THE "SMART" APPROACH

Key return measures: Return relative to liabilities (or solvency return)

At the highest level, CIOs must track annualized growth in the surplus (defined
as the difference between the annualized return on assets minus the annualized
return on liabilities), on an intra-year basis (even daily). *This is the true measure of
return for pension funds, and one can make a similar case for insurance companies;
endowments and sovereign wealth funds would be benchmarked to some spending
policy or the achievement of some social goal that has a target rate of return.* In an
ideal world, where a pension fund starts with 100 percent solvency (i.e., an asset-to-
liability ratio of 100 percent), total immunization of the liabilities may be feasible as
long as the asset returns equal liability returns, otherwise the result is an insufficient
hedge, as opposed to a "Japanese hedge". When solvency is less than 100 percent,
or when the pension fund seeks to increase the buffer on solvency, then asset
returns must exceed liability returns, but this incurs risk.

Cost-adjusted returns

Typically, CIOs are benchmarked to SAAs that include allocations to various
asset classes that are not easily and/or costlessly replicated, while the benchmark
assumes constant, costless rebalancing. Therefore, the liability should be replicated
with an easy-to-track, "costlessly" rebalanced portfolio of financial assets; and
more important, the assets in the SAA should be chosen so they broadly represent
the market, and can also be traded in futures markets (as this is the lowest cost,
most efficient way to gain transparent asset class exposure with minimal credit
risk)[45], as addressed below.

---

[45]   Muralidhar (2001), Appendix to Chapter 6, argued for such indices. Japanese investors suffer
       from the same problem with respect to the Nomura BPI local bond index.

Risk-adjusted returns

Typical risk measures for solvency should include:

(i)   Measures that relate to volatility of the surplus (i.e., the tracking error of the excess between assets and liabilities);

(ii)   Drawdowns of the surplus, as this could lead to a contribution event; and

(iii)   Semi-moments (downside deviation, ratio of good/bad risk).

Ideally, a Board should articulate a risk budget relative to the liabilities they delegate to the CIO, as this can help in assessing the probability of meeting some solvency target over given time horizons. In addition, one may use the same procedures highlighted below for risk-adjustment in the asset-only space.

The asset-only framework of hiring and evaluating internal staff or external managers should use the M^3 risk-adjusted performance measure. Chapter 2 has already covered the M^2 measure, but in the principal-agent space, M^3 is the appropriate risk-adjusted performance measure, as it adjusts for all the risks and also provides guidance on optimal portfolio construction across cash (leverage), beta assets (the benchmark), and alpha (external manager). The calculation of risk-adjusted returns (3.1) highlights the key function of this measure, and Appendix 3.1 gives a more detailed solution with some background on various risk-adjusted measures, and then demonstrates how M^3 is calculated and how it eclipses other measures.[46]

Consider $r(CAP)$ for external fund manager 1:

$$r(CAP\text{-}1) = a*r(1)+(1\text{-}a\text{-}b)*r(F)+b*r(B), \qquad (3.1)$$

where $r(CAP)$ is the M^3 risk-adjusted portfolio return, F is the risk-free rate, and B is the benchmark.[47] Investors select a and b, such that

$$\sigma^2_{CAP-1} = \sigma^2_B \qquad (3.2)$$

and

$$TE(CAP) = TE(\text{target}). \qquad (3.3)$$

---

[46]   See Muralidhar (2000), (2001), on the Skill, History, and Risk-Adjusted (SHARAD) measure.
[47]   The terms "benchmark" and "market portfolio" are used interchangeably.

The solution for a and b, as described in Appendix 3.1, is:

$$a = +\sqrt{\frac{\sigma_B^2(1-\rho_{T,B}^2)}{\sigma_1^2(1-\rho_{1,B}^2)}} = \frac{\sigma_B}{\sigma_1}\sqrt{\frac{(1-\rho_{T,B}^2)}{(1-\rho_{1,B}^2)}} \qquad (3.4)$$

$$b = \rho_{T,B} - \rho_{1,B}\sqrt{\frac{(1-\rho_{T,B}^2)}{(1-\rho_{1,B}^2)}}. \qquad (3.5)$$

Adjusted for Skill and History (Time)

Traditionally, when a pension fund manager has to choose between two external managers - one with a seven-year track record and another with a five-year track record - if both managers generate similar returns per unit of risk, the bias has been to hire the one with more experience. But this tendency does not account for the fact that, typically, risk and return numbers, and longevity of experience, are wildly different, thereby blurring the right decision. For example, is the manager with the longer track record preferred to the one with less experience despite a lower annualized excess return over the benchmark? Generally, the selection favors the manager with the higher excess return, regardless of the length of their track record. Investment managers encounter a similar problem when they have to choose between competing investment strategies, where often the availability of data (or lack thereof) determines the period over which rules can be tested. Placed in such a quandary, investors often consider dropping "excess data" to make an "apples-to-apples" comparison, but a decision that disregards available data is flawed, as it penalizes the manager or strategy with the longer track record.

A new measure, the SHARAD (Skill, History, and Risk-adjusted performance), which is the product of the confidence in skill and M^3, resolves this issue.[48] It exploits the fact that "$C(S)$" is a probability measure (equation A.2.4) dependent on the time horizon of the data series, and that the M^3 measure provides appropriate risk adjustment, guidance on portfolio construction, and expresses risk-adjusted performance in basis points. As a result, the SHARAD measure, by definition, is a probability-adjusted performance measure (or an expected risk-adjusted measure) for an active strategy 1 with a given tracking error budget, as:

$$\text{SHARAD}(1) = C(S_1) * r(\text{CAP-1}). \qquad (3.6)$$

The "S" measure relates to the confidence that the CAP returns are skill-based (as opposed to using raw returns), and $C(S_1)$ is the cumulative probability of a unit

---

[48]   Muralidhar (2001).

normal with the standard deviation of *S*. This revised measure has all the attractive properties of M^3, yet it accounts for time through the $C(S)$ term, consistent with the evaluation of skill.[49] For managers with identical data histories, this adjustment does not impact their rankings, but different data histories yield interesting results, as shown in Muralidhar (2000)

From the various risk-adjusted performance measures, let us now turn our attention to the choice of benchmarks, as performance measures can be effectively used only if the benchmarks are transparent, easily monitored and managed, and available at low cost.

THE CASE FOR AN INVESTIBLE LIABILITY PORTFOLIO

The principal challenge in developing an optimal policy for managing the assets-to-liabilities ratio (called the funded ratio) has more to do with understanding liabilities than developing innovative investment policies. To explore how innovative investment policies can be used to ensure that the funded ratio grows over time, it is important to first develop a simple process by which liabilities can be understood and monitored on an intra-year basis. Moreover, performance statistics used to manage pension funds need to be changed from asset returns to solvency measures, and the evaluation of asset managers needs to shift from excess returns over benchmarks and information ratios to M^2 and M^3 risk-adjusted performance.[50]

The renewed interest in asset-liability matching is mainly due to the rapid decline in interest rates, which has led to an increase in most pension fund liabilities on a mark-to-market basis. Unfortunately for most pension funds, the decline in rates coincided with a downturn in many stock markets as well as in the performance of hedge funds and private equity investments. The simultaneous decline in the value of assets and increase in the value of liabilities led to a dramatic drop in the ratio of assets to liabilities – which occurred previously in 2000, with a complete reversal of the technology boom. The asset-liability ratio is often what regulators, CFOs, and members of pension funds consider when assessing whether a pension plan is "safe" or solvent. Further, new accounting standards imply that pension fund losses can affect the corporate pension fund sponsor. As a result, many pension plans worldwide are adjusting their investment and hedging strategies to reduce the impact of a declining and volatile funded ratio.

Pension funds often find it difficult to elucidate to their asset managers the desired approach and implementation of LDI strategies, which would enable the

---

[49] For the sake of argument, *S* is an equality rather than an inequality, and the rankings need not be identical with skill rankings, as shown later.

[50] Thanks to David Deutsch for this point.

managers to design optimal products. In an industry that lacks innovative products, the CIO has to be a key innovator. The main problem that pension fund managers encounter is in setting an appropriate investible benchmark that reflects the liabilities.

The liability is the projected pension cash flow that needs to be serviced and hence is the basis for all investment decisions. In other words, the investment plan needs to be designed to meet the objective of servicing liabilities, at the lowest possible cost and with minimal contribution volatility.[51] Several recommendations have been published to protect pension fund solvency through the immunization of liabilities. These recommendations range from the approach of the Boots Pension fund, which converted the entire portfolio of assets into fixed income assets (since revised to include a small allocation to non-fixed income assets), to completely abandoning the strategic asset allocation policy in favor of a totally tactical policy, to duration extension combined with 'portable alpha'.

TRADITIONAL APPROACH

The traditional approach includes a simple simulation from the actuaries, whose output is often no more than a series of quasi-deterministic, once-a-year cash flow estimates. Figure 3.1 charts a typical projected cash flow for a European pension

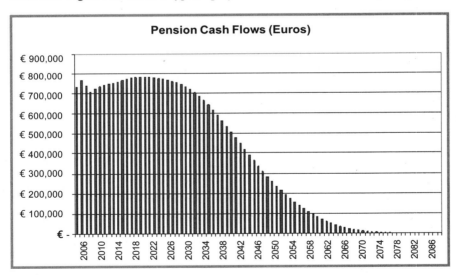

Figure 3.1. Typical projected pension fund cash flow.

---

[51]   The author thanks David Deutsch for this clarification. Cost can be viewed from two perspectives: (i) the lowest possible contribution rate; and (ii) the lowest cost of managing the investment operation. Both perspectives are used here.

fund.[52] The hump-shaped profile is common across all major developed countries, indicating the aging population.

Typically, these simple cash flow projections are introduced into an ALM model, in an attempt to develop an SAA to reduce ALM risks. Pension funds (i.e., CIOs and the Boards) deal with many issues vis-à-vis these projections. The simplest criticism is attributed to Mulvey (1994), who highlights that the use of deterministic projections of liabilities is incorrect, as liabilities are influenced by various inflation and interest-rate projections. However, the bigger questions, as highlighted in Muralidhar and van Stuijvenberg (2006), are:

- How should assets be managed against this set of cash flows? To effectively manage a pension fund, one needs to measure and monitor these nominal liabilities.
- How does one measure and monitor liabilities relevant to investment decisions that have to be made? Previously, an annual assessment was sufficient, but in today's world a more frequent valuation is needed, especially if the funding ratio is to be managed effectively on an intra-year basis.
- How does one deal with the challenge of such a schedule, namely, the challenge of translating the above cash flows into quoted market instruments? Though the standard approach for developing a benchmark is relatively simple (see below), it is more difficult to implement in practice, compelling managers to either accept a high tracking error or incur very costly implementation.

Figure 3.1 presents a typical example of projected pension benefit cash flows from actuaries. For ease of explanation, the analysis is restricted to nominal liabilities. Effectively, future cash flows are nothing but a zero coupon bond with a given maturity. From this viewpoint, the manager needs to invest in such bonds in the appropriate notional amount. For example, if the estimated cash flow due in 2016 is € 750,000, then the manager needs to find a zero coupon bond with that maturity and invest the relevant amount to earn an equal payout. Today, the relevant invested amount to achieve such a payout in December 2016 would be determined by the zero coupon bond rate for that maturity.

Using the cash flows charted in Figure 3.1, and logged in Table 3.1, one can conclude that the present value of liabilities is € 15 billion, with a duration of 15.14 years. However, the snag in this approach is that such pure instruments do not exist; hence, either a theoretical zero coupon portfolio is constructed but not implemented, or an alternative portfolio needs to be constructed from a zero coupon

---

[52]   Thanks to Roland van den Brink of Bedrijfstakpensioenfonds Metalektro in the Netherlands (PME) for this data.

as well as coupon-bearing bonds (or by boot-strapping the zero coupon curve implied by these bonds).

It is not difficult to construct such a portfolio for any set of liability cash flows from the universe of government bonds in any market, although inter/extrapolation techniques would have to be used for 30+ year cash flows. The theoretical bond portfolio can be marked-to-market daily, thereby giving clients an effective estimate of their intra-year liability performance. The difficulty is, with many cash flows, over multiple years and moderate amounts, the traditional liability benchmark involves small allocations to multiple securities, making the benchmark unwieldy and therefore difficult for the average board member. Managing a tailor-made portfolio of 50 zeros does not seem to exceed current computing power. The crucial drawback is that the zero coupon bond approach does not lead to clean, transparent pricing and would also be costly to implement. Furthermore, the obtained benchmark, relying on the valuation of (zero coupon) bonds, may contain a credit spread element (there being no unique Euro zone government yield curve, because different issuers have marginally different credit qualities) and hence are less objective than standard benchmarks.[53]

INNOVATIVE APPROACH

A simple, stable, and accurate benchmark mimics liabilities based on daily available swap indices,[54] and the work done at the PME Pension Fund is used to make the case. The only input needed is the projected annual liability cash flows. For the issues highlighted above, PME adopted a different approach from the zero coupon approach, instead using the most liquid fixed income markets instruments: swaps. The pricing benchmark of the Euro market is the swap curve and therefore the best starting point for index construction. The plain vanilla (coupon-bearing) interest rate swaps market offers excellent benchmarks. For instance, each of the Lehman/Barclays Bellwether indices has long track records. If the above cash flows could be replicated by using a set of these indices, an objective, investible benchmark can be achieved. Under the swap method, an optimization technique is used to determine optimal weights to a portfolio of Lehman/Barclays indices, such that the swap portfolio mimics the performance of liabilities. In such a situation, a chosen set of indices is used to find an optimal mix and, typically, the swaps are standard, plain vanilla coupon-bearing with maturities of one-year, two-year, five-year, 10-year, and

---

[53]   Tim Barrett raises an interesting idea - break out liability into two components - retired and active - and manage the pools accordingly. This paradigm applies to all the concepts presented in the following pages.

[54]   Previously offered by Lehman Brothers, and now offered by Barclays. Similar indices can be constructed for the U.S. and other developed market clients.

20-year. To determine the weight of each Lehman index in the liability benchmark, one simply needs to use historical yield curve data and find the portfolio that gives sufficiently low tracking error relative to the valuation of liabilities. In the case of the pension cash flows modeled in Figure 3.1, optimal weights to the various indices are as shown in Table 3.1.

TABLE 3.1 Modeling liabilities as a portfolio of swaps

Instrument	Optimal Weights	Optimal Notional
012M SWAP	-6.29%	-€ 946,585,328
024M SWAP	7.82%	€ 1,176,410,795
060M SWAP	3.55%	€ 534.557.087
120M SWAP	16.50%	€ 2,496,188,497
240M SWAP	23.10%	€ 3,473,746,096
360M SWAP	27.29%	€ 4,103,839,938
480M SWAP	18.98%	€ 2,854,444,211
600M SWAP	6.92%	€ 1,041,095,121

Daily Tracking Error	0.019%
Tracking Error Annualized	0.303%
R-Squared	99.83%

Duration Liabilities	15.14
Duration Mimic Portfolio	15.00

This simple portfolio of some key liquid instruments is more likely to be accepted by a Board. The portfolio of swap indices has an annualized tracking error of 0.30 percent relative to liabilities over the historical simulation period. An alternative check is to compare durations of both portfolios – and, as shown in Table 3.1, there is minimal difference. It may be argued that it is better to optimize weights over some future simulations, using a Monte Carlo technique, but such a proposal alters only the method, not the approach to estimating an appropriate liability benchmark.

A few other caveats require mention. Sometimes, such an optimization can provide negative weights to certain swap maturities (e.g., the 12-month/one-year recommended allocation), which sophisticated clients can see is either a short position or a forward starting swap. Another issue with portfolios using swap indices is that they include credit risk; hence, as in the recent market meltdown, credit spreads can widen, with the unintended consequence of making the current value of liabilities appear lower than they are in reality. The 15+ year discount rate (inclusive of a credit spread) in the accounting treatment of liabilities in the United States led to a substantial reduction in "estimated" liabilities, because credit spreads "blew out" during the 2008 crisis. The economic liability remained unchanged, but the accounting liability was dramatically reduced. Such constraints notwithstanding, the annualized growth in the surplus can now be tracked, on an intra-year (or even daily) basis, as the difference between annualized return on assets minus annualized return on liabilities. *This is the true return measure for pension funds, and risk measures must relate to the volatility, drawdown, and semi-moments of this yardstick.* [55]

An additional benefit of using the swap-based approach embedded in the ILP is that negligible capital is required to hedge liabilities. Many pension funds mandate setting aside capital for hedging liabilities (through fixed-income investments) or return generation (through equity or alternative investments). Then, because fund managers suspect the imposition of a leverage constraint (i.e., the weights allocated to these instruments have to add up to 100 percent), they react as if the objectives were beset with contradictions. Of course, this is not the case. The real concern should be overall funding risk. The ability to effectively hedge liabilities with derivatives is an attractive proposition that frees up capital to generate returns. Leverage for risk reduction is not as insidious as the reputation it has earned because of bad decisions by asset managers.

This section demonstrates how innovative pension plans can convert actuarial projections of pension benefits into an appropriate investible benchmark, allowing plan sponsors a better measure of performance of liabilities (and assets) on an intra-year basis and a transparent, simple index that can be tracked by the Board. This ILP is used in Chapters 5, 6, and 8 to demonstrate effective implementation of LDI strategies. In addition, it highlights new solvency performance and risk measures, with the goal of designing strategies to ensure effective achievement of these objectives within tolerable levels of risk measures. Now the discussion shifts to how beta assets should be selected, followed by a discussion on how they should be managed effectively (Chapters 4 and 6).

CREATING EFFECTIVE, LIQUID, LOW-COST, TRANSPARENT ASSET BENCHMARKS

Muralidhar (2001) treated low-cost benchmarks tangentially, appending the discussion to a chapter on the effective use of derivatives in managing pension funds. However, the recent market turmoil underscores that this issue is probably more critical than the SAA itself, as poorly chosen benchmarks cause CIOs to take unintended tracking error, preventing dynamic managing and hedging of beta.

---

[55] This is explained in more detail in Muralidhar (2001), Chapter 4.

The most pressing problem that irked pension fund managers worldwide is that the indices used in the SAA, to which they were benchmarked, were not easy to replicate by using futures. For example, Lehman/Barclays Aggregate, MSCI World, MSCI Kokusai, Nomura BPI, etc. are common benchmarks, but they generate unnecessary tracking error in replication through futures, making it problematic for pension funds to make low-cost, effective shifts if assets were not favored temporarily or if the View-Neutral, rebalancing shifts had to be made periodically.[56] The rationale for benchmarking to more complex indices was that most investment managers used these standard benchmarks to manage assets, and these indices cover the broader investment spectrum of sectors.

Smart pension funds should use only indices based on liquid futures, as these capture broad asset class performance and volatility (typically modeled in ALM studies). Though such a practice may exclude certain market segments, such as credit in bond indices today, this tendency is attributed more to badly-designed market instruments than to an inability to provide this product. It may be confidently assumed that investment banks would be ever-willing to create a futures-based index on credit if it were requested by CalPERS, CalSTRS, and other major corporate pension funds. This has not been the case, however, leaving the field clear for investment banks to absorb profit from creating exposure through illiquid, over-the-counter swaps. On the other hand, the existence of an S&P 500 equity index, and even an MSCI EAFE and MSCI Emerging market futures index, demonstrates that it is trivial for banks to create a futures contract on the Lehman/Barclays Aggregate Index or the Citigroup World Government Bond Index. It is time that CIOs request such products, and that banks become more proactive in providing what institutions need, instead of capturing disproportionate rents by exploiting an incomplete market.

It is obvious that the performance of these futures-based indices is not biased in any way towards underperforming regular indices on an *ex-ante* or *ex-post* basis. Table 3.2 provides basic statistics on a futures-based index for international investments (i.e., composed of a weighted average of multiple country equity benchmarks) and compares it to the actual performance of the MSCI EAFE cash index. The latter is a typical index used by U.S. pension funds to benchmark international investments. Clearly, these indices are virtually indistinguishable from one another, but the futures index composite (i) is more liquid than an MSCI or alternative vendor-based index; (ii) is based on the primary equity indices traded in every country; (iii) has maximum transparency and visibility; and (iv) has the lowest cost to trade.

---

[56] See Muralidhar (2001), Chapter 6, Appendix.

With liquid indices represented in the SAA, and liabilities captured as a portfolio of swaps, an increase in the correlation of assets to liabilities through dynamic management of the SAA and liability hedging becomes much easier to implement. Now, liabilities are hedged when it is optimal to do so (Chapters 5 and 6), and many more decisions are available to manage the funds (i.e., all the rebalancing in the SAA), as shown in Chapter 7.

The variety of liquid benchmarks makes the actual implementation of transactions extremely cost-effective, and it can be easily delegated to a futures/derivatives execution agent. Chapter 9 demonstrates the use of futures to replicate broad asset class exposure and thereby shows how a simple change in implementation can save participants in DC plans as much as 50 basis points annually – a significant saving that leads to a much higher pension.

TABLE 3.2 Monthly statistics for MSCI EAFE and a futures-replicating basket (06/00- 02/09)[57]

	EAFE Futures Basket	EAFE USD (BMK)	Futures Basket - BMK
Mean	-0.29%	-0.36%	0.065%
Standard Error	0.49%	0.50%	-0.011%
Median	0.60%	0.41%	0.194%
Standard Deviation	5.03%	5.15%	0.111%
Sample Variance	0.25%	0.26%	-0.011%
Kurtosis	1.72	1.81	-0.10
Skewness	-0.85	-0.97	0.12
Range	31.86%	31.92%	-0.059%
Minimum	-20.15%	-21.00%	0.858%
Maximum	11.72%	10.92%	0.798%
Count	106	106	

---

[57] Thanks to Brian Baker for this table.

SUMMARY

This chapter has shown how the focus on asset returns masks both the key norm of a CIO's performance and the ineffectiveness of peer comparisons. It also highlighted the method for calculating risk-adjusted (M^2 and M^3) and skill-adjusted (SHARAD) performance. Finally, the discussion presented a new approach to benchmarking and monitoring of assets and liabilities – an approach that uses futures and swaps. Once assets and liabilities are replicated by these liquid instruments, CIOs can easily and effectively (at low cost) implement the desired change in portfolio. Clear, liquid, transparent benchmarks, and clearly articulated solvency goals and risk measures empower the CIO to manage the fund in the most effective manner. Subsequent chapters demonstrate how SMART management of assets and liabilities improves solvency and lowers ALM risk.

APPENDIX 3.1 Risk-adjusted Performance

Practitioners and academics recognize it is meaningless not to adjust performance for risk. Of the various risk measures used to adjust performance, the two most commonly used measures are the Sharpe ratio and the Information Ratio (also known as the differential Sharpe ratio).[58] Newer variations of these measures have been proposed. This appendix develops and evaluates a series of inter-related measures.

SHARPE RATIO AND INFORMATION RATIO

The Sharpe ratio effectively adjusts performance above the risk-free rate by the volatility of excess returns (where excess return is the portfolio return minus the risk-free rate). The Information Ratio (A.2.3) is a variation of the Sharpe, and it adjusts the excess of benchmark performance by the volatility of the excess return series. Logue and Rader (1997) suggest that the Sharpe ratio is the best way to adjust for risk.

THE M² MEASURE

Modigliani and Modigliani (1997) make an important contribution by showing that the portfolio and the benchmark must have the same risk for a comparison in terms of basis points of risk-adjusted performance. They propose that the portfolio should be leveraged or deleveraged, using the risk-free asset. If B is the benchmark being compared to portfolio 1, the leverage factor d is defined as follows:

---

[58] Sharpe (1994).

$$d = \sigma_B/\sigma_1 . \tag{A.3.1}$$

This creates a new portfolio, called the risk-adjusted portfolio (RAP), whose return $r(RAP)$ is equal to the leverage factor multiplied by the original return plus 1, minus the leverage factor multiplied by the risk-free rate. Thus, if portfolio F is the riskless asset with zero standard deviation and is uncorrelated with other portfolios, the risk-adjusted return is:

$$r(RAP) = d*r(\text{actual portfolio}) + (1-d)r(F), \tag{A.3.2}$$

where

$$\sigma_{RAP} = \sigma_B. \tag{A.3.3}$$

The correlation of the original portfolio to the benchmark is identical to the correlation of RAP to the benchmark, as "leverage/deleverage" (using the risk-free rate) does not change the correlation characteristics. Correlation is normally less than unity. Correlation of 1 could lead to a riskless arbitrage. Figure 2.1 provides the chart for the M^2 measure.

The M^2 adjustment makes the returns from the benchmark and the RAP an "apples-to-apples" comparison, because now both have the same volatility. This adjustment turns peer rankings of mutual funds and managers on its head. The rankings are identical when using the Sharpe ratio measure, as the principle is similar. The M^2 measure, however, is preferable, as it expresses RAP in terms of basis points of outperformance and provides guidance on assets allocated to the external manager (allocation of d) and the risk-free asset (allocation of $1-d$). The Modiglianis also discard the Information Ratio, as it could lead to incorrect decisions. For example, portfolios could have a negative Information Ratio, but would have a risk-adjusted performance greater than the benchmark. Graham and Harvey (1997) propose a variation of this method, assuming the riskless asset need not be uncorrelated with other assets. This only leads to different allocations across funds rather than suggesting a new approach.

The M^2 adjustment makes the comparison in terms of basis points of outperformance by ensuring that all portfolios have the same variance as the benchmark. The only major shortcoming is that two funds, normalized for benchmark volatility, could have different benchmark correlations and hence different tracking errors. This is also shown in Figure 2.2. The tracking error is important to investors, especially institutional investors, because it provides a measure of variability of a manager's returns around the benchmark. All else being equal, investors prefer funds with lower tracking error (and hence greater predictability in returns). Hence, these rankings can provide investors with incorrect information about the relative risk-adjusted performance of funds.

THE M³ METHODOLOGY – ADJUSTING FOR DIFFERENCES IN CORRELATIONS

An investor relies on available data to make future projections. Assuming historical distributions are preserved, one has to synthesize the three-dimensional problem of a comparison of returns, standard deviations, and correlations, into a simple two-dimensional space of risk and return.[59] In mean-variance space, the riskless asset is portfolio F (with returns $r(F)$), and it can be used to leverage or deleverage the desired mutual fund/manager. In tracking error space, the only portfolio with zero tracking error is the benchmark portfolio, as it is perfectly correlated with itself (where $\rho = 1$, $TE = 0$, as $\sigma_B = \sigma_1$). Therefore, combining active mutual funds/managers with passive benchmarks, the riskless asset can be used to alter the overall standard deviation of the portfolio and its correlation with the benchmark.

To create measures of correlation-adjusted performance, the investor has to invest in the active strategy, the riskless asset, and the benchmark to ensure: (i) the volatility of this composite is equal to that of the benchmark (Modigliani and Modigliani 1997); and (ii) the tracking error of the composite is equal to the target tracking error (Muralidhar 2000). The M³ measure recognizes that the investor has to consider basis points of risk-adjusted performance after ensuring that correlations of various funds versus the benchmark are also equal.

THE M³ MODEL

Hammond (1997) states that, to establish performance-related thresholds for managers, the investor must set a target tracking error and compare funds to the target. Litterman, Longerstaey, Rosengarten, and Winkelman (2001) propose a similar approach.

Assume the investor is willing to tolerate a certain target annualized tracking error around the benchmark, say, 300 bps (TE(target)).[60] The investor essentially wants to earn the highest risk-adjusted alpha for a given tracking error and variance of the portfolio. Now define a, b, and $(1-a-b)$ as the proportions invested in the mutual fund, the benchmark, and the riskless asset, respectively. Let CAP be the correlation-adjusted portfolio. Then the returns of a CAP are:

$$r(CAP) = a*r(1) + b*r(B) + (1-a-b)*r(F). \qquad (A.3.4a)$$

---

[59] These are bold assumptions, to say the least. Expected outperformance, variability of performance to achieve this outperformance, and correlations between portfolio and benchmark returns have to be forecast. Historical performance is one way of making forecasts, but the M³ measure is independent of the forecasting technique. In addition, one has to assume that markets are inefficient to conduct such analyses.

[60] This measure is independent of the tracking error, and hence is applicable across all tracking error targets.

As is apparent, this is an extension of the M^2 measure. Further, the investor must hold appropriate proportions of each asset to ensure that the final portfolio has the target tracking error and standard deviation of the benchmark. For a specific mutual fund, say, mutual fund/active strategy 1, with a risk-adjusted return $r(CAP\text{-}1)$, equation (A.3.4a) can be re-written as:

$$r(CAP\text{-}1) = a*r(1) + (1-a-b)*r(F) + b*r(B), \qquad\qquad (A.3.4b)$$

where the coefficients of each portfolio represent the optimal weight of that specific portfolio to ensure complete risk adjustment. In addition, from the constraint on tracking error, a unique target correlation is apparent between the CAP and benchmark B. As demonstrated in Muralidhar (2000), this target correlation of the portfolio with that of the benchmark ($\rho_{T,B}$) is given by the equation for tracking error when $\sigma_B = \sigma_1$; namely,

$$\rho_{T,B} = \frac{1 - TE(target)^2}{2^* \sigma^2_{B}} \qquad\qquad (A.3.5)$$

By maximizing the $r(CAP)$ subject to the condition that the variance is identical to the benchmark, and its correlation to the benchmark equal to the target correlation, for mutual fund 1,

$$a = + \sqrt{\frac{\sigma_B^2(1-\rho_{T,B}^2)}{\sigma_1^2(1-\rho_{1,B}^2)}} = \frac{\sigma_B}{\sigma_1}\sqrt{\frac{(1-\rho_{T,B}^2)}{(1-\rho_{1,B}^2)}} \qquad\qquad (A.3.6)$$

$$b = \rho_{T,B} - a * \frac{\sigma_1}{\sigma_B}\rho_{1,B} = \rho_{T,B} - \rho_{1,B}*\sqrt{\frac{(1-\rho_{T,B}^2)}{(1-\rho_{1,B}^2)}} \qquad (A.3.7)$$

The details of these calculations are provided in Muralidhar (2000). The allocation to the benchmark is independent of variances and is only a function of the correlation terms. While b and $(1-a-b)$ may be greater than or less than zero (negative coefficients being equivalent to shorting the futures contract relating to the benchmark and borrowing at the risk-free rate), a is constrained to being positive, as it is not currently possible to short mutual funds.[61] However, with active management strategies, a can be positive and negative.

---

[61] This trend may change with the development of exchange-traded funds (ETFs) on active portfolios. In some cases, it may be difficult to short the benchmark as well, and then b will have to be constrained to being greater than or equal to zero. This would not change the analysis of the measure. Generally, most benchmarks can be shorted through either their futures contract or a swap.

This method is preferred to the M^2, as it: (i) expresses risk-adjusted performance in basis points; (ii) gives advice on portfolio construction – specifically between the risk-free asset, the benchmark (passive investing), and the active portfolio (active management); and (iii) provides rankings identical with those based on skill for equal time horizons. This measure also has the attractive property of keeping a constant annualized tracking error target over all time horizons. However, M^3 falls short when two funds have different time periods of data.

4

The Case for SMART Management of Portfolios

"To hell with the public! I'm here to represent the people." A New Jersey senator[62]

BACKGROUND

The year 2008 was a turning point for the fund management industry, revealing the flaws in past portfolio management theory and practice. Difficult performance trickled into the first quarter of 2009 and even into the first half of 2010. *Pensions and Investments*, a leading U.S. pension publication reports, "The median plan in the BNY Mellon U.S. Master Trust Universe returned -6.07 percent in the first quarter, up 7.03 percentage points from the fourth quarter of 2008, but still the sixth straight quarter of negative returns. Ninety-seven percent of plans in the universe posted negative returns for the first quarter."[63] Sadly, in the United States, this was on the heels of a stormy period for pension solvency as, "[F]or information years ending in 2007, PBGC received filings for 119 controlled groups covering 313 plans. These plans reported total liabilities of $253.3 billion and total underfunding of $67.2 billion (both measured on a termination basis)."[64]

The solvency of pension funds declined globally, and the unforeseen downturn in solvency was coupled with a severe cash crunch, as illiquid assets demonstrated that liquidity could dry up and cause a plethora of problems. Many pension funds (and endowments and foundations in the United States) that had invested in private equity funds on the assumption that capital calls could be met by maturing

---

[62] Petras (2001), page 136, quoting a New Jersey senator.

[63] See *http://www.pionline.com/apps/pbcs.dll/article?AID=/20090515/DAILYREG/905159994/ 1034/PIDailyUpdate.* The universe comprises 578 corporate and public pension plans, Taft-Hartley and health-care plans, foundations, and endowments, with a combined $888.9 billion in assets as of March 31, 2009.

[64] Testimony of Charles E.F. Millard, Director Pension Benefit Guaranty Corporation, before the Committee on Education and Labor, United States House of Representatives, October 2008.

investments found that existing investments could not be liquidated while capital calls still needed to be met. In an attempt to generate cash, clients could not exit hedge funds (which instituted gates[65] at the worst possible time), could not sell out of fixed income (which had ostensibly been maintained for their liquidity), and therefore sold the most liquid asset – equities. This led to a further decline in equity markets. In addition, many Dutch pension plans implemented static, fully currency-hedged international investments, at the suggestion of the DnB and the advice of ALM consultants, and they had to liquidate investments to meet cash margin calls from hedges that impaired performance from a weakening Euro in 2008-2009. To compound problems, differences in (accounting) valuation cycles between public and alternative assets caused havoc in portfolios, as alternatives grew to a disproportionate percentage of typical portfolios, necessitating even more drastic rebalancing measures. *In short, the 2008 economic meltdown proved that the static portfolio management approach to dynamic markets is a prescription for disaster, especially when the storm hits.*

DYNAMISM – OLD WINE FINALLY UNCORKED

"Nobody goes there anymore. It is too crowded." Yogi Berra[66]

The experience of the Dutch, Japanese, and U.S. funds underscored the need for change in the pension fund management paradigm to deal with dynamic markets. One may also assume that the experience of other major markets, such as Australia, Asia (Singapore, Hong Kong, and Korea), Canada, the Middle East, and the UK, with large pools of capital in institutional funds, are similarly fraught with problems. To cope with this, some clients have embarked on a strategy termed "Risk Parity" whereby portfolios are selected based on levering the fixed income component to ensure that the marginal contribution to risk of each asset class is equalized. There is little theoretical basis to this approach which has been actively promoted by Bridgewater to market one of their products. The flaws in this approach have been highlighted by others: Montier (2010) attacks it for ignoring valuations in the risk equalization process, and Sullivan (2010) faults it for being based more on hope than a theoretical basis, and because leverage may expose funds to undue risks not highlighted in the simple calculations. Our critique would be based on the fact that it is old wine being repackaged in new bottles and suffering from the same problems of any static approach.

---

[65] See Muralidhar (2009b).
[66] See Petras (2001), page 143, quoting Yogi Berra as to why he did not want to go to a particular restaurant for dinner.

Instead, smart clients globally are asking key questions, including: (a) Does it make sense to have a static SAA? (b) Should there be a long-term and a medium-term SAA? (c) How do investors make the rebalancing decision? (d) How should investors decide on the correct currency hedge? (e) How does an investor account for illiquidity in returns and risk? and (f) What is the best approach to rebalancing portfolios allocated to illiquid assets? [67]

The current market situation is possibly the best time to introduce a "new" approach, as there is a lot of soul-searching globally; regrettably, the focus on exotic hedge funds and alternatives over the past four years distracted the industry away from simple pension fund ALM issues using liquid assets. None of what follows is entirely new in presenting the SMART (Systematic Management of Assets using a Rules-based Technique) paradigm.[68,69] The same processes and techniques can be applied by other institutional investors as well.

Brock (2005) provides the most succinct explanation of this approach, namely, that the paradigm of Optimal Portfolios needs to be substituted with Optimal Strategies, or what he refers to as Passive Beta Management. "A strategy is defined as a rule that specifies, for an investor of a given risk attitude, the best portfolio to hold in any particular 'state'. If there are 12 different states, then there will be 12 state-dependent optimal portfolios." Mulvey (1988) provides an alternative explanation, but a similar focus, namely, "At each stage, the investor must attempt to maintain his long-range goals, while simultaneously adjusting to short-run market swings. This...takes into account the dynamic nature of pension plan investment decisions." It is remarkable that Prof. Mulvey's observation was made 20 years ago, but the market is only just beginning to understand its relevance. The next section explains why this approach is important, especially in the context of the assumptions on correlations made by pension funds or consultants in setting up the SAA and rebalancing policies for funds.

UNDERSTANDING THE BET TAKEN IN CORRELATION ASSUMPTIONS

While there has been considerable introspection on expected return assumptions and volatility, relatively little attention is paid to the correlation statistic.[70] Swensen

---

[67] Tai Tee Chia is credited for simplifying the debate into the much simpler set of questions posed here.

[68] It has been developed through the work of Barrett (2006), Brock (2005), Hodgson (2006), Mulvey (1988), Mulvey (1994), Arikawa et al (2005), Muralidhar (2007), and Muralidhar and Muralidhar (2009).

[69] Mulvey (1994) refers to SMART as Surplus Management and Risk Technology which can also be applied in this context.

[70] For growing literature on the impact of correlations on portfolio diversification, see Fernholz (2005) and Hight (2009).

(2009) devotes some attention to the topic of correlations, demonstrating how historical correlations may not be appropriate for asset allocation studies and discussing how "the Investments Office adjusted the correlation matrix to reflect the staff's informed judgments regarding expected correlations."[71] In effect, the Yale Investment Office is takin° a **static** correlation bet. Approaches such as the Black-Litterman model have gained so much credence in promoting an investor's implied market views[72] that several asset management firms have built investment processes based on it without questioning a major assumption:[73] in trying to reverse-engineer asset allocation decisions, the Black-Litterman model ignores the fact that the investor may take a bet on volatilities and correlation – the simplest reason for doing so is that it is practically impossible to solve for these implied parameters, hence ignoring a pertinent factor, to the investor's detriment.

CIOs must initially overlook the fact that correlations across two assets may be dynamic (Swensen 2009), and focus on a much simpler problem - understand the implied bet in choosing a correlation value. This blunt statistic masks the relationship of assets to various factors (i.e., a low correlation between stocks and bonds is caused by the fact that they respond differently to the price of oil, interest rates, etc.). Therefore, in setting an SAA and assuming specific correlations (and expected returns), pension funds are betting on these economic relationships – *it is inconsistent to neglect their use in the implementation and management of a portfolio*. In making the case against market timing, Swensen decries the same daunting, bewildering array of factors that implicitly impact asset returns and correlations.

For example, a client provided data on two currency managers labeled Manager 102 and Manager 117. A historical correlation analysis suggested that the correlation of the manager returns was 0.06, and hence a good case could be made to include both of them in a portfolio. But the questions that arose are: what caused the low correlation, and could it be explained by evaluating the managers' performance relative to some market factors?

A series of factor-based regressions were run, using factors known to influence the performance of currency managers, such as interest rate differentials, yield curves, implied volatilities, commodity prices, and economic data.[74] The resulting analysis provided valuable insight into why these managers performed differentially

---

[71] Page 119.
[72] See Black and Litterman (1992, 1999). See also Lee (2000) and http:// www.blacklitterman.org/.
[73] Bob Litterman indicated, during a job interview with the author in 1999, it is easier to forecast volatilities – an assumption that can be contested after 2008 – and hence the focus solely on implied return views. But holding correlations and volatilities constant can be shown to be severely flawed, as investment processes often take on volatility risk unwittingly. See Muralidhar and Neelakandan (2002).
[74] See Chapter 8 for a more detailed list of these factors.

over time. Figure 4.1 highlights the cumulative growth of a dollar invested in Manager 102 (white line) and Manager 117 (dark line), along with the EUR/USD Option Implied Volatility from October 2002 to January 2007. The figure clearly indicates – also evident in the factor analysis – that the performance of Manager 117 had a positive impact, with an increase in the EUR/USD Option Implied Volatility (lagged for the purpose of the factor analysis), whereas the performance of Manager 102 had a negative impact, and vice versa. Yield curves revealed similar sensitivity. While no prior information was available on these managers' styles, it was obvious that, when volatility rose, good performance suggested a trend-based portfolio management style, whereas the opposite is true in the case of a short volatility position (both of which are profitable in the long run, but in different market environments).[75]

Therefore, over a long cycle, while the two managers may be uncorrelated, understanding the impact of evolving market parameters on manager performance has important implications for portfolio management. A cursory glance at the chart suggests that, rather than a static Markowitz-type optimization of portfolio weights, in November 2004, a prudent investor would have chosen to tilt the portfolio in favor of Manager 102 when volatility started to decline, and thus would have done better than the static mix.[76]

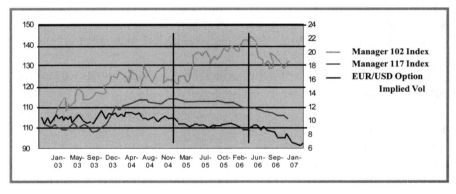

Figure 4.1. Explaining manager correlations using market factors.

It is only the beginning of the process to choose two assets (individual securities, asset classes, managers, etc.) on the basis of some historical or forecasted correlation. *For consistency, first a factor analysis should be used to analyze the factor sensitivity bets implied in the correlation assumption and then to manage the portfolio dynamically as the factors evolve over time.*

---

[75]   See Muralidhar and Neelakandan (2002).
[76]   Alternatively, as shown in Muralidhar and Neelakandan (2002), new products based on options could have been used as an overlay on managers to exploit these relationships. Credit to Roger Paschke for implementing such a unique options overlay-on-an-overlay.

MOVING TO THE "SMART" PARADIGM

Historically, the approach to asset allocation has been very static – and SEI (2009) confirms this assertion. This section reviews the traditional practice of static SAAs and static rebalancing and then suggests an innovative alternative.

TRADITIONAL APPROACH

The SAA was considered the lynchpin of the investment portfolio and was conducted over a long-term horizon (usually with a 5- to 10-year perspective). As a result, the SAA, including the newly proposed "Risk Parity approach", was completely static and not modified either intra-year or at regular intervals over many years for any reason. The exceptions are a few research studies that suggest adjusting the SAA annually, relative to the funded status to improve solvency risk (addressed in Chapter 5). Simple examples of these SMART approaches, highlighted in Muralidhar (2001), include basic formulae such as:

Allocation to Equity = 20% + 0.4*Funded Status.[77]   (4.1)

Therefore, starting with 100 percent solvency, the initial allocation to equity would be 60 percent; but if the funded status rose to 110 percent, the fund could increase its risk-taking ability, and increase the scope for higher investment in risky assets (up to 64 percent). This approach is referred to as "*View-Neutral* Dynamic SAA", as these rules were not based on the market perspective but rather on the solvency of the fund. Typical ALM models can easily simulate these rules, adjusted annually at the start of the year, and can generally be proved no less effective than the oft-applied static SAA approach, from the perspective of solvency and contribution policy. According to *Investments and Pensions Europe*, the ABN AMRO Pension Fund applied such rules more frequently in 2008 with distinctive success, managing to retain solvency at about 105 percent, when most other pension funds in the Netherlands suffered serious setbacks.[78] This is one of the simplest forms of SMARTs. Yet, this technique has been utilized more as the exception than the rule, as it was not given credence, even though research in 1997 showed its efficacy (Muralidhar 2001). However, ABN AMRO's positive implementation in 2008 attests its advantages (Chapter 5 includes the case study). There has been little work done by other analysts to demonstrate the value of a View-based approach where the SAA adapts to changing market valuations. Thus, a dynamic, evolving SAA, using a View-Neutral and View-based SMART process, is clearly preferred over the static SAA alternative (discussed in greater detail in Chapter 5).

[77]   *http://www.wealthmanagementexchange.com/articles/14/1/Managing-Your-Portfolio-Frequent-Rebalancing-Helps-Maintain-Allocation-Targets-/Page1.html*

Rebalancing

The next issue facing plan sponsors, after setting the long-term SAA, is to rebalance the portfolio as daily market movement shifts the actual allocation away from the SAA. Many consultants and pension fund managers adopt a rebalancing policy that typically involves returning the asset allocation to the target allocation/ SAA at regular intervals (e.g., monthly, quarterly, or annually). Alternatively, portfolio managers may use a "range-based" approach whereby the triggers or ranges are typically 3-5 percent from the target, based on the volatility of asset classes. Lim (2008) and Lim (2009) provide good examples of rebalancing for retail investors, based on the practices of institutional investors. In fact, the well-respected CIO of the Yale Endowment, David Swensen, has repeatedly affirmed the value of this programmatic rebalancing for institutional and retail investors.[79] To quote from Swensen (2005), "Rebalancing involves taking action to ensure that the current portfolio characteristics match as closely as is practicable the targeted portfolio allocations......Rebalancing represents supremely rational behavior.....When markets exhibit excess volatility, rebalancing enhances portfolio returns....Moreover, real-time rebalancing tends to cost less, as trades generally prove accommodating to the market....Yale's trading activity during the fiscal year ending June 30, 2003, provides some insight into the potential magnitude of rebalancing profits....Careful investors rebalance....investors position portfolios to satisfy long-term investment goals."[80]

Variations of this formalistic rebalancing approach fall somewhere within these allocation ranges, or they use periodic cash flows to move the asset allocation of various assets closer to what a rebalancing action would attempt. Often such approaches are a move towards a practical maintenance of strategic weights, a trade-off between managing transactions costs and tracking error relative to the benchmark.

Such approaches may be called 'static rebalancing' because limits are set ahead of time; however, the *portfolio still drifts within the bands,* as most policies are silent about what actions staff or Boards should take within these bands. In effect, ***pension funds take implicit bets within the range***, as shown in Figure 4.2. Even Swensen (2005) acknowledges, "Perhaps the most frequent variant of market timing comes not in the form of explicit bets for and against asset classes, but in the form of passive drifts away from target allocations. If investors fail to counter market moves by making rebalancing trades, portfolio allocations inevitably move away from desired target levels."[81] The proposed approach towards traditional rebalancing

---

[78]   Chapter 6. Sections of this material and other references to Swensen (2005) are repeated *verbatim* in Swensen (2009).

[79]   Page 21.

[80]   Petras (2001).

[81]   Page 21.

mirrors that of a congressional candidate in Texas who commented, "That lowdown scoundrel deserves to be kicked to death by a jackass – and I am just the one to do it."[82]

David Swensen's rationale thus explained, "Strong evidence exists that markets exhibit mean-reverting behavior, a tendency for good performance to follow bad and bad performance to follow good." A recent paper by the Nobel Prize winner, William Sharpe (2009) highlights the flaws in traditional rebalancing policies. The fallacy in Swensen's approach is evident in a number of simple observations: (i) it does not provide any evidence of the frequency (i.e., the time over which) and amplitude (i.e., the size) of mean reversion, rendering invalid the arbitrary claim of mean reversion; (ii) if an investor truly believes that markets mean-revert, then a more intelligent mean-reverting strategy should/can be developed (such as a SMART strategy), as opposed to a naïve range-based or "real time" rebalancing strategy; (iii) mean reversion of a single asset class is not relevant, but rather all assets in the portfolio are significant, as the frequency and amplitude of different assets are different; (iv) the likelihood of an optimal static rebalancing policy, given other choices, is close to zero for a mean-reverting market; and (v) one must be concerned with relative asset performance, as portfolio weights are influenced by relative performance and not the absolute performance of a single asset class.

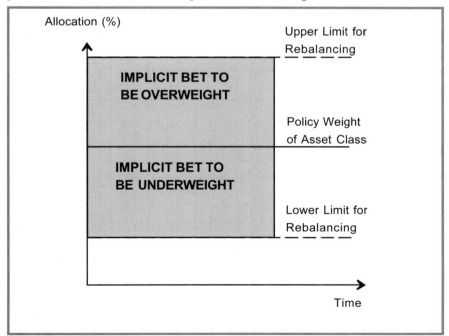

Figure 4. 2. Implicit bets in rebalancing (either time- or range-based).

---

[82] Petras (2001).

The other disconcerting problem for pension funds (or individual investors) is that rebalancing policies were recommended to keep tracking error low relative to the SAA, but they have little relevance to liabilities. This potentially increases ALM risk and typically leads to large drawdowns in performance, as experienced by pension funds globally in 2008-2009 and earlier in 2001-2002. SEI (2009) provides an overview of the practices adopted by 119 institutional investors in the U.S. and Canada, showing how pension funds have struggled with this concept. More troubling, however, are the suggestions offered by the SEI (2009) authors on how to deal with this critical issue, given its importance as highlighted by MetLife (2009).

Table 4.1 provides an analysis of a simple simulation: Assume an investor has 60 percent allocated to the S&P 500 and 40 percent to the Citi World Government Bond Index(noted as BMK for benchmark in Table 4.1),The evaluation shows the performance of different rebalancing strategies, assuming a one-sided transaction cost of 10bp for both assets, for 2008. A multi-asset portfolio is not required to show the insidious nature of blind rebalancing.

TABLE 4.1 The performance of "naïve" rebalancing strategies in 2008

Strategy		Annualized Returns (%)	Annualized Standard Deviation (%)	Annualized Return-Risk Ratio	Worst Single Negative Performance (%)	Maximum Drawdown (%)	Ratio of Good/ Bad Risk	Success Ratio (%)	Annual Turnover (%)
Daily Rebalancing	BMK	-18.97	23.81	-0.80	-5.33	-31.08	1.02	N/A	N/A
	Strategy	-19.16	23.81	-0.80	-5.33	-31.18	1.03	N/A	N/A
	Excess	-0.19	0.02	-9.50	-0.01	-0.2	0	1.15	121.15
Weekly Rebalancing	BMK	-18.97	23.81	-0.80	-5.33	-31.08	1.02	N/A	N/A
	Strategy	-19.62	23.58	-0.83	-5.33	-31.44	1	N/A	N/A
	Excess	-0.65	0.61	-1.07	-0.43	-0.76	0.52	31.31	49.71
Monthly Rebalancing	BMK	-18.97	23.81	-0.80	-5.33	-31.08	1.02	N/A	N/A
	Strategy	-20.15	22.59	-0.89	-5.17	-31.28	0.97	N/A	N/A
	Excess	-1.18	1.65	-0.72	-0.89	-1.36	0.59	46.18	20.52
3% Range Rebalancing (back to SAA)	BMK	-18.97	23.81	-0.80	-5.33	-31.08	1.02	N/A	N/A
	Strategy	-19.42	23.7	-0.82	-5.37	-31.32	1.01	N/A	N/A
	Excess	-0.45	0.6	-0.75	-0.26	-0.76	0.71	49.62	26.71
5% Range Rebalancing (back to SAA)	BMK	-18.97	23.81	-0.80	-5.33	-31.08	1.02	N/A	N/A
	Strategy	-19.66	23.61	-0.83	-5.56	-31.5	1	N/A	N/A
	Excess	-0.69	0.86	-0.80	-0.28	-1.18	0.94	48.47	11.99
3% Range Rebalancing (back to mid point)	BMK	-18.97	23.81	-0.80	-5.33	-31.08	1.02	N/A	N/A
	Strategy	-19.7	23.48	-0.84	-5.43	-31.43	1	N/A	N/A
	Excess	-0.73	0.73	-1.00	-0.32	-0.99	0.54	51.53	14.66
5% Range Rebalancing (back to mid point)	BMK	-18.97	23.81	-0.80	-5.33	-31.08	1.02	N/A	N/A
	Strategy	-19.27	22.9	-0.84	-5.34	-30.93	1	N/A	N/A
	Excess	-0.3	1.14	-0.26	-0.44	-0.79	0.73	49.62	12.11

What is noteworthy, but not shocking, is that all naïve rebalancing approaches lost money in a period when the SAA also declined, as seen by the negative values in the "Annualized Return" column. The success ratio (penultimate column) was above 50 percent in only one case (the 3 percent mid-point) – equivalent to

---

[83]   These policies are actively recommended by consultants but can be tested only in a two-asset case. In a multiple asset portfolio, there is no unique solution and, hence, the policies cannot be tested without assuming qualitative judgment.

underperforming a coin toss! Increasing turnover does not necessarily reduce loss, as shown in the "Annualized Turnover" column. The biggest problem is that the maximum drawdowns (in absolute terms) of all but one naïve rebalancing option are worse than the drawdown of the BMK. In short, naïve rebalancing policies acted like an anchor tied to the leg of the captain of the *Titanic*!

Static LDI

Finally, in an attempt to lower ALM risk, many funds increased their duration to match liabilities. This strategy was promoted aggressively by asset managers and derivatives overlay advisors. "LDI focuses specifically on the duration gap arising from interest rate mis-match between assets and liabilities. In broad terms, it is the mechanism for matching the two in order to improve solvency over time."[84] Many asset managers created duration pools and convinced clients to invest in these pools to extend their duration. Using the example in Table 3.1, this involves extending the asset portfolio's duration to 15 years (considerably longer than the typical duration of bond funds that pension funds invest in, which are typically 4-5 years). "Typically, funds need to invest 20-25 percent of their assets into the LDI pools to fully hedge the interest rate risk of their liability, leaving the fund with a significant portion of assets invested in a diversified return portfolio."[85] While this approach is appropriate, it is once again a static approach, and extending the duration is a timing decision (much like the rebalancing decision). Hence, the point at which a pension fund extends the duration (when rates are perceived to decline) and the point at which it reduces the duration (when rates are expected to rise) can be a source of additional value, while hedging interest rate risk. Lowering volatility of the asset-liability ratio does not fulfill the complete objective, as it focuses only on the risk and not on the return differential.

Extending the duration may be a meaningless measure, as the return on assets has to match, and even exceed (depending on the funded status), the return of liabilities. With yields at current levels, long duration bonds do not have the potential to provide adequate returns relative to liabilities.

Chapter 6 addresses the issue of dynamic liability hedge management, after demonstrating the basic premise of SMART.

INNOVATIVE APPROACH

In an attempt to discredit "market timing", an exercise that Swensen indirectly engages in through his mean-reverting rebalancing trades, Swensen (2005) states,

---

[84] See Watts (2006).
[85] See Watts (2006).

"Maybe investors keep to policy asset allocations because they recognize the futility of consistently making the relative asset class valuation assessments necessary for market timing success, particularly when such assessments rely on a bewildering collection of unknowable economic and financial variables."[86] This comment precedes the commendation of his "sophisticated team of investment professionals [that] manages the funds on a day-to-day basis, providing the staff support needed for management intensive activities."[87]

Not satisfied with this criticism of market timing, Swensen (2005) continues, "[A]ctive market timers usually fail. Market-timing requires taking relatively few, generally undiversifiable positions. Timing decisions involve the large questions of asset-class valuations, forcing short-term asset allocators to develop views on an impossibly broad range of factors...Serious investors avoid entering the market-timing morass."[88] Swensen (2009) contains a similar unsubstantiated diatribe.[89] Such a tirade, expressed in such dismissive language, is inexplicable, especially when it is obvious that the CIO of a major fund should invest time and resources, especially with a sophisticated (and possibly highly paid) team at their disposal, to discern the factors that affect the relative movement of assets which form the core asset allocation, which by Swensen's own admission is the most important decision. Moreover, SMART rebalancing addresses the fundamental misunderstanding that the CIO needs to be correct only 52-53 percent of the time in making these tilts, and therefore does not need a whole array of factors to make these decisions, but only those that can be reliably modeled by using economic logic and clean and consistent data.

SMART Rebalancing and LDI[90]

Dynamic SAA based on market factors is recommended. It can be alternatively termed as "The View-based SAA" and can be implemented after allowing for the View-Neutral dynamic SAA described above. More important, the dynamism is not intended to keep tracking error low or to raise the Information Ratio, but *ideally to help assets outperform liabilities while increasing the correlation* (thereby lowering the ALM risks). Chapters 5, 6, and 8 demonstrate the application of these concepts. To clarify, "portfolio insurance", which has been discredited purely on the price movement of assets, is not being proposed.[91]

Though we live in a dynamic world, most academic work, portfolio management techniques, and even risk budgeting approaches seem to have fallen short of the

---

[86]   Page 20.
[87]   Page 197.
[88]   Page 151.
[89]   Pages 52, 53, and 64.
[90]   This section leverages Muralidhar and Muralidhar (2009).
[91]   Leland and Rubinstein (1998).

practical problems encountered by plan sponsors. Proposed approaches are usually static, and assumed optimal even in the long term, which is rarely any manager's time horizon. The industry favors an over-reliance on "optimization" approaches which assume that long-term returns and risk can be reasonably guesstimated to structure long-term portfolios. Though such approaches derive an acceptable "starting point" for portfolio structure and asset allocation, the subsequent commitment to maintaining this structure/allocation over different economic cycles and investment regimes has definite shortcomings. In many ways, this is akin to building a heating/air-conditioning system that operates at an average temperature year round, while ignoring the actual outside temperature and seasonal changes. For example, static recommendations such as "purchase an asset management product to match the liability cash flows", or "hire portable alpha managers and statically replicate the beta", and "rebalance your portfolio back to the benchmark weights at the end of the quarter or when some range has been reached" have severe limitations that presume the pension fund sponsor can relax after making these "crucial" decisions.

Such approaches are often marketed as "silver bullets" that require a single action of hiring an external manager, with little thought to allocation in each period; or of implementing a rebalancing policy and ignoring it for many periods until some target (calendar period or range) is met. Therefore, the portfolios that result are sub-optimal, and it should be apparent that such naïve recommendations are inadequate at the least, and can potentially jeopardize the pension fund at the worst. Good governance of multi-asset, multi-manager portfolios requires a disciplined approach to the selection of assets/managers and periodic determination of appropriate asset allocation to these assets/managers. Figure 4.1 for two asset managers (and similar analyses for all asset classes) clearly shows how assets are influenced – by investors who have good economic market intuition or by the knowledge of managers or occasionally by something that may be unbeknownst to even the managers themselves (e.g., most currency managers did not realize they were long volatility when creating their portfolio management products).[92] Investors with good intuition or knowledge of managers can exploit these relationships in the ongoing allocation decisions.

Most important, assets included in a portfolio (i.e., asset classes and even managers), as modern portfolio theory has taught us, are ideally uncorrelated with each other (or at least have low correlation). Swensen (2009) advises, "[B]y identifying high-return asset classes that show little correlation with domestic marketable securities, investors achieve diversification."[93] The logical extension of the

---

[92] Muralidhar and Neelakandan (2002).
[93] Page 63.
[94] See also Appendix to Chapter 2.

assumption of low correlation is, in any given period (whether determined by market regimes, economic cycles, or calendar periods), some assets will perform better than others in the portfolio. There will also be times when assets outperform their expected returns, and still others underperform these expectations. The static/naïve approach to asset allocation assumes (or hopes) that these pluses and minuses will even out over short windows of time and should not be a concern in the ongoing asset allocation decisions. The economic crisis of 2008 proved the fallacy in that argument, severely threatening solvency and forcing major corrective actions. Moreover, many ongoing asset allocations are necessary, as a result of cash flows generated by the pension management fund by way of dividends, coupon payments, private equity distributions, as well as contributions and disbursements to meet ongoing pension obligations.

SMART portfolio management takes the view that periodic variation in asset performance in a fund demands that responsible asset managers make asset allocation decisions to best position their portfolio for these regimes/cycles/market conditions and, by doing this expertly and systematically, greatly improve the return/risk and eliminate, in large part, knee-jerk, emotional decision-making that cannot be explained to a wider audience (or in this case – the principal). After all, CIOs expect at least as much from their external asset managers, and it would therefore be only logical to extend this same responsibility one decision level up to the portfolio's internal managers.

Asset and manager returns constantly move up or down daily, simultaneously resulting in changes in the weights of assets and managers in the portfolio. Such fluctuations can be expected due to volatility and correlation assumptions in SAA studies. In addition, the decision of CIOs (often relatively *ad-hoc*) on what to do with contributions or which assets to liquidate to pay pensions also influences performance. *Many pension funds consider that if they do not take an explicit decision about a manager or an asset weight, they will not have a bet on the markets.* In fact, the opposite is true! If a CIO adopts a static approach to hiring a manager with an initial allocation, and lets that allocation change over time due to market movements, they are opting for considerable risk. If the manager performs well, their weight in the portfolio increases, and avoiding a reduction in the weight implies a view that the CIO assumes that the manager will continue to outperform other managers.

The same analysis applies to assets (or beta) that may have drifted in allocation above the long-term strategic weight because of strong recent performance. To desist from making an explicit decision implies subscribing to the view that the asset will continue to outperform. Similarly, triggering an *automatic* rebalancing decision to reduce (increase) the weight of an asset back to its benchmark weight at the end of a quarter, because a particular day has been reached, implies subscribing to the view that the asset will do worse (better) than other assets – otherwise committing to such a decision would seem contradictory. In addition, a rebalancing decision makes the assumption that the benchmark allocation is most desirable at *all* times (under all market conditions), and hence managing back to this asset allocation benefits the portfolio, regardless of current market conditions, and, more important, liability growth. However, all CIOs must realize that every decision, whether to overweight/underweight asset classes or managers, or continue to allow the portfolio to drift, are active decisions – whether they are made explicitly or implicitly.

Having addressed the implicit bet in rebalancing portfolios, the discussion now shifts to the impact of currencies on portfolio performance and risk. The decision on optimal currency hedge has been sorely neglected, as most consultants who were not well-versed with currency issues refrained from expressing a view explicitly while, nonetheless, expressing a view implicitly. Most currency hedging studies acknowledge that currencies are volatile but have zero expected return. Therefore, the choice of a static passive hedge is a bet on the market direction of all currencies relative to the base currency – this can be a very dangerous bet to take in global markets.

For effective asset management, a pension fund should be run like a professional company, with staff using market intelligence and *SMARTs to make implicit bets in a portfolio explicit and improve solvency*. After all, the correlation of these assets (used in the SAA) reflects multi-factor relationships across assets. Hodgson (2005) makes an eloquent case for such a process.

This SMART approach, therefore, involves the following steps:

1. Identify all asset allocation decisions (and possibly currency) made in the portfolio.
2. Develop investment rules to guide desired asset allocation tilts in the portfolio. These rules define whether assets should be over- or under-weighted relative to the target allocation, based on levels of certain market or economic factors, typically sourced from finance or academic journals. These factors will be measures of valuation (whether an asset class is over- or under-valued), economic activity (different economic conditions favor different asset classes), seasonality, momentum, market sentiment (fund flows, risk aversion, volatility, volume etc.). *After all, these economic relationships result in a blunt correlation statistic, rendering such analysis critical to the potential for exploiting the implications of low correlation.*

For example, Campbell and Shiller (1998a) state that the price-earnings (P/E) ratio and dividend-price (D/P) ratio are useful forecasting variables for the long-term price return of stocks. They suggest:

- A low P/E implies stock price growth will increase (as P adjusts) over the long term, and
- A low D/P implies price growth will decline in the long term.

These parameters can help a SMART investor develop a formal process to tilt allocations between Stocks and Cash.

In the case of the two currency managers highlighted in Figure 4.1, a more formal rule can be specified as follows (Figure 4.3), relative to a static, constantly rebalanced 50-50 mix. In this example, the SMART rule calibrates an automatic reaction to an evolution of the underlying parameter. Notice the simplicity of the rule and lack of over-optimization of choice of triggers. In short, this rule states that if the historical EUR/USD implied volatility exceeds 1 standard deviation from the mean (Z-score), then the allocation to Manager 102 should be rebalanced to 49 percent, and the allocation to Manager 117 increased to 51 percent (the actual size shifts depending on liquidity, but 1 percent is used merely to calibrate the model). The opposite is true when implied volatility falls; and in the middle range, no tilt needs to be taken, as it avoids decision-making until parameters are reasonably stable and clear on information content (as opposed to arriving at a decision on noise).[94]

Description	EUR Option Implied Volatility: When this factor is low, overweight Manager 102 and underweight Manager 117
	IF {(*Historical Z-Score* Of Euro Zone, Implied Option Volatilities, EUR/USD 1 year, Ask, Close, EUR <-1)}
	THEN Allocate 51% of Smart Currency Fund-Manager 102
Criteria Description	ELSE IF {(*Historical Z-Score* Of Euro Zone, Implied Option Volatilities, EUR/USD 1 Year, Ask, Close, EUR >1)}
	THEN *Allocate 49% of Smart Currency Fund-Manager 102*
	ELSE Allocate 50% of Smart Currency Fund-Manager 102

Figure 4.3. Example of a simple, SMART rule, based on the EUR/USD implied volatility – what to do, when, how much, and why.

The process to develop the rules is:

- Quantify the historical performance of such an asset allocation approach to understand the risk/return profile of each factor model and possibly fine-tune the selection of various factor-based rules to ensure they meet the investment objectives or constraints. In the case above, the rule was tested for October 2002-December 2005 (Figure 4.4), for an out-of-sample evaluation. This rule is interesting because, given the short time span it covers, it does not have a high rate of success (48 percent), but the confidence in skill is high (89 percent). However, a one percent allocation tilt results in four bps of excess, indicating that a 10 percent allocation tilt would generate 40 bps.

---

[94] See also Appendix 2.1.

- Combine many such factor-based rules into a diversified strategy that provides a net indication of the relative attractiveness of each asset class and currency, to mitigate the risks of making decisions on a single economic factor.

- Implement these asset allocation recommendations in a disciplined way (just as with static rebalancing). The weights for each of these rules can be dynamic, but it is adequate for this level of dynamism of asset allocation to be based on factors.

- In case an investor tends to believe they must be correct in every decision they make or equivalently a 100 percent success ratio (as already argued in the context of Swensen's comments), the data tabulated in Figure 4.4 shows, even being right only 48 percent of the time, the SMART rule adds value with high confidence that performance is based on skill. Combine this with other rules to get a higher success ratio (which need not exceed 55 percent) outperforming the static, constantly rebalanced naïve approach. (This is covered in greater detail in Chapters 6 and 8.)

In short, it does not take a genius to do better than the rebalanced benchmarks because of the embedded bets, and SMART portfolio management provides the structure and process to manage assets (and liabilities) effectively.

Performance Summary							
Total Period							
		Annualized Return	Annualized Standard Deviation	Annualized Return-Risk Ratio	Maximum Drawdown	Confidence in Skill	Sucess Ratio
Total	BMK	7.52%	5.51%	1.36	-4.16%	N/A	N/A
	Rule	7.56%	5.54%	1.36	-4.17%	N/A	N/A
	Excess	0.04%	0.06%	0.73	-0.04%	89.59%	48.72%

Figure 4.4. Summary results of shifting 1 percent of assets relative to a 50-50 mix of Managers 102 and 117 (October 2002-December 2005).

SUMMARY

Pension funds cannot adopt static policies in dynamic markets because static policies imply unmanaged bets. To improve solvency, CIOs should incorporate four levels of dynamism in managing assets: (i) View-Neutral Solvency-based Beta Adjustment (Chapter 5); (ii) Dynamic LDI (Chapter 6); (iii) View-based SMART Beta Management (Chapter 6); and (iv) SMART Alpha Management (Chapter 8). These techniques embody the concepts underlying Arikawa et al (2005), Brock (2005), Hodgson (2005), and Mulvey (1994).

Rules need to be clearly articulated to indicate "What to do; When to do it; How much and Why." Explicit factor analysis and exposition of these rules exploit the correlation assumptions underlying ALM studies and lend themselves to transparency and good governance, whereas optimized portfolios are derived from black boxes where the investor is not sure whether the decision is driven by the return, correlation, or volatility.

5

SMART View-Neutral LDI: Two Approaches

"This strategy represents our policy for all time. Until it's changed."
Marlin Fitzwater[95]
"There may be a recession in stock prices, but not anything in the nature of a crash." Irving Fisher[96]
"Stock prices have reached what looks like a permanently high plateau."
Irving Fisher[97]

BACKGROUND

Money was pouring into less liquid and more complex strategies pre-2008, and pension funds, especially in the United States, drifted towards endowment-based investing (Swensen 2009), potentially ignoring the ALM perspective. Institutional investors had benefited from high returns to capital and ignored the Hyman Minsky paradigm – the more things look good, the worse they will get. However, the recent global financial turmoil and palpable hesitation over the fundamental justification of these high returns have tempered expectations going forward.

Increasingly, enlightened regulation in countries such as the Netherlands has focused on pension plan solvency as the determinant of success. The United States lags far behind in giving its regulators teeth and guidance to help pension funds achieve solvency. While the U.S. Pension Protection Act (PPA) requires corrective action vis-à-vis contributions, it falls short of the three-pronged response (raising contributions, lowering benefits or indexation, and reducing asset risk) required by the Dutch National Bank (DnB). Even though pension plans became more sophisticated in determining their investment strategy (increasingly looking for "alternative" opportunities), they missed the

---

[95] Petras (2001), page 95, quoting Marlin Fitzwater, White House spokesperson on national security strategy under President George H.W. Bush.
[96] Petras (2001), page 52, quoting economist Irving Fisher, six weeks before the 1929 crash.
[97] Petras (2001), page 52, quoting economist Irving Fisher, nine days before the 1929 crash.

opportunity to lock in their previous asset gains and preserve solvency. In addition to extending into non-marketable asset classes, pension plans contemplated derivative strategies on their assets.

This chapter focuses on certain innovative SMART solvency-enhancing strategies, and the Appendix compares one specific SMART View-Neutral (VN) strategy to the simplistic option-based strategies that investment banks have traditionally sold to pension funds. The analysis also provides a brief overview of an alternative, though related, View-Neutral approach that would have protected solvency in 2008. The chapter describes situations under which each strategy can lead to efficiency gains for pension plans in an ALM context. Further, the choice of a fixed income portfolio (traditional short duration, with credit, versus liability matching) may lend itself to effective SMART management of solvency. It thereby becomes apparent that relatively simple strategies can be instrumental in ensuring ongoing solvency.

IMPLEMENTING DYNAMIC SAA: THE SMART VIEW-NEUTRAL APPROACH

The 1997 analysis, conducted in the context of a DB pension plan, is somewhat dated, but its robust conclusions remain relevant.[98] Simply put, the plan makes annual benefit payments many years into the future and has inflows due to contributions made by the plan's sponsor and participants. The act of withdrawing/ adding funds to a pension fund compels a CIO to make rebalancing decisions, annually, at a minimum (without the use of derivatives, etc.). It is clear that when a simple, rigorous rule, based on the funded status, is applied to annual cash flows to help revise the SAA – as opposed to naively rebalancing to a static SAA – it promotes future solvency. This SMART rule was provided in Chapter 4 (equation 4.1).

Since pension plans usually have a long-term investment horizon, innovative strategies in the simulation are evaluated over a period of nine years. The choice of horizon is merely for simplicity and does not affect the results; however, it is assumed that plans review their investment policy annually. (Appendix 5.1 covers a more elaborate menu of strategies that can be implemented if Boards permit leverage to determine optimal solvency-protecting strategies.) This discussion demonstrates that consultants/pension plans often take an implicit bet unintentionally, in conducting SAA studies, when they intentionally prevent leverage.[99] This may be

---

[98]   Muralidhar (2001). Thanks to Ronald van der Wouden for his hard work, contributions, and partnership in this case study.

[99]   See, for example, Peskin (1997) and Boender (1998). Interestingly, many public pension plans have considered adding leverage to their funds in 2010, but the use of leverage appears to be driven by a desire to achieve a return on the asset portfolio that is close to the rate at which liabilities grow (as opposed to a way to manage risks).

a reflection of the fact that some countries preclude leverage in asset allocations, as misguided regulations impose unusual conditions that can impact solvency.

Although pension plans have become more sophisticated and regulation is more solvency-focused, the practice of examining assets and liabilities in concert is not fully integrated in the decision-making process.[100] It may be argued that this shortcoming afflicts endowments and foundations in particular, as the liabilities are not clearly articulated. The presence of liabilities is the only reason for the existence of pension plans; hence, ignoring liabilities altogether would lead to an inadequate, potentially incorrect analysis. To highlight the importance of liabilities, Figure 5.1 provides the growth of aggregate assets and liabilities of pension plans in the United States covered by the Pension Benefit Guarantee Corporation (PBGC) between 1980 and 1996.

These graphs demonstrate that although, on aggregate, pension plan assets rose impressively in the two decades from 1980, the funded ratio declined dramatically. In a more recent analysis, "Wilshire Consulting's eighth study covering defined benefit plans sponsored by S&P 500 Index companies notes that DB pension assets for S&P 500 Index companies declined by $310.2 billion – from $1294.3 billion to $984.1 billion – while liabilities increased $21.9 billion, from $1199.7 billion to $1221.6 billion. As a result, *the aggregate funding ratio (assets divided by liabilities) for all plans combined decreased from 107.9 percent to 80.6 percent, and a $94.6 billion surplus at the beginning of the year turned into a $237.5 billion deficit.* Wilshire's analysis of the 323 companies in the S&P 500 that maintain DB plans indicates that 92 percent of those plans are underfunded, notably higher than the 62 percent reported for the previous year. Moreover, the median (50th percentile) corporate funded ratio is 73.3 percent, a decline from 96.6 percent in the previous year." [101]

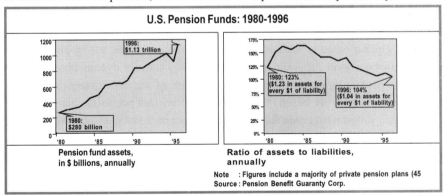

Figure 5.1. Important to develop an effective ALM policy.

---

[100] A number of pension plans still develop their policy decisions on mean-variance types of analyses, or a consensus benchmark such as the average asset allocation of their peer group.
[101] Plan Sponsor Daily email – April 20, 2009. Emphasis added.

The data on the Dutch pension system (provided earlier) is equally troubling, as regulations require pension plans with funded ratios less than 105 percent to implement corrective measures that include increases in contributions, less asset risk, and a reduction in benefits. Though all plans in the Wilshire study may not have experienced this outcome, one has to question the suitability of the investment policies of some of these plans, given their liability structures. It is surprising that even after the decline in solvency in 2001-2002, many pension plans were unprepared for the 2008 recession.

To ensure that plans are not subjected to such uncertainty in the future, and to emphasize the importance of liabilities, the following analyses use a framework in which investment decisions are integrated with revised liability valuations and hence depend on funded status.[102] Interestingly, even Frank Russell endorses this approach (Collie and Gannon 2009). The principles can be more broadly applied to any investment problem – whether for an insurance company, a central bank managing reserves, or an endowment/foundation seeking to achieve a spending target.

THE STRATEGIES

Before making a simple comparison between a static SAA and a simple, SMART View-Neutral SAA, the stage must be set for the analysis to describe the assumptions on the economy and the pension plan (investment and contribution policy). Three critical distinctions for strategies are highlighted: (i) static versus dynamic investment policies; (ii) portfolios with/without options; and (iii) leveraged versus unleveraged portfolios. The static investment strategy proposes a fixed allocation throughout the investment horizon, whereas the dynamic investment strategy focuses on the ability to revise the asset allocation from one period to the next. The adjustment can be daily, but for simplicity it is assumed that decisions are made once a year on January 1. Option-based investment strategies focus on acquiring a long-put position on the portfolio's domestic equity portion (either on a static or dynamic basis), in an attempt to protect against a decline in the value of assets. Finally, leveraged investment strategies are based on the ability to construct portfolios that leverage cash or other investment grade fixed income (either on a static or dynamic basis).

Appendix 5.1 analyzes (ii) and (iii). This section focuses on the simple SMART View-Neutral strategy that can be adopted immediately by clients globally. Other strategies may require regulatory revisions or changes in investment policies on

---

[102] Ideally, pension plans should jointly optimize contribution policy and investment policy. This is covered in greater detail in Krishnamurthi, Muralidhar, and van der Wouden (1998 a, b), and Dert (1995).

the use of derivatives, leverage, etc., but SMART strategies can be easily implemented (at low cost) if CIOs adopt the basic concepts of liability and asset replication highlighted in Chapter 3.

The Investment Environment

This section highlights the economic environment for the analyses, plan-specific issues, and assumptions made on asset returns, correlations, and volatility. In addition, the assumptions on policy issues deal with the restrictions and freedom of the pension plan in constructing the portfolio. Policy assumptions are necessary for practical, realistic investment policies.

Plan-Specific Issues

The experiments are based on the demographic profiles (length of employment, life expectancy, salary growth) of participants in a pension plan. These profiles help to simulate a hypothetical DB plan (entitling the employee to a replacement rate of approximately 70 percent of final salary after 35 years of service – in keeping with the Aon (2008) replacement rate study). Benefits are unconditionally indexed to price inflation, and the plan's liabilities are measured under the Closed Group method.[103] Further, a discount factor of 4 percent real is used to value liabilities.[104]

Sensitivity to an assumed 125 percent initial funded ratio, where many funds were probably situated prior to 2008, is calculated. The maturity of the plan, measured by the ratio of assets to total salary, is around 10. For simplicity, the policy horizon of the fund's Board of Trustees is assumed to be nine years, with an annual review. The time horizon and frequency of review do not affect the results.

Different scenarios of the economic environment were created to deal with the uncertainty and impact of asset returns. Each scenario represents the development of returns over the chosen nine-year plan horizon. An investment policy is evaluated for each scenario, and the impact of this particular investment policy is captured by solvency risk measures (Chapter 3), taking into account the policy's behavior in all the scenarios. Scenarios are generated by a model that assumes each economic factor follows a random walk. In addition, the simulations preserve the

---

[103] None of these assumptions has an impact on the generic results of the analysis. Estimation under the Closed Group method means liabilities are the value of benefits expected to be paid, with both salaries and service projected to expected dates of termination or retirement, including benefits in payments. This is equivalent to valuation on a Projected Benefit Obligation (PBO) basis, reflecting expected future service.

[104] This is different from the discount rate for U.S. corporate plans which use a long-term corporate bond yield.

statistical relationships among the economic factors.[105]

Table 5.1 shows the most important characteristics of the scenarios generated.

Table 5.1 Characteristics of economic variables

	Annual Expected Nominal Return (Arithmetic)	Standard Deviation (Annual Volatility) %
Price inflation	4.0	3.0
U.S. equity	10.5	15
U.S. fixed income	6.5	5.2
High-yield bonds	8.0	9.8
Real estate	7.0	18.0
Private equity	10.5	27.0
Cash	5.2	1.4

It assumes an expected real risk-free rate of 1.2 percent (the difference between cash and expected inflation), a real bond return of 1.3 percent (the difference between fixed income and cash), and an expected real equity risk premium of 4 percent (the difference between the expected return on equity and fixed income). Further, the estimation of correlations among these asset classes use historical data of 10 years (see Table 5.2). In 1997, when the analysis was first conducted, the data on expected returns and correlations was cross-checked with major consultants and asset managers to ensure they were reasonable; however, no attempt was made to examine the correlation data as described in Chapter 4.

Table 5.2 Correlations among asset classes

	US EQ	NUS EQ	US FI	NUS FI	HY	EM EQ	PE	RE	PI	Cash
U.S. equity	1									
Non-U.S. EQ	0.5	1								
U.S. fixed income	0.4	0.2	1							
Non-U.S. FI (hedged)	0.4	0.3	0.4	1						
High-yield bonds	0.5	0.2	0.3	0.3	1					
Emerging markets EQ	0.3	0.3	0.3	0.3	0.2	1				
Private equity	0.4	0.1	0	0	0	01	1			
Real estate	0.1	0.1	0	0	0	0.1	0	1		
Price inflation	-0.3	-0.2	-0.1	-0.2	-0.3	-0.2	-0.2	0	1	
Cash	0	0	0	0	0	0	0	0	0.3	1

---

[105] Dert (1995) presents a technical discussion which explains the use of standard simulation techniques to conduct such analyses.

Policy Issues

The two major tools available for pension fund management are the investment policy and the contribution policy.[106] This book focuses on asset strategy, and shows how contribution policy is a tool to ensure solvency through the revision of the amount of money injected by the plan sponsor into the fund. Restrictions on the use of these tools have been incorporated in the analysis to prevent the policy from becoming unrealistic.

Investment Policy

The proposed pension fund has been allowed to invest in nine different asset classes (Table 5.1), a fair representation of current investment opportunities for U.S. pension plans.[107] In addition, the allocation to several classes is fixed from one period to the next, at a certain percentage, to avoid significant allocation changes in illiquid asset classes.[108] An alternative route to a similar result would be to increase transaction costs, or even exclude them completely from the evaluation (as suggested in Chapter 3). However, when this study was originally conducted in 1997 and futures-based indices were proposed, it gained little endorsement. Table 5.3 gives an overview of which asset classes are fixed and at what level.[109] The assumption that pension plans today have invested up to 15-20 percent of the entire fund in these assets (and possibly other alternatives, such as hedge funds) is not unrealistic.

Contribution Policy

In general, pension plans and individuals (as shown in Chapter 9) can revise the contribution rate from one year to the next. The rate is the percentage of the total salary of the active (contributing to the pension plan) workforce. This rate is often determined by either actuarial projections or accounting rules. In occupational pension plans, contributions are made by the employer and, in some plans, by the employee. Generally, the employee's portion of this amount is a fixed rate, whereas the employer's part may be flexible and has therefore to be determined from one

---

[106]   The method of specifying and jointly optimizing these two policies is provided in Dert (1995). The implication of such joint optimizations for pension plans is covered in Krishnamurthi et al (1998 a, b).

[107]   "Hedge funds" are excluded as they are not an asset class but rather an investment strategy.

[108]   Given the expected returns and volatility of these asset classes, attention must be paid to rebalancing, but constraining allocations restricts the problem within practical limits.

[109]   This is not a buy-and-hold strategy; in order to rebalance to the same allocation, transaction costs need to be considered. However, in the case of Real Estate and Private Equity, portfolios are infrequently marked-to-market, rendering rebalancing difficult. In High Yield and Emerging Equity, rebalancing is affected by cost and delay in liquidating positions.

[110]   http://www.pbgc.gov/media/pension-legislation/content/page15921.html

period to the next. However, the flexibility and levels of these contribution rates have practical limitations. For most organizations, it is difficult to accept a significant increase in the contribution rate, as it jeopardizes other activities. In other cases, pension regulations determine the contribution when solvency declines below 100 percent (see the U.S. PPA).[110]

TABLE 5.3. Fixed and floating allocations

	Fixed/Floating	Allocation (if fixed) %
U.S. equity	Floating	
Non-U.S. equity (unhedged)	Floating	
Emerging markets equity	Fixed	5.0
U.S. fixed income	Floating	
Non-U.S. fixed income (hedged)	Floating	
High-yield bonds	Fixed	2.0
Real estate	Fixed	7.0
Private equity	Fixed	3.0
Cash	Floating	

As pointed out earlier, the initial funded ratio of the hypothetical pension plan is 125 percent. The contribution policy is planned so that, at this funded ratio, the basic total contribution rate is 7 percent,[111] which can be seen as the fixed portion of the employees' contribution. If the funded ratio falls below 110 percent, the contribution rate is increased; if the funded ratio rises above 140 percent, the contribution rate will be decreased. Once the contribution rate exceeds the basic 7 percent, the plan does not allow more than 5 percent increases in the contribution level from one year to the next. In addition, the contribution level is restricted to be no higher than 25 percent.[112]

---

[111]   One can argue that contributions are not necessary for a high funded ratio. This assumption is applied when the funded ratio is less than 100 percent and it removes the need to normalize for different contributions.

[112]   In the analysis, negative contribution rates are allowed in order to make the comparisons simpler to understand. Most plans do not allow for negative contribution rates (i.e., liquidating the pension fund's assets to return monies to the company or individuals) for regulatory reasons.

The use of this contribution policy is critical to show that dynamic strategies are effective, and it becomes more evident later in this chapter.

Methodology

STATIC AND DYNAMIC INVESTMENT STRATEGIES

Since the strategies are evaluated in a multi-period framework, the investment strategy can be revised from one period to the next. Static investment strategies are evaluated, where the portfolio is rebalanced every year back to an initial allocation. The SMART View-Neutral (or dynamic) approach permits the asset allocation to change to a new optimal allocation every year, based on the plan's funded ratio.[113] The logic behind this method is that, if a pension plan's financial situation improves (i.e., the funded ratio increases), then the ability to rebalance to a more risky portfolio is enhanced because of the increase in the plan's risk-bearing capacity. Consequently, by taking on a more risky position, the ability to generate more returns increases. The intuitive reader recognizes this as a form of delta hedging the solvency option, using asset rebalancing (since solvency options are either not provided by investment banks or are exorbitantly expensive).

Objectives and Targets

The first step is to set targets that indicate the achievement of a plan's solvency objectives. A funded ratio of 100 percent indicates that current assets in the plan are equal to liabilities. Ratios less than 100 percent indicate a shortfall and that the plan is underfunded, whereas a ratio higher than 100 percent indicates that the plan has a surplus. Once the funded ratio drops below 100 percent, asset returns must exceed the "return" on liabilities to ensure a return to full solvency.

Consequently, the probability that the funded ratio in any year is lower than 100 percent is used as a measure of risk borne by the plan. However, this measure does not indicate the extent to which the funded ratio is below this threshold. To capture this, downside deviation is employed as a risk measure. Downside deviation represents volatility of the shortfall when the funded ratio is lower than the threshold.[114] The objective is to minimize downside risk.

---

[113]   See Boender (1998) for a description and empirical results on this strategy.

[114]   The downside risk of a decline in the funded ratio below a threshold is analogous to the downside deviation of portfolio returns. See Sortino and van der Meer (1991). The equation for this would be: $Downside\ Risk = \left[\int_{x=-\infty}^{x=0} x^2 f(x)dx\right]^{1/2}$, where x is a (negative) surplus and $f(x)$ the probability that a surplus occurs of the size x.

This chapter focuses primarily on the downside deviation risk measure and the probability of not achieving a 100 percent threshold for the funded ratio. Being generic measures for all plans, they can be used to make comparisons across plans, unlike comparisons of investment returns that do not normalize for different liabilities.

While the main objective is to minimize the occurrence and extent to which the plan's funded ratio is lower than 100 percent, CIOs must try to maximize wealth and minimize the contributions made by the plan sponsor. These objectives are, in some sense, opposed to each other; however, in selecting the "right" investment strategy, a Board must make a trade-off between these objectives.

In general, three clear objectives may be defined for CIOs of a pension plan: (i) maximizing the funded ratio (or maximizing the plan's wealth); (ii) minimizing the contribution level and volatility; and (iii) minimizing occurrences of underfunding (or minimizing downside risk).

Framework for comparison – A neat trick!

This section describes the method for comparing different investment strategies. Pension plans must control the volatility of contributions, as it is not feasible for plan sponsors to cope with huge increases in the contribution rate from one year to the next. This objective is incorporated in the analysis by constraining annual increases to 5 percent, once the contribution rate reaches levels higher than the basic rate of 7 percent. Further, in order to reduce the complexity of viewing the problem in a multi-dimensional space, the additional assumption is that the contribution rate may be negative (i.e., the sponsor can extract the surplus and liquidate assets to repay itself and/or participants). This simple modification ensures that maximizing the wealth objective now indirectly appears in the average contribution rate. This follows because maximizing wealth implies that the funded ratio of the plan will be as high as possible. If it is assumed that the surplus is returned to the plan sponsor once the plan's surplus reaches a certain level, then the wealth of the plan is maximized by maximizing the amount to be paid back to the plan sponsor (or minimizing the contribution level). Therefore, the objective is reduced to minimize the contribution rate for every level of risk or minimize the risk for every level of the contribution rate.

Figure 5.2 provides a framework for comparing different strategies, with the plan's risk depicted on the vertical axis and the average contribution rate on the horizontal axis. The ball in this plane represents a particular investment policy. As is clear from the graph, implementing this strategy implies a certain risk level for the plan (downside deviation is about 3 percent), and the expected annual contribution rate, when the strategy is imposed, is 0 percent. A three-standard deviation equivalent of the downside risk would imply that, when the funded ratio is below

100 percent, the respective confidence interval denotes a funded ratio of 91 percent. Further, better strategies are defined as those with either a lower risk level and/or a lower average contribution rate.

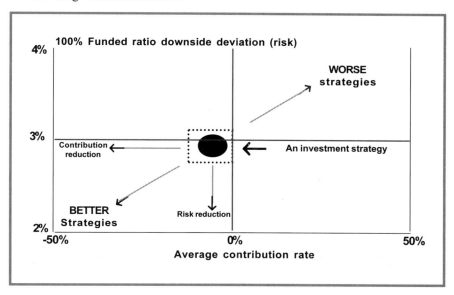

Figure 5.2. ALM framework for comparing strategies.

Results

STATIC INVESTMENT POLICY

The results of the first strategy are used as a benchmark in comparing the efficiency improvements of the SMART View-Neutral strategy. Figure 5.3 presents the efficient static investment policies for the plan and highlights a frontier that connects different portfolios with minimum risk, given an average contribution rate. This frontier has been created by conducting a hybrid simulation/optimization procedure, described in Boender (1997).

Figure 5.3 demonstrates that the plan's downside deviation risk ranges from nearly 0 percent to about 7.5 percent. Investment policies with low risk (or the policies with low downside deviation and high contribution rates) have a negligible amount allocated to equities, whereas the high-risk policies allocate the maximum allowable percentage to equities. In addition, the average contribution level over the horizon decreases as the plan's risk and expected return increases, which is an intuitively reasonable result.

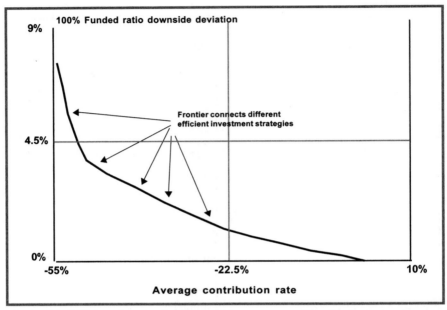

Figure 5.3. Efficient frontier for the static investment policy (basic strategy).

SMART VIEW-NEUTRAL INVESTMENT STRATEGY

The SMART View-Neutral Rebalancing rule is applied on arbitrage-free simulation paths; hence, the change in allocation from bonds to stocks, and vice versa, is not based on market factors but on solvency. Chapter 9 demonstrates the absurdity of a "Naïve View-Neutral Rebalancing", as current TDFs, with the blessing of the U.S. Department of Labor, are *shifting allocations based on the age of participants rather than solvency*! Generally, a pension plan can experience efficiency gains by changing the asset allocation to a more risky (conservative) portfolio when the plan's funded ratio increases (decreases).[115] For example, a simple SMART View-Neutral Rebalancing rule would be:

Equity Percentage at time T = 15% + 0.5*Funded Ratio at T - 1.[116]   (5.1)

Figure 5.4 allows a comparison between a SMART strategy and the basic investment policy, and shows the conditions under which the dynamic strategy

---

[115]   See Boender (1998) and Krishnamurthi et al (1998).
[116]   In a truly dynamic framework, the intercept and coefficient are time-dependent. In this example, a linear relationship is given between the funded ratio and allocation to equity; however, these relationships can also be non-linear or discrete.

dominates the commonly adopted static strategy. The frontier that represents the dynamic SMART investment strategy connects policies that optimize the rebalancing rule. Figure 5.4 clearly shows that the ability to revise the asset allocation will result in significant efficiency gains in certain regions (A-B). These efficiency gains are apparent for each risk level up to a point where the maximum allowable allocation to equity is reached (B).

Since the SMART strategy increases (decreases) its allocation to risk when the plan is most (or least) able to bear risk, risk-taking, and hence efficiency, increases relative to a static investment strategy that may take risk when there is no risk-bearing capacity. In short, it is easy to show how a solvency-based rebalancing policy can do better than the traditional static SAA. The trick lies in specifying a SMART rule to guide asset allocation.

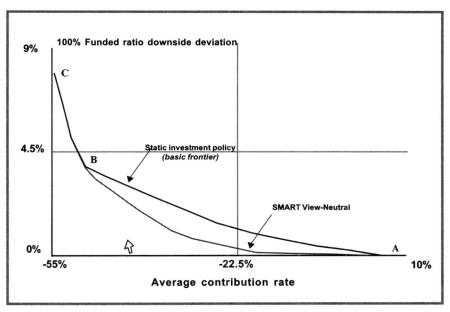

Figure 5.4. The SMART View-Neutral rebalancing compared to a static strategy.

Extensions

Initial Funded Ratio

This case study assumes an initial funded status of 125 percent. The conclusions were also tested for initial funding ratios of 85 percent and 100 percent. The results appear relatively robust initially, though the magnitude of the efficiency gain and points of inflection (e.g., point B) may differ. An interesting point is, in the case of the 85 percent initial funded ratio, the derivative strategies in Appendix 5.1 end up being too costly for the expected gains, as the goal is to attempt to ensure a 100 percent target funded ratio.

Importance of Correlation Assumptions

The strategies are largely driven by the correlation assumptions (Chapter 4), and recent experience has shown that, in times of market distress, correlations tend to unity. Hence, such strategies may be risky in the short term, but would be stable if long-term correlation estimates are accurate. This is why View-based Rebalancing of the SAA gains favor over any View-Neutral allocation changes. (Chapter 6 addresses this in greater detail.)

THE SMARTER "SMART" VIEW-NEUTRAL REBALANCING

As Head of ABN AMRO Structured Asset Management, Cees Dert proposed a more intelligent approach to the same problem.[117] He began by creating a liability-replicating portfolio (along the lines highlighted in Chapter 3) and then made an intelligent allocation between that portfolio and a risky portfolio based on current solvency. His approach lent itself to more appropriate hedging in times of stress and could also be conducted more frequently than once a year. However, this approach required the use of liquid futures-based benchmarks and effective swap-based representation of liabilities – otherwise the cost would be exorbitant.

SMARTER VIEW-NEUTRAL CASE STUDY: DUTCH PENSION PLAN

In the Netherlands, when funding falls below 105 percent, the DnB requires immediate corrective action. The background on the case study assuming a Dutch pension plan is:
- Initial funded ratio: 110 percent.
- Asset mix: 50 percent equity, 50 percent fixed income (5-year duration).
- 1st year return on assets:
  - between -13 percent and +27 percent with 95 percent certainty, expected return 5.2 percent.
- Funded ratio after 1 year:
  - between 93 percent and 135 percent with 95 percent certainty, expected return 111 percent.
  - less than 105 percent with a probability of 29 percent.

---

[117]   Cees Dert, "Risk Budgeting and Liability Driven Investments," IIR Conference on Professional Risk Management for Pension Funds,   December 12-14, 2006.

The outcome of the ALM study is liability-driven; but as assets are managed relative to the MSCI World Index (equity) and the Citigroup European Global Bond Index (EGBI) for fixed income, there was a mis-match between the SAA and liabilities. Liabilities resurface only when the next ALM study is conducted, and the asset mix is essentially Buy-and-Hold until then, assuming an annual SAA. This annual Buy-and-Hold SAA, commonplace in the Netherlands, was driven in large part by consultants who did not exercise control for shorter time periods in the simulation model. The question is: Can the CIO benefit from taking into account liabilities between annual ALM studies? Figure 5.5 highlights the impact on solvency of the worst scenarios in this ALM model. Table 5.4 provides additional details of the impact of asset returns and liability returns on solvency.

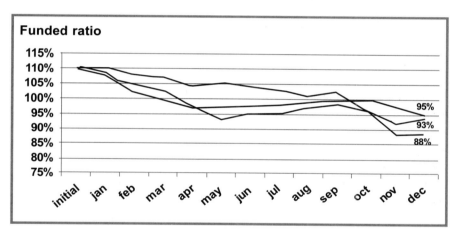

Figure 5.5. Evaluating the worst funding/solvency scenarios.

TABLE 5.4. Digging deeper into the worst solvency simulations

Funded ratio after 1 year (%)	88	93	95
Asset Return (%)	-16	-13	-10
Liability Return (%)	4.7	3.7	4.8

In many cases, it takes more than a single bad month to cause a bad year. What if the asset mix can be adjusted to reduce the funded ratio risk from both causes?

Let us consider a smarter SMART View-Neutral (SMART VN) Rebalancing, such that the objective is to maximize returns relative to liabilities, subject to:

- The tracking error limit on the return of assets relative to the return on liabilities (Chapter 3).
- Probability of the funded level dropping below 105 percent.
- CIO to monitor risk and allocate risk budget relative to liabilities.

Risk is caused by market exposure (beta) and active exposure (alpha). Counter-intuitively, a passive portfolio of 50 percent MSCI World and 50 percent Citigroup EGBI, which used to be considered "safe", is risky because of the implied bet relative to liabilities. The SMART rule that follows is simple:

1. Invest in the MSCI World and in a cash flow stream that matches the projected benefit payments (the Investible Liability Portfolio).
2. At the end of each month, invest a percentage in equities proportionate to the surplus over 105 percent.
3. Apply the following formula:

Allocation to Equity = 30% + 1.5*(Surplus)   (5.2)

Intuitively, as in the previous example, the CIO invests more in equities when the funded ratio is higher and more in a matching portfolio when the funded ratio is lower. *This is feasible only if the asset manager explicitly accounts for the liabilities and monitors their value development; hence the requirement for specification and creation of an Investible Liability Portfolio, as detailed in Chapter 3.* As Figure 5.6 and the following case study demonstrate, a simple policy such as the one highlighted in equation (5.2) achieves effective results.

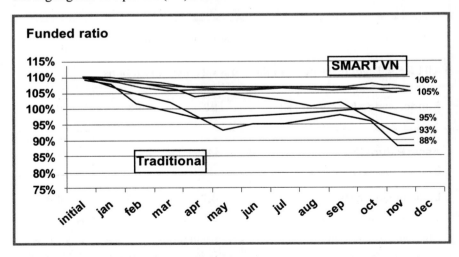

Figure 5.6. Comparing smarter SMART View-Neutral to static SAA.

Figure 5.7 and Table 5.5 validate the supremacy of the smarter SMART over a static SAA! The startling result is that the SMART policy has the same expected funded ratio as the traditional mandate, with less volatility.

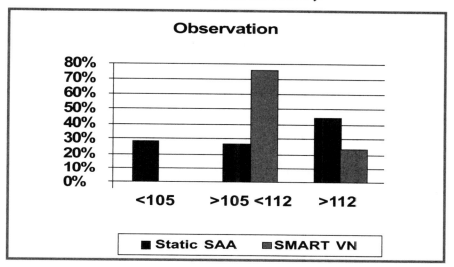

Figure 5.7. Smarter SMART View-Neutral versus Static SAA – distribution of outcomes.

TABLE 5.5. Smarter SMART View-Neutral versus Static SAA – distribution of outcomes

Funded Ratio (%)		
	SMART View Neutral	Traditional
Average	111	111
Lower Bound 95% Confidence	105	93
Upper Bound 95% Condience	135	133

CASE STUDY: ABN AMRO PENSION FUND
(Cees Dert and Geraldine Leegwater)

The Board of Trustees of the ABN AMRO Pension Fund (AAPF) determines investment policy. Their decisions are expected to reflect a fair trade-off between the interests of the fund's stakeholders. The Board is supported by an Investment Committee and by the ABN AMRO Pension Bureau. The Pension Bureau is also responsible for implementation of the investment policy by hiring external asset managers on behalf of the pension fund.

Decision process – strategic investment policy

The decision-making process of the AAPF's strategic investment policy is well-governed by the Advisors to the Board of Trustees, who play an important role in an annual process which consists of four steps. First, the Pension Bureau, together with the Investment Committee, prepares the input for an ALM study. Second, after approval of the inputs by the Board of Trustees, the Pension Bureau prepares an annual ALM study. Strategies, or a combination of a low-risk matching portfolio (a return in line with the return of liabilities) and a return portfolio composed of a variety of risky investment categories, were simulated. Both static strategic and dynamic investment strategies are evaluated.

Third, the AAPF discussed the results of the study with the Investment Committee. They judge whether selections achieve the Board's various goals and evaluate whether the strategies can be implemented. This results in a selection of approximately 10 strategies to present to the Board.

The fourth step occurs during an interactive "strategic investment policy workshop." This two-hour workshop presents the results of the strategies in terms of their impact on funded status, consequences for the sponsor, and indexation ambition. This is particularly relevant for Dutch plans, as pension funds can offer indexed benefits, but only as long as there is adequate solvency. This implies that the Board of Trustees can really focus on their goals instead of on the policy tool – the investment policy – ensuring that the Board is not distracted by the need to review the investment strategies themselves. Any prejudice with respect to the investment categories or instruments cannot play a role in such a set-up.

During the first workshop in the autumn of 2007, the Board decided on an investment policy with high potential for indexation and the least possible risk. This resulted in a dynamic investment strategy, and the Board also decided to review the strategy annually. The latter is important because changes in external circumstances can lead to a situation in which the chosen strategy no longer reflects an optimal trade-off between the interests of the stakeholders in the pension fund.

CHARACTERISTICS OF THE DYNAMIC INVESTMENT STRATEGY

The main characteristics of the dynamic investment strategy are:

1. The amount of risk taken in the investment portfolio depends on the solvency of the pension fund, and risk tolerance of the Board depends upon the

amount of assets in excess of liabilities. A clear scheme describes, for each solvency position reflected in the coverage ratio (or funded status), how much needs to be invested in the matching portfolio and how much in the return portfolio.

2. The allocation to these two portfolios is managed dynamically: as the coverage ratio changes over time, the portfolios need to be adjusted according to the scheme decided on by the Board. It implies a physical or synthetic transition from one sub-portfolio to another.

3. The actual coverage ratio is calculated only on certain predetermined dates during the calendar year. Thereafter, the size of the portfolios is measured to determine whether a transition is required, avoiding excessive trading between portfolios.

As a consequence of this investment policy, the AAPF gradually reduced risk as of March 2008. As compared with holding a static asset mix with the same expected return, the strategy resulted in a 10 percent point higher funded ratio by the end of 2008.

Implementation in practice

In practice, both the return portfolio and the matching portfolio are composed of sub-portfolios managed by several external managers: the matching portfolio has sub-portfolios assigned to three different fixed income managers; and the return portfolio is composed of four investment categories, managed by more than 10 investment managers. This implies that a transition from one normal portfolio to another is a complex operational process. Therefore, the AAPF hired two rebalancing managers to implement the (potential) periodic transitions. Their role is to devise a clear strategy on how to efficiently implement the required moves between the two portfolios. Depending on criteria such as costs, operational complexity, operational risk, and the remaining portfolio composition, this can result in physical and synthetic transitions, with one or more of the underlying transition managers.

Results

At the end of 2007, the AAPF introduced an innovative decision-making process for their strategic investment policy. The process resulted in the selection and implementation of a dynamic investment strategy, which integrated the management of asset/liability risk. In essence, this meant the pension fund had to steer away from the more traditional asset allocation approach, towards a course in which rebalancing occurred with a direct link to the solvency and risk tolerance of the pension fund.

SUMMARY

This chapter evaluated two types of SMART VN Rebalancing rules: one where the SAA is composed of traditional assets, and the second where the benchmark-replicating portfolio is treated as an asset to replace the traditional fixed income allocation. In both cases, the allocation to "risky" assets was predicated on the fund's solvency. (This is contrasted in Chapter 9 with a policy where the allocation to risky assets depends on the age of the plan, and further analysis reveals the extreme danger inherent in such an approach.)

This chapter demonstrates that dynamic strategies can be more efficient than static investment strategies, depending on the fund's current position and restrictions on asset allocation. Further, it has been established that the View-Neutral hedging of liabilities can also be very effective.

When asset-liability markets are incomplete, ALM strategies outperform asset-only strategies, and this dynamism is seen as the delta hedging of the solvency option. (Chapter 6 takes this analysis one step further by demonstrating the benefit of SMART View-Based Asset Rebalancing; Chapter 8 extends the analysis by including a case study that incorporates SMART Liability Hedging with SMART Rebalancing and SMART Manager Allocation.)

APPENDIX 5.1 Evaluating the impact of option and leveraged strategies

Muralidhar (2001), Chapter 4, encompasses additional strategies with the simple static and dynamic SAA. These strategies included: (i) a static put derivative strategy; (ii) a dynamic put derivative strategy (where the derivative exposure depends on solvency); and (iii) leverage opportunities on the static and dynamic SAA. For simplicity, the report below is restricted to the results of all the strategies in aggregate, and Figure A.5.1 summarizes these results.

The efficient frontiers of the six different strategies are shown. The following conclusions may be drawn from Figure A.5.1 for a given funded status:

1. Imposing a static one-year put strategy does not provide efficiency gains for the pension plan. This approach was adopted by some pension plans, largely to the benefit of the investment banks that offered them.

2. The dynamic put strategy could improve the plan's performance when total exposure to equity is larger than 50 percent (beyond B).

3. Although the dynamic put strategy can provide efficiency gains for the pension plan, the SMART/dynamic strategy, which allows the asset allocation to be revised from one year to the next, outperforms these option strategies.

4. Leverage results in more investment opportunities and hence expands the efficient frontier. Consequently, investment strategies for more risky utility functions can be optimized by allowing leverage (rather than opting for a constrained sub-optimal allocation).

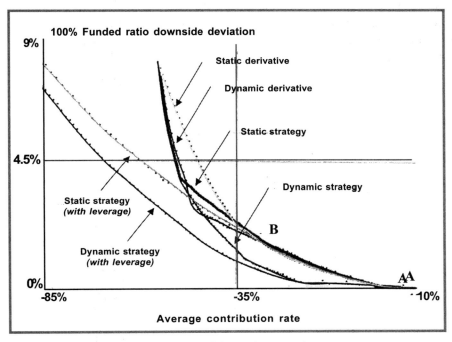

Figure A.5.1. Dominance of leveraged dynamic strategies.

5. As total allocation to equity exceeds 50 percent, the leveraged portfolios gain in efficiency. This is a function of the funded ratio and not a constraint imposed in the research.

6. The dynamic investment approach, with the ability to have short positions, offset by compensating long positions, is clearly the most efficient investment approach, regardless of the risk tolerance level of the plan.

For simplicity, the option strategies evaluated have a one-year maturity period. Further, the use of options is limited to a long-put position on the domestic equity allocation. An extension of this strategy to international equities can increase the (small) efficiency gains that have been detected with the dynamic derivative strategy. In addition, it can be preferable for pension plans to consider other types of derivatives (e.g., zero cost or exotic derivative strategies).[118] Finally, the cap on total derivatives in the dynamic strategy can be raised above 10 percent, but this is not expected to significantly affect the results.

A critical result is that permitting leverage expands the efficiency frontier and makes it preferable to the unleveraged case. Permitting leverage is preferred for two reasons: first, it allows an increase in expected returns and, second, it permits greater exploitation of the correlation matrix in a manner different from that described in Chapter 4.

---

[118] For instance, a pay-later derivative has the positive characteristic of a simultaneous premium payment and pay-off – a feature that could be preferable to pension funds, since cash flows are arranged conveniently.

6

The Case for SMART View-based LDI and Rebalancing

*"There are basically two types of people. People who accomplish things
and people who claim to accomplish things. The first group is less crowded."*
Mark Twain

BACKGROUND

Managing liability risk is the most critical aspect of pension fund management. Even a very innovative client, Client X, saw its assets under management dip by 1.4 percent in the first three months of 2009, as an earlier move to protect the fund against falling interest rates instead damaged its returns. The cover ratio dropped three percentage points to 87 percent by the end of March 2009, on the heels of a further fall in equity prices and pressure from long-term interest rates. Subsequent decisions to reduce fixed income allocation, from 60 percent to 54 percent at the end of 2008, and dilute equities from 20 percent to 17 percent, were intended to provide an 8 percent allocation to protect against interest rate cuts; however, this move actually doubled the fund's loss, as its returns would have been only -0.7 percent had it not tried to limit potential losses against its liabilities.[119]

Renewed interest in asset-liability matching is mainly due to the rapid decline in interest rates, which led to an increase in most pension fund liabilities on a mark-to-market basis. Unfortunately for most pension funds, this decline in interest rates coincided with a slump in many stock markets and waning performance of hedge funds and private equity investments. The fall in the value of assets, when the value of liabilities was increasing, led to a dramatic downturn in the ratio of assets to liabilities. Therefore, it is all the more inexplicable that pension funds were not advised (by academics, asset managers, and consultants) to adopt innovative approaches after the collapse of the technology bubble. As a result of this

---

[119] Adapted from an *Investments and Pensions Europe* article. The exact date and title of the article are withheld to protect the client's name.

negligence, funds are frantically scrambling to beef up their balance sheets. One reason for this inertia was probably the allure of the so-called "absolute return strategies" which took on a form of religious fundamentalism. Such distortions may, in large part, have been an attempt to outdo innovative endowments that loudly professed their ability to outperform markets through alternatives and then derided the folly of CIOs who dabbled in plain-vanilla assets or, alternatively, recommended and implemented a blind mechanical rebalancing of the SAAs in their portfolios.[120]

The ratio of assets-to-liabilities is often the focus of CFOs, pension fund members, and regulators engaged in estimating whether a pension plan is "safe" or solvent, since this ratio indicates whether there is a shortfall that must be made up.[121] During an economic recession, there is minimal scope for plan sponsors to fund pensions. Nowhere in Europe is this more apparent than in Ireland, the Netherlands, and the United Kingdom, where companies face the biggest competitive disadvantage due to pension liabilities from sponsoring DB pension schemes (Aon 2009). It is precisely for such troubled periods, when sponsors have the onerous responsibility of topping up their funds, that pension funds have to be smart about designing static and dynamic strategies. Further, new accounting standards, especially in the United States, imply that pension fund losses can impact corporate pension fund sponsors. As a result, many pension plans worldwide adjust their investment portfolios and hedge strategies to reduce the impact of a declining, volatile funded ratio. Recent attempts by the U.S. Department of Labor to soften the cash flow impact of declines in solvency to corporations sets a dangerous precedent, as it solves the immediate cash flow problem by dramatically reducing required contributions but, in so doing, threatens the long-term solvency of the fund.

Moreover, as mass-scale production in asset management led to healthy profits, asset managers were loathe to develop customized solutions for clients, and CIOs were given minimal staff to conduct this essential research themselves. The industry consequently suffered a lack of innovative products. This reinforces the recommendation that pension funds are better off hiring good staff than paying high asset management fees to external third parties.

Up to this point in the book, the stage has been set for the optimal process and innovation to ensure future pension solvency – namely, helping CIOs take advantage of asset price/security (including the ILP) cyclicality in managing fund solvency through effective management of liability hedges and SAA. It has been clarified that assets and liabilities need to be replicated through the most liquid instruments (Chapter 3) to ensure their daily tracking, but they may also be allocated into and out of the portfolio at minimal cost and without friction. The discussion has also

---

[120]   Swensen (2009) and Swensen (2005).
[121]   An alternative measure is the ratio of Salaries to Liabilities, as it provides an indication of
        the degree of contribution sensitivity the fund implies. See Muralidhar (2001), Chapter 4.

clearly demonstrated how pension funds can develop factor-based SMART Rules (Chapter 4), and now progresses to applying this principle to hedging liabilities intelligently, or SMART LDI, as well as SMART Rebalancing (or the Beta Engine). Chapter 8 addresses how SMART manager allocation or Alpha Engine can further enhance the solvency profile of a pension fund, as manager selection and allocation are just another set of decisions to achieve solvency goals. *However, the key message is: there is no single product that can solve the problems of CIOs worldwide, and hence our emphasis has been on improving pension fund process that would enable each CIO to design the optimal approach for their fund, given their respective liabilities and objectives.*

SMART LDI

The old approach – static LDI

Chapter 4 showed how static LDI products are simplistic and naïve and do not achieve the objectives of pension funds. Though the "duration pool" approach may seem appropriate, it is a static approach, unnecessarily utilizing cash when the same exposure could have been achieved by availing of relatively simple derivatives, as in the ILP in Table 6.1. Most important, extension of duration is a timing decision, and deciding when, and how much, to hedge can be a source of additional value and risk management over a static hedge. SMART LDI does not have to be right 100 percent of the time to be successful, but clearly the operation lends itself to the rules-based approach. *Lowering volatility of the asset-liability ratio by increasing correlation between assets and liabilities is an incomplete objective, as it focuses only on the risk and not on the return differential.*

Another piece of new research that is somewhat misleading is the case for investing in 20-year bonds instead of trying to capture the ephemeral equity premium (Arnott 2009). To quote liberally (in order to avoid misinterpretation), "A 2.5 percentage point advantage over two centuries compounds mightily over time. But it's a thin enough differential that it gives us a heck of a ride… Stocks for the long run? L-o-n-g run, indeed!… Over this full 207-year span, the average stock market yield and the average bond yield have been nearly identical. The 2.5 percentage point difference in returns had two sources: Inflation averaging 1.5 percent trimmed the real returns available on bonds, while real earnings and dividend growth averaging 1.0 percent boosted the real returns on stocks… Our research on the Fundamental Index® concept, as applied to bonds, underscores the widely held view in the bond community that one should not choose to own more of any security just because there's more of it available to us… As investors become increasingly aware that the conventional wisdom of modern investing is largely myth and urban legend, there will be growing demand for new ideas, and for more choices." *How true – except that the new idea is dynamic management of assets, <u>not Fundamental Indexing</u>®! And pension funds need not hire an asset manager to adopt this "new" idea.*

TABLE 6.1 The Investible Liability Portfolio (ILP) for a Dutch client

Index Maturity	Benchmark Allocation
Liability Index 003M	0 %
Liability Index 006M	10 %
Liability Index 012M	10 %
Liability Index 024M	20 %
Liability Index 060M	10 %
Liability Index 120M	10 %
Liability Index 240M	5 %
Liability Index 360M	5 %
Liability Index 480M	15 %
Liability Index 600M	15 %

Not so implicit in Arnott's paper is a pitch to create a market for bond ETFs – no doubt, in the course of being constructed by his "bond-offering heavy" employer. It is surprising that Arnott did not make the additional leap of faith that, given the duration of liabilities, this could be the perfect hedge for liabilities – injudiciously, the case was made from an asset basis alone. The argument is so lax that Arnott himself shows that, over extended periods, one asset dominates the other – and *hence the only take-away for a smart reader is the need to allocate dynamically to assets, instead of anchoring their portfolios to the pitfalls of static allocation.*[122]

---

[122]   Thanks to Hideo Kondo of DIC Pension Fund for sharing this research with us.

Extending the duration of a fund may unfortunately be a hollow measure, as the return on assets has to match, and sometimes even exceed (depending on the funded status), the return on liabilities. With yields at current levels, and the likely prospects of high inflation (in view of the degree of liquidity injection into the system), far from providing adequate returns relative to liabilities, long-duration bonds may actually damage a pension fund's portfolio. Hence Arnott's (2009) recommendation is questionable.

SMART LDI SIMPLIFIED

The dilemma of dealing with LDI, in Japan and the United States, is that the economic liability (or the set of proposed cash flows to be financed) has to be offset against the funding liability and the accounting liability, or the valuation implied by local regulators. A keen understanding of these parameters is important, since well-intentioned regulation can often have unintended consequences. A case in point is the U.S. corporate pension fund problem that, due to accounting gimmicks, runs the risk of making the AIG bailout look like a walk in the park.

John Osborn of Russell Investments kindly shared his convictions: "There are two key liabilities that DB plans are concerned with – accounting and funding.

Accounting – The discount rate is set by company management, as recommended by the actuary, in accordance with FAS/IAS GAAP guidelines – 'High quality corporate curve' generally interpreted to be AA corporates. Actuaries are now recommending their own proprietary interpretation of this. For example, Mercer publishes their Pension Discount Yield Curve and Index Rates monthly on their website. Another actuary has stated that "Barclays Capital Long Aa Credit and the Merrill Lynch High Quality 10+ and 15+ indexes" are most closely correlated with their rate. Historically, many plans used Moody's Long-Term Corporate Bond Yield. A better, more general proxy is the Citigroup Pension Discount Curve and its related Citigroup Pension Liability Index; sadly, there is no one unique benchmark that all corporate funds can use.

Funding – With the adoption of the PPA in the United States, the Internal Revenue Service (IRS) has also moved to a high quality corporate curve. Plans have the choice of a 24-month average "segmented" curve or a "spot" full yield curve (actually a 1-month average). Given the recent debacle to liabilities and what happened to rates in 2008, a new provision allows plans to look back a few months (e.g., for 12/31/08 valuations, plans can look back to October '08), thereby providing a huge element of funding relief (but not addressing the long-term underfunded situation). The IRS publishes these yields monthly. Many complain that their methodology is not transparent and the resulting curve cannot be replicated in practice.

"During good economic times, companies emphasized accounting measures, in part because many plans were in surplus and generating pension income (non-cash profit and loss items), and were taking contribution holidays. My sense is that the pendulum is shifting back towards cash, as funded status has collapsed, and PPA is much more stringent in requiring contributions at a time that companies are cash poor. Many street analysts ignore pension-related income and expense. Some in the industry argue that a Treasury curve should be used to calculate the true economic liability. No plans that I know of do this, and obviously right now this would be extremely onerous."

Some of the more innovative clients and consultants (Frank Russell has advised at least one other corporate fund on this approach) provide CIOs and implementation agents (e.g., The Clifton Group) with a menu indicating the acceptable extent for hedging liability, based on the level of interest rates (*and possibly credit spreads*). While such a stance may, in effect, be successful, it is a bet by the consultant and the CIO on the likely movement of rates once they pass certain thresholds – i.e., it implies a view on the markets.

Figure 6.1 shows a hypothetical chart of what such a Marginally SMART LDI operation may resemble and it assumes a continuous reaction function whereas, in practice, given the realities of swap transactions, the function may need to be made more discrete. In this SMART approach, the rule clearly specifies how much liability should be hedged, based on the level of nominal interest rates and credit spreads. As shown in Figure 6.1, when credit spreads are high, a 2.5 percent nominal long-term rate implies a 25 percent hedge (top line). When credit spreads are low, a move to the same liability hedge requires a 3 percent nominal rate (bottom line).

THE SMART VIEW-BASED APPROACH

Though the previous approach is merited with simplicity and clarity of action, and can be considered a SMART LDI approach, it implies mean reversion of rates and credit spreads in the liability hedge. Further, this chart assumes that hedges will be added and lifted, though in real-life implementation there may be a tendency to only increase hedges, in the mistaken perception that 100 percent hedged is a low risk alternative. The analogy to the full currency hedge espoused by the DnB should be obvious. Such an approach is subject to a changing mean, fluctuating time horizon of mean reversion (much like was demonstrated as the problem with

Swensen's (2005) and (2009) rebalancing approach), and a potential lack of clarity on the particular market factor that currently spurs the liability hedge.

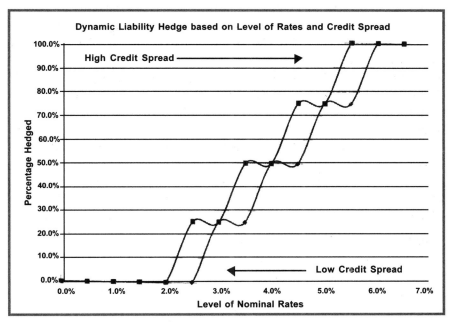

Figure 6.1. The simple/marginal SMART liability hedge – the U.S. case.

The absence of a clear understanding of risk factors driving the LDI hedge does not allow an overburdened CIO to be decisive at short notice. SMART LDI requires a study that defines when extending/shortening duration is preferable to doing nothing, thereby reserving such decision-making only for propitious times. In the detailed factor-based approach, the basis for believing that rates can mean revert is driven by market factors.

Consider a relatively simple liability profile for a Dutch pension fund, as highlighted in Table 6.1. For the sake of exposition, Figure 6.2 provides a slightly

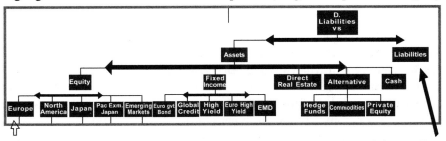

Figure 6.2. The SMART IDP – liability matching portfolio as a potential "asset".

revised Investment Decision Process (IDP) for the CIO, where every branch in the hierarchy is an opportunity for SMART decision-making.[123] To some degree, this IDP resembles the PME and Vervoer Pension Fund IDPs, and possibly many other Dutch funds. The only difference across pension funds is likely to be in the weights of each portfolio decision (PD) and possibly the index to which the PD is measured. Two aspects of this chart are highlighted – the first is the liability hedging box made up of the securities in Table 6.1 (marked with an arrow at the top level of the IDP in Figure 6.2). Put differently, a traditional investment policy can be seen as a 100 percent allocation to the SAA and a zero percent allocation to the ILP. For simplicity, assume the sum of the assets and the liability hedge can exceed the total AUM (i.e., swaps can be used to hedge liabilities and can be traded on a notional, rather than a funded basis). The second are the possibilities for SMART Rebalancing (horizontal arrows at the next two levels of the IDP in Figure 6.2) to be applied to enhance the return and risks of the overall fund – primarily, across the asset class level in the portfolio; and secondarily, within the major asset classes.

TABLE 6.1. SAA for hypothetical Dutch fund

Asset Class	Allocation (%)	Index
Equities	45	Rolled up composite
- *Europe*	*20.25*	*MSCI Europe*
- *N. America*	*18.00*	*Frank Russell 1000*
- *Japan*	*2.25*	*FTSE All World Japan*
- *Pacific ex-Japan*	*1.35*	*FTSE All World Asia ex Japan*
- *Emerging markets*	*3.15*	*FTSE All World Emerging*
Bonds	40	Rolled up composite
- *Euro government*	*12.00*	*Barclays Euro Agg Govt*
- *Global credit*	*12.00*	*Mernill Lynch EMU Corporate*
- *High yield*	*6.00*	*Merrill Lynch High Yield II Master*
- *European high yield*	*4.00*	*Merrill Lynch European High Yield*
- *Emerging debt*	*6.00*	*JP Morgan Emerging Market Bond +*
Real estate and alternatives	15	Direct Real Estate Index + Global Fixed Income + 1%

Table 6.1 shows the distribution of SAA for this hypothetical fund. The basic statistics on both the ILP and the SAA (2001-2006) provided in Table 6.2 demonstrate that the annualized ILP return was 6.83 percent (with 4.5 percent volatility), exceeding the SAA return of 6.03 percent (with 8.42 percent volatility). Other statistics are included to provide a feel for the distribution of returns (average when positive, average when negative, worst single performance, and the ratio of good-to-bad risk) and the degree of decline in value (maximum drawdown). The table shows that

[123] Chapter 8 adds external/internal managers to this IDP.

a typical SAA has an enormous drawdown – validated by the exigencies of 2008, and hence solvency risk is likely to have a similar profile. Further, the drawdown on the asset portfolio is approximately four times the drawdown of the ILP! The most fascinating statistic is not provided: that the correlation of the SAA to liabilities is zero. This has significant implications for drawdowns of the surplus.

TABLE 6.2. Statistics for ILP and SAA:hypothetical Dutch fund (2001-2006)

Portfolio Decision	Annualized Return (%)	Annualized Standard Deviation (%)	Annualized Return-Risk Ratio	Average Return When Positive (%)	Average Return When Negative (%)
Assets	6.03	8.42	0.72	1.73	-2.36
Liabilities	6.83	4.51	1.52	1.39	-0.91
Portfolio Decision	Worst Single Negative Performance	Worst Negative Performance Occurred On	Maximum Drawdown (%)	Maximum Drawdown Occurred On	Ratio of Good/Bad Risk
Assets	-6.95	6/28/2002	-21.16	3/31/2003	0.64
Liabilities	-2.33	3/31/2006	-5.46	6/30/2006	1.01

It is assumed the SAA study was conducted with estimates of expected returns for 10 years, but typically these studies come up short, as one is not sure where the actual returns may manifest themselves. The fact that the asset-liability returns are so close after the first five years should be cause for jubilation, given the difference in asset-liability volatility. A naïve interpretation of the table would please some analysts, since no case is made for dipping into the equity pond, given the drawdown, returns, and volatility.

Therefore, though a typical consultant may be anxious about the return differential between ILP and SAA, and deem the 0.8 percent difference to be the required annualized alpha to cover the gap, what is lost in this simplistic objective setting is that, typically, the ILP's volatility at 4.5 percent is 55 percent of the asset portfolio's volatility, indicating that the plan sponsor has to bear enormous risk – not to mention other deterrents, such as the worst single performance, maximum drawdown, and ratio of good/bad risk, implying the imminence of high ALM risk. With everything fixed in terms of a choice of assets and liabilities, the only flexible parameter is dynamic allocation.

In this example, a set of rules framed in 2005 were applied to the portfolio.[124] For simplicity, the assumption is that decisions are made only once a month at the end of the month. A more practical, effective method would be to allow decisions to be

---

[124] Muralidhar (2005a) and Muralidhar (2005b) describe the dynamic investment process in detail.

made daily, though SMART rules may not actually trigger every day – in fact, a smart CIO can design the program to work on an individualized, desired frequency. For this example, monthly decision-making is made on the basis that, at a minimum, pension funds review asset allocation decisions at month-end, to act thereafter on cash flows.

The following economic/financial factors are used to help decide whether or not to recommend an allocation to implement a liability hedge (by buying the ILP). Each of the four rules (factors listed below), originally used to help with rebalancing across assets, is applied here to show that the factors are not data-mined and will be used across the two key levels of decision-making. By using derivatives to gain liability exposure, "leverage" may actually curtail risk and, as shown in the M^2 measure, leverage is beneficial when deployed appropriately. Four simple factors used to decide whether or not to hedge are listed below, and each is arbitrarily equally weighted at 25 percent to register no further factor data-mining. The resulting analysis demonstrates that exploiting the assumptions underlying the correlation matrix is not rocket science, but rather a simple application of economic intuition to asset class performance, and a more detailed factor analysis could easily generate better results.

- o *Baltic Dry Index*: Economic activity is measured by shipping goods across markets, and one measure of shipping activity is the Baltic Dry Index. When this index of global economic activity rises above (falls below) a historic threshold, it tends to be mean reverting. Economic growth tends to be inflationary; hence, one would not seek to extend duration when inflation has the potential to rise.[125]

- o *Oil*: If the price of oil rises, it is typically inflationary and not a favorable indicator for extending duration.[126]

- o *Seasonality*: During the summer months, investors avoid risk, but at all other times they seem to opt for risk. A CIO benchmarked to an SAA (and not the ILP), should discard the hedge in the summer but keep it on otherwise.[127]

- o *Momentum*: For simplicity, use the trend of the 10-year swap index in the ILP, as an indicator of the ILP's general trend. If the performance of fixed

---

[125] Thanks to Patrick Groenendijk, Roland van den Brink, and Philip Menco for pointing out this statistic as far back as 2003.

[126] This is basic economic intuition and a frequent topic of discussion, including in the daily editions of the *Wall Street Journal*.

[127] Jacobsen and Bouman (2001). Also known as the "Sell in May and Go Away" strategy (Ned Davis Research).

income assets shows improvement, the CIO should allocate to the ILP – otherwise do nothing.

Figure 6.4 shows the resulting allocation to the liability hedge (jagged line above zero). For attribution reasons, an offsetting negative position to a zero return portfolio is shown.

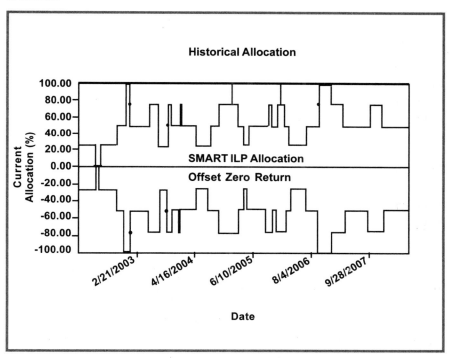

Figure 6.4. Historical allocation of the liability hedge.

Table 6.3 demonstrates that each rule individually adds value relative to a "Do Nothing" approach, and a combination of these four rules leads to a comfortably diversified strategy (weighted combination of the four rules). For example, the momentum-based liability hedge is the most effective and generates a 4.06 percent annualized return (for 3.75 percent volatility) versus doing nothing. Equally weighting all four rules provides 2.31 percent annualized excess versus not hedging. To be precise, if three rules say "Do Nothing" and the fourth says "Full Hedge", the CIO interprets it as a 25 percent hedge, using the ILP. As more rules click into place, the hedge ratio increases. Table 6.3 shows the results were not optimized, as the annualized return-risk ratio of the strategy is less than that of the best rule, and includes the Oil Rule even though it performed poorly.

TABLE 6.3 Value of SMART LDI rules and strategy versus doing nothing (2002-2008)

Performance Summary			
	Annualized Return	Annualized Standard Deviation	Annualized Return-Risk Ratio
Total Period			
Strategy Excess	2.31%	2.47%	0.9333
SMART LDI Oil			
Excess	0.09%	2.50%	0.0372
SMART LDI			
Summer Excess	1.11%	2.01%	0.5493
SMART LDI Baltic			
Excess	3.50%	4.02%	0.8691
SMART LDI Trend			
Excess	4.06%	3.75%	1.0809

However, if this SMART LDI strategy does not combine well with the SAA, adding value proves inadequate, as ultimately the purpose is to ensure that the sum of all portfolio decisions achieves the solvency goals within acceptable risks. Table 6.4a presents the results of the SMART LDI plus the SAA (titled "Strategy" in the Table) in comparison with the SAA (titled "BMK") from 2002-2006; and Table 6.4b provides the same comparison for 2002-2008. The most critical outcome is that adding the liability hedge left overall volatility unchanged (8.42-8.51 percent, and 7.42-7.54 percent over the two periods, respectively), whereas adding excess returns would potentially enhance overall solvency from a return perspective. One needs to evaluate how these parameters compare with the liability, and ascertain whether a trade-off has been made between enhanced asset returns and lower correlation to ILP.

An additional level of sophistication that can be applied to the SMART LDI strategy is to dig deeper into each ILP maturity component and then manage the allocations and positions relative to the ILP. Therefore, CIOs or investors with strong capabilities to manage the duration and convexity risk implied in the ILP have the wherewithal to extract additional value from the ILP hedge.

TABLE 6.4a Performance of SMART LDI strategy versus SAA benchmark (2002-2006)

Performance Summary					
	Annualized Return	Annualized Standard Deviation	Annualized Return-Risk Ratio	Average Return when Positive	Average Return when Negative
Total Period					
BMK	6.03%	8.42%	0.7167	32.91%	6.03%
Strategy	9.50%	8.51%	1.1158	55.36%	9.44%
Excess	3.46%	2.53%	1.3673	22.45%	3/41%

Comparing the performance of the ILP with that of the SMART LDI strategy clearly shows that adding the dynamic hedge allows the portfolio to outperform liabilities – something a pure LDI strategy would not have achieved, especially if the plan started out underfunded.

BETA ENGINE

A dynamic SAA, based on market factors, and alternatively termed a View-based SAA (after allowing for the View-Neutral dynamic SAA in the previous chapter and the SMART LDI), is highly recommended.

TABLE 6.4b Performance of SMART LDI strategy versus SAA benchmark (2002-2008)

Performance Summary			
	Annualized Return	Annualized Standard Deviation	Annualized Return-Risk Ratio
Strategy	4.62%	7.42%	0.62.20
BMK	2.31%	7.54%	0.3061
Excess	2.31%	2.47%	0.9333

More important, the dynamism is not intended to keep tracking error low or raise the information ratio, but *ideally to help assets outperform liabilities while increasing the correlation* (thereby lowering the ALM risks). The case study provides an example of how SMART Rebalancing can be used to improve solvency. Once again, SMART Rebalancing rules were established in 2005, and the post-2005 results are out-of-sample.[128]

---

[128] Thanks to Roland van den Brink (PME and Mn Services) and Patrick Groenendijk (formerly with PME, currently with Vervoer) for their assistance in this analysis.

As in the SMART LDI portion of this analysis, the following economic factors were converted into rules. Again, little more than economic intuition was applied to this analysis, and hence this is well within the realm of the average CIO.

o *Baltic Dry Index:* When this index of global economic activity rises above/falls below a historic threshold, it tends to be mean reverting. Economic growth/recession tends to benefit stocks/fixed income, respectively. Hence one would invest in stocks/bonds when global economic activity improves/declines, respectively.

o *Oil:* If the price of oil rises, this is typically bad/(good) for stocks (bonds) relative to bonds (stocks) and vice versa.

o *Seasonality:* During the summer months, investors avoid risk, but at all other times they take on risk. It has been shown, in 37 out of 39 countries, that the seasonality rule of avoiding stocks in the summer is profitable.

o *Dividend Yield:* Research has shown that investors favor stocks when dividend yields are high and vice versa. Here, only the S&P 500 and Eurostoxx dividend yields are used as indicators.

o *P/E Ratio:* When the P/E ratio is low, the market is undervalued and vice versa.[129]

o *Fed Model:* When the yield of stocks is greater than that of bonds, favor stocks and vice versa.[130]

Table 6.5 reports the excess return of each rule individually, along with its tracking error, and then does the same for a strategy that equally weights each rule at 100 percent, indicating if one rule says overweight stocks by 1 percent and another says overweight bonds by 1 percent, the two cancel each other out and the portfolio is maintained at the benchmark. Again, the combination of many simple rules adds value, as does each idea individually. The fact that the post-2005 results are out-of-sample is evidence of the durability of good economic intuition when combined with SMARTs. The order of magnitude here is much smaller than in the SMART LDI case because most funds restrict policy ranges around the SAA to no more than +/-5 percent. As a result, there is little room to maneuver. However, Muralidhar and Muralidhar (2009) have shown, from an asset-only perspective, clients opting for higher absolute risk by restricting rebalancing policy ranges - this point was first made by Barrett (2006) and supported actively by Allan Martin of New England Pension Consultants as the correct way to manage a pension fund.

PUTTING IT ALL TOGETHER – CAN ONE TRULY IMPROVE SOLVENCY?

Previous sections have attempted to show how SMART LDI and SMART Rebalancing add value relative to the SAA. The economic factors and SMART

---

[129] Campbell and Shiller (1998a).
[130] O'Higgins (1999).

Rules utilized to elucidate the case had been set in 2005; hence, even with simple examples, the out-of-sample results have been astounding and durable. Though one may criticize this approach for generalizing, based on a simple case study (as these rules could have easily underperformed over a different time window), the emphasis is on process rather than specific factors.

TABLE 6.5 Performance of SMART rebalancing vs. SAA benchmark (2002-2008)

Performance Summary			
	Annualized Return	Annualized Standard Deviation	Annualized Return-Risk Ratio
Total Period			
Strategy Excess	0.43%	0.45%	0.9611
SMART LDI: Eq v FI-Dividend Yield Excess	0.03%	0.05%	0.5170
SMART LDI: EQ v FI - FED Model Excess	0.11%	0.19%	0.5498
SMART LDI: EQ v FI - Summer Effect Excess	0.07%	0.12%	0.5586
SMART LDI: EQ v FI - Oil Rule Excess	0.13%	0.13%	1.0587
SMART LDI: EQ v FI-P:E Ratio Excess	0.03%	0.13%	0.2307
SMART LDI: EQ v FI - Baltic Dry Index Excess	0.07%	0.13%	0.5332

As has been pointed out from the opening chapters, the intrinsic value is the implication for solvency of the pension fund. Hence, this section directs all possible strategies to the most vital benchmark – liabilities. The parameters used to gauge the efficacy of each strategy are highlighted in Chapter 3. For simplicity, assume the current funded status is 100 percent. This raises the question – given the generous current funded status, and historical annual growth in surplus and volatility – what is the probability of the funded status exceeding 105 percent at the end of a calendar year?

After a brief overview of the various approaches, Table 6.6 summarizes all the results from an ALM perspective. Interestingly, when the same rules and principles are applied to the Vervoer Pension Fund (with updated data through April 2009), with no additional customization for different benchmarks, the conclusions are confirmed, validating this approach for a broad swath of pension funds in the Netherlands (at a minimum) and in other countries as well. Transaction costs are ignored because the degree of annualized turnover indicated by any of these strategies is trivial, as compared with the value they add. Moreover, many of these strategies are implemented by using exchange-traded futures which have the greatest liquidity and transparency, and lowest cost-to-trade, as indicated in Chapter 3.

o   *Static Asset Allocation:* This is merely the constantly rebalanced asset portfolio.

o   *Add SMART LDI:* This is the SAA with the View-based SMART LDI hedge overlay.

o   *Add SMART Rebalancing;* This is the SAA with the SMART LDI hedge overlay combined with a restricted (in terms of ranges) form of SMART Rebalancing.

o   *Annual Rebalancing:* For comparison, the SAA is allowed to drift intra year, per the recommendation of many ALM consultants in the Netherlands.

o   *Three Percent Range Rebalancing:* Another alternative, common in other countries in the Anglo-Saxon world and Japan, is to set ranges around the SAA and allow the portfolio to drift until a range is hit and then the assets are rebalanced back to the SAA weights.

TABLE 6.6 The Solvency Perspective – comparing all strategies (2002-2008)

Case	Solvency growth %	Volati- lity %	Correlation of portfolio with liability	Draw- down of Surplus (%)	Confi- dence in skill (%)	Success ratio (%)	Prob. funded ratio < 105% at the end of 1 year
(1a.) Static SAA	-2.69	9.73	-0.27	-28.45	20.2	49.37	78.54
(1b.) Add SMART LDI	-0.04	8.53	-0.11	-24.31	40.91	55.7	72.27
(1c.) Add SMART rebalancing	0.02	8.55	-0.05	-23.12	45.89	56.9	71.99
(2.) Annual rebalancing	-2.51	9.41	0.01	-27.57	21	50.63	78.76
(3.) 3 percent range rebalancing	-2.65	9.73	-0.02	-28.42	20.54	50.63	78.41

The best outcome for each category is shaded in grey. The focus is exclusively on SMART View-based decision-making, whereas a creative client takes the best of SMART View-Neutral LDI, View-based LDI, and Rebalancing to truly optimize the fund's results.

o The average SAA is poorly correlated with liabilities. This has been the greatest pitfall of ALM in recent years, and experience has shown that no amount of dynamism can rectify a poorly designed SAA.[131]

o Adding successive layers of SMART decision-making, where portfolios are already dynamic, increases the likelihood that a portfolio will outperform its liability benchmark with minimal risk. In the case study, the potential value that can be generated from additional layers of rebalancing within Equities and Fixed Income were not considered and, needless to say, this would further improve the ALM profile.

o Interestingly, SMART portfolios not only have low absolute volatility, but can also help manage surplus volatility. Chapter 8 includes a Japanese case study that allows for dynamic manager allocation and goes the additional step to select SMART Rebalancing rules with a unique correlation property vis-à-vis liabilities, providing even more fascinating results.

o The drawdown of the surplus (or the likelihood of a big contribution injection) is minimized by including SMART LDI and SMART Rebalancing (and can be reduced further by adding intra-equity rebalancing and intra-fixed income rebalancing).

o The success ratio (i.e., percentage of times the portfolio beats the liability benchmark) is also highest when SMART LDI and SMART Rebalancing are employed. Interestingly, the success ratio is less than 50 percent in all cases and the fund can still experience positive solvency growth.

o In this hypothetical example, the probability of being under the DnB mandated 105 percent funding ratio target (usually in 3 years, but in this case it is assumed after 1 year) is lowest when using the SMART LDI and Rebalancing approach.

SUMMARY

Pension funds should incorporate many levels of dynamism in managing assets to improve solvency. This chapter focused on SMART VB LDI and SMART Rebalancing to accomplish this goal. It also showed how an integrated approach of

---

[131] Lester Siegel is credited with this observation.

SMART LDI and SMART Rebalancing helps to improve solvency and lower the probability of being under any regulatory thresholds while, at the same time, keeping all emotional and financial risk management parameters at the safest end of all currently implemented rebalancing strategies. SMART decision-making can be applied to every level of a portfolio IDP. Hence, adding more layers of decisions can only improve the solvency profile.

The book digresses briefly to discuss risk budgeting and external manager compensation before demonstrating the efficacy of an integrated SMART LDI, Beta Engine, and Alpha Engine.

7

Skill, Risk Budgeting, and Risk-adjusted Performance Fees

"All animals are equal, but some animals are more equal than others."
George Orwell
"We made too many wrong mistakes." Yogi Berra [132]

BACKGROUND

George Orwell's reference to animals is a popular quote from contemporary literature, but lest one wonders about its relevance to finance, this chapter turns to the topic of risk budgeting, which has become very popular. Recent experiences with presentations at conferences (including a case study at a CFA Seminar in Japan in 2006),[133] analyses for pension funds conducted by third parties (including asset managers and consultants), and even software offered to clients and so-called risk management companies by asset managers[134] suggest that pension funds (or other investors) may not be getting sound advice. The three areas where current approaches seem to be inaccurate are: (i) conducting risk-budgeting analyses on an asset-only basis, instead of helping pension funds budget risk on an asset-liability basis; (ii) focusing unduly on *static* external manager allocations instead of allocating risk based on dynamic decisions made by the fund (allocations to various assets, investment styles, and managers) and then which managers allocate to (Waring et al 2000); and (iii) focusing on tracking error as a measure of risk instead of on other measures, such as absolute volatility and maximum drawdown. These shortcomings have hampered pension plans, causing regulators to question the ability of pension funds to manage risk.[135]

---

[132] Petras (2001), page 62, quotes Yogi Berra on why the New York Yankees baseball team lost the 1960 World Series.
[133] See, for example, Gentry (2006), *http://www.effas.com/pdf/18th_Joint_Seminar.pdf*
[134] These are risk measurement companies, as they do not advise the investor on the investment decisions that would improve the fund's risk profile.
[135] *http://www.ipe.com/news/Pension_system_risks_underestimated_DNB_31172.php*

The one consistent feature in the extensive literature on risk budgeting and risk management[136] is that tracking error is used as a measure of risk relative to a benchmark. However, this measure is used in its totality as a composite number without further evaluation of the components of this calculation.[137] In this chapter, attention is focused on only the tracking error, assuming for the sake of the argument that it is the crucial risk measure, though previous chapters show this is not always the case.

Chapters 2 and 3 have demonstrated that the tracking error is closely connected to confidence in skill; hence, the means by which it is generated can have different implications for how much confidence an investor has in an investment manager's skill.[138] This chapter explains why smart investors should not be indifferent between two equal tracking errors (assuming excess returns are identical), and indicates they would do well to specifically instruct their active managers on how to take risk in creating portfolios to outperform benchmarks. This analysis is conducted on an *ex-post* basis, but it is apparent the results apply on an *ex-ante* basis. The additional proposed analyses should help investors choose an optimal benchmark, a tracking error target, and a period over which the evaluation is carried out, as these may influence the final result. The entire argument is based on the premise that investors intend to compensate their managers for skill- and risk-adjusted performance.[139] The chapter concludes with a novel proposal for compensation to managers on the basis of their risk- and skill-adjusted performance.

DECOMPOSING TRACKING ERROR

Assuming an investor hires a single manager (as extending to multiple assets and multiple managers does not change the results) and that the tracking error of portfolio 1 versus the benchmark is defined as the annualized standard deviation of excess returns, its formulation will be as in equation (A.2.2). The justification for this, as being the appropriate measure for risk when an external manager is compared to a benchmark, is elegantly clarified in Ambarish and Siegel (1996).

---

[136] The most notable of these papers would be, in alphabetical order, Arnott (2002); Berkelaar et al (2006); Blitz and Hottinga (2001); Chow and Kritzman (2001); Grinold and Kahn (1999); Hammond (1997); Lee and Lam (2001); Litterman et al (2001); Litterman, R. et al (2003); Rahl (2000); Sharpe (1994); Sharpe (2002); and Sherer and Martin (2005).

[137] Work has been done on marginal contributions to tracking error as in Muralidhar (2001), but this still ignores the more important issue discussed here.

[138] Cornell (2008) proposes an alternative measure for skill, but Ambarish and Siegel (1996) is much more elegant and simple (with a clear connection to elucidate why the tracking error is the relative risk measure).

[139] Muralidhar (2009a).

Assume the manager beats the benchmark by 1.5 percent annualized. The annualized Information Ratio (IR) is equal to the annualized excess return divided by the annualized tracking error [equation (A.2.3)]. Outperformance over a benchmark, unfortunately, does not tell the investor whether the external manager or mutual fund manager is skillful (Modigliani and Modigliani 1997). Nor does it provide the investor with a measure of confidence that the alpha is generated by skill-based processes. Critical factors involved in answering the Luck versus Skill question include time, desired degree of confidence, investment returns of the portfolio and benchmark, standard deviation of the portfolio and the benchmark, and the degree of correlation between the two [equation (A.2.4)]. The problem, as pointed out in Chapter 2, is that performance data includes considerable noise, and the more volatile the portfolio and a manager's excess return series, the greater the noise, and hence the more time needed to resolve this issue. (Appendices 2.1 and 3.1 provide the details of these equations.)

Implications for Risk Budgeting and Portfolio Management

For simplicity, the results are presented in graphs, though it is apparent the implications for how tracking error is created through benchmark volatility, portfolio volatility, and correlation, and their impact on confidence in skill can be derived through a series of equations.[140] Therefore, this section starts with a simple experiment (Base Case) and assumes a 2 percent annualized tracking error, a benchmark annualized standard deviation of 10 percent, and a 2-year track record. This 2 percent tracking error can be achieved by multiple combinations of portfolio volatility and correlation for a given benchmark volatility.

For a given tracking error, Figure 7.1 plots the correlation (left vertical axis and square dots), the portfolio's volatility (right vertical axis and diamond-shaped dots), and confidence in skill (horizontal axis). For every confidence in skill level, there is a single correlation and portfolio volatility combination. As Figure 7.1 shows, an investor who is anxious about confidence in skill is not indifferent to the portfolio that the manager creates relative to the benchmark. This parabolic shape is consistent across all simulations.[141] *A smart investor would require the manager to have a high correlation to the benchmark and, as a result, potentially more volatility than the benchmark.* In other words, the preference for a manager with this simple objective is path-dependent. The more attractive portfolios have a higher confidence

---

[140] Differentiating between various parameters and holding others constant.
[141] The parabolic shape should come as no surprise to those who do the math.

in skill (moving from 82.4 percent to 88.8 percent), and this is the primary method that shows that not all tracking errors are equal. After all, only a naïve investor would choose the portfolio with the lowest confidence in skill, all else being equal.

This result has interesting implications for Modigliani and Modigliani (1997), as now an investor who conducts their portfolio normalization for risk adjustment (called the M^2) may make a sub-optimal portfolio decision based on skill.[142] Muralidhar (2000) extended Modigliani and Modigliani (1997) to make a case for creating

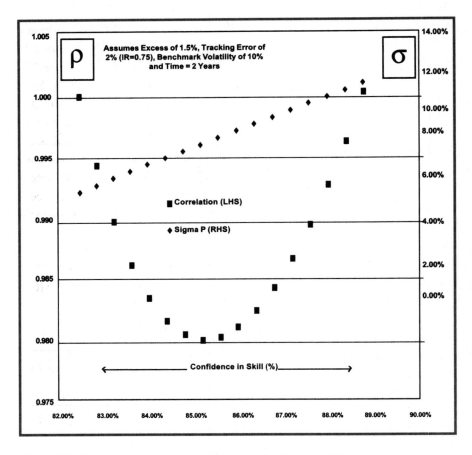

Figure 7.1. Base case – higher correlation and higher volatility are better.

---

[142]   In fairness, Modigliani and Modigliani (1997) assume that volatility is the measure of risk, and hence they normalize only for volatility of the portfolio relative to the benchmark. But an investor who is worried about relative risk and uses Modigliani and Modigliani (1997) could make a mistake, as leveraging/deleveraging the external manager by using risk-free cash does not change the correlation relative to the benchmark.

correlation risk-adjusted performance portfolios (M³) by ensuring portfolio volatility is set equal to benchmark volatility – which, in turn, implies a specific target correlation. *The analysis here suggests the M³ approach may be sub-optimal, even though Muralidhar (2001) claims that rankings based on the M³ measure of performance are consistent with rankings based on skill.*

For ease of exposition, Table 7.1 highlights four simple simulations that draw attention to the parameters being changed in each simulation and the resulting conclusions.

Where tracking error is the same but simulations have two different benchmark volatilities, the same 4 percent range for portfolio volatility (5-9 percent versus 8-12 percent) is also plotted. In this example, at low portfolio volatilities (Figure 7.2), *confidence in skill for the 7 percent benchmark volatility is higher than in the 10 percent benchmark volatility case,* but as volatility increases, confidence in skill rises to just 87.98 percent (i.e., lower than the equivalent Base Case portfolio). As the correlation declines from 1 (at the low end of portfolio volatility), confidence in skill in the Less Benchmark Risk Case is higher; this continues until the correlation rises beyond a threshold (correlation exceeds 0.992), at which point confidence in skill is lower than in the Base Case. This case is examined as clients have a choice of benchmark (e.g., in the United States, equity between the Russell 3000 and the

TABLE 7.1 Highlights of various simulations

Simulation	Tracking Error (%)	Time (years)	Std. Deviation of Benchmark (%)	IR
Base Case (Fig. 7.1)	2	2	10	0.75
Less Benchmark Risk (Fig.7.2)	2	2	7	0.75
More Tracking Error (Fig.7.3)	3	2	10	0.5
More Time (Fig. 7.4)	2	3	10	0.75

Wilshire 5000) for a given tracking error budget, and this analysis again suggests they need not be indifferent between two benchmarks with similar market coverage.

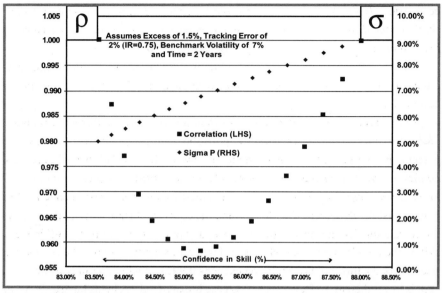

Figure 7.2. Less benchmark risk - ambiguous results.

The next case (Figure 7.3) is simple, as an increase in tracking error has the most direct impact on lowering the Information Ratio. All else being equal, this shows up as an immediate decline in confidence in skill, relative to the Base Case – this is obvious from the skill equation.

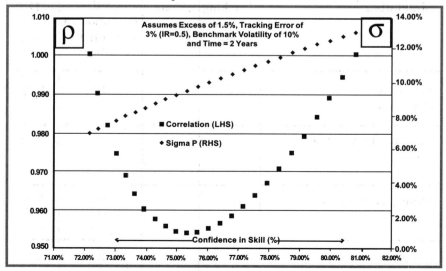

Figure 7.3. Increase in tracking error - confidence declines.

The final case (Figure 7.4) is quite trivial – the longer the track record (or "time"), all else being equal, the skill equation shows that confidence increases.

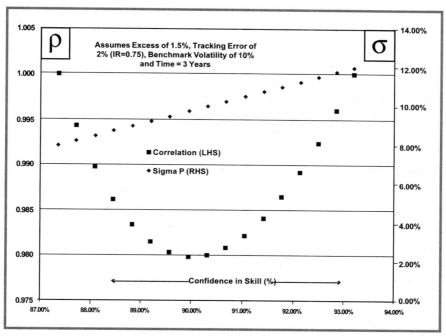

Figure 7.4. Adding time – confidence increases.

All Tracking Errors are Not Equal

Chapter 2 emphasized that investors hiring external asset managers have to be vigilant about managers' skills or they risk paying fees that are disproportionate to the managers' efforts. One of the provisions of the new Capital Relative Asset Pricing Model was that the principal had to state the target risk budget and ensure that the portfolio lies on the appropriate iso-confidence curve. The analysis clarified that an investor who focuses on confidence in skill is not indifferent to the manner in which a manager creates risk relative to the benchmark. For a given tracking error budget, *a smart investor requires the manager to have a high correlation to the benchmark and, as a result, potentially more volatility than the benchmark.* Therefore, this requires a re-examination of all previous analyses on relative risk, risk budgeting, and optimal allocation of risk.

Another condition needs to be added to existing research, namely, emphasis on a minimum correlation/volatility of portfolio combination, and re-examination of the result in this light. This approach assumes the investor does nothing to modify volatility and correlation characteristics of the risk-adjusted portfolio (à la the M^2 and M^3). Moreover, increasing the tracking error and decreasing the time factor have a negative impact on confidence in skill, and an ambiguous impact on volatility of the benchmark.

To return to the Animal Farm analogy, at the end of the novel, one of the pigs emerges upright from the farmhouse, carrying a whip. The animals had never seen anything more shocking! It goes against everything they had been taught. Just as it seemed some animals might object, the sheep broke into a deafening chorus of "Four legs good, two legs better."[143]

Compensating Asset Managers on a Risk- and Skill-adjusted Basis

After clarifying how risk budgets need to be allocated to control manager behavior, it is pertinent to deal with the subject of appropriate compensation for managers, as inadequate compensation schemes could pressure managers into taking unintended risks. Recent scandals over pay for executives at financial intermediaries begs the question whether fees in the investment management industry adjust appropriately for the risk involved and encourage long-term alignment of interests, leading to the conclusion, generally, that compensation fees for investment managers and investment staff are not long term and *do not* adequately adjust for skill and risk. The three primary fee structures are based on: (i) assets under management (50 bps per annum on assets under management); (ii) absolute returns (2 percent + 20 percent of performance); and (iii) outperformance relative to some benchmark. In the interest of full disclosure, this author receives compensation from clients on a fixed and performance-fee basis – without adjusting for risk (addressed later).

Incredibly, Modigliani and Pogue (1973, 1975) wrote seminal papers on this subject in response to changes in SEC rules on investment compensation. They highlighted the need for performance fees to be adjusted for risk to ensure appropriate compensation and regulatory oversight. They proposed and evaluated a few simple fee structures, but a "Google" search for more updated proposals shows a paucity of practical recommendations on this topic. Of the numerous theoretical papers on principal-agent fee structures for this industry, the most practical suggestions are given by Raymond (2008) who reports on how the Canadian Pension Plan Investment Board structured fees in an attempt to pay only for skill, not luck. In the investment management industry, the principal-agent relationships are pervasive and tiered, providing some useful theoretical ideas with no real practical benefit. Moreover,

---

[143]   *http://www.online-literature.com/orwell/animalfarm/10/*

risk-adjusted compensation is pointless in the absence of effective risk-adjusted performance measures. It is no surprise then that Modigliani and Modigliani (1997) created a new risk-adjusted performance measure called the M^2, which opens the door to a rational discussion on risk-adjusted compensation for investment managers and investment professionals in pension funds, endowments, foundations, asset managers, hedge funds, etc. But, surprisingly, the late Prof. Modigliani did not connect his work on risk-adjusted performance to his work on risk-adjusted compensation, and this chapter attempts to fill that gap.

For simplicity, the discussion begins by assuming fully funded mandates with clearly articulated benchmarks.[144]

PRINCIPAL-AGENT RELATIONSHIP RECAP

Chapter 2 showed the asset management industry has many layers of principal-agent relationships, and often pension fund/endowment CIOs/staff are both principal and agent. Individual principal-agent relationships are analyzed, but the approach is generic so the compensation schemes can be stacked and are applicable at multiple levels of a fund.

What are some of the issues that the extensive principal-agent literature deal with, and do they offer any guidance on risk-adjusted compensation? When a principal hires an agent and delegates decision-making authority to them, this results in typically asymmetrical information, as the principal does not know if the agent is skilled (or informed, as in theoretical literature) and, more important, whether they are willing to exert the required effort to perform in the best interests of the principal. The agent would have to incur cost to expend the requisite effort and, as the principal cannot observe the effort, they need to find a way to monitor the agent to ensure that the principal's objectives are achieved.[145] In short, the situation is fraught with adverse selection and moral hazard problems, as also the need to design incentive-compatible contracts to encourage optimal behavior, given the asymmetric information and inability to clearly observe effort.

The investment business assumes the investor (or asset owner) hires a manager to outperform a clearly specified benchmark because of a perceived comparative advantage in favor of the manager. The asset owner expects the manager to outperform the benchmark within certain risk guidelines (as excessive risk-taking could lead to the loss of capital that does not impact the manager but penalizes the principal). Therefore, typically, the only worthwhile parameter reported to the asset owner is the periodic performance of the portfolio versus the benchmark. This data

---

[144] Seigel (2003) provides a comprehensive overview of benchmarks.
[145] See Woodbury and Neal (1999) and Das and Sundaram (1998).

is used to calculate performance and *ex post* risk statistics, but the drawback is that performance data is noisy – i.e., it does not clearly demonstrate how much of the performance is truly from skill and not luck (Appendix 2.1). The asset owner obviously wishes to pay the agent only for skill-based performance, but this issue is baffling, as often the number of periods of data needed to make such estimations can be overwhelming.[146]

The theory of optimal contracts, with its focus on absolute risk aversion parameters, exponential utility functions, and convex payoff functions, is too abstract for effective, practical application in the investment industry. However, there is general consensus that the viable structure of fees is a combination of a fixed fee (to cover the costs for the agent) and an element of variable fees (linked to performance of the portfolio). In the interest of simplicity, the focus is on the performance-based component and shows how effective risk-adjusted performance must capture all risks incurred in managing a portfolio while, at the same time, providing some indication of skill. This approach assumes selection of the correct benchmark for performance and risk evaluation by the asset owner, as this is a fundamental tenet of the entire argument (raised by Modigliani and Pogue 1975),[147] and it addresses the difficulties encountered in evaluating assets that are not easily benchmarked .

BACKGROUND LITERATURE ON RISK-ADJUSTED PERFORMANCE FEES

The literature on risk-adjusted performance fees appears to be limited to Modigliani and Pogue (1975) and the response from Magrabe (1976). All the subsequent literature is on main-line performance fees (Davanzo and Nesbitt 1987, Kritzman 1987, Raymond 2008). Schliemann and Stanzel (2008) provide an extensive overview of the entire gamut of performance-based fees and their characteristics (e.g., options such as payoffs, high-water marks, reset periods), review the extensive principal-agent literature, and yet mention risk-adjustment only in passing without developing any concepts, except to state, "In practice, it would be necessary to use a multidimensional performance measure like the Information Ratio to control the

---

[146]   Ambarish and Siegel (1996).
[147]   Admati and Pfleiderer (1997) examine, theoretically, the use of benchmark portfolios in the compensation of privately informed portfolio managers. They find that the use of a benchmark, and particularly the types of benchmarks often observed in practice, cannot be easily rationalized. Specifically, commonly used benchmark-adjusted compensation schemes are generally inconsistent with optimal risk-sharing and do not lead to the choice of an optimal portfolio for the investor. Moreover, benchmarks do not help in solving potential contracting problems such as inducing the manager to expend effort or screening out uninformed managers.

possibility of increased or decreased risk-taking due to performance fee incentives. Simple return measures do not account for this specific problem."[148] Interestingly, even a recent article by Arnott (2005), which summarizes all the issues relating to performance-based fees, does not refer to compensation for risk-adjusted performance!

Schliemann and Stanzel (2008) identify the key aspects of performance fee structures, namely, (i) the benchmark, which could be a zero return or LIBOR; (ii) the base or flat fee; (iii) the hurdle rate over which performance fees are paid; (iv) the high-water mark (typical of fee structures that have an asymmetric payoff); (v) the participation rate (or the percentage of profits to be shared with the investment manager); (vi) the resetting period over which any high-water mark may be limited; and (vii) a fee cap. This chapter presents a simple risk-adjusted compensation structure without looking into high-water marks, reset periods, and caps (these are addressed in the discussion on extensions).

Modigliani and Pogue (1975) highlight three different fee structures based on (a) assets under management (e.g., 50 bps per annum); (b) absolute returns (e.g., 2 percent + 20 percent of performance); or (c) outperformance relative to some benchmark. They quickly reject the first two as irrelevant, as these do not align the asset owner's interests with the manager's, as neither one adjusts for risk. They consider two different performance fee arrangements that attempt to adjust for risk.

Plan 1 is used in current practice:performance is measured by comparing the return of the fund directly with that of a market index, such as the Standard and Poor's 500 Stock Composite Index. Plan 2 employs the "market line"-type of risk adjustment usually associated with CAPM, where performance is measured by comparing the fund return with that of a risk ("beta")-adjusted market portfolio.[149,150] Modigliani and Pogue (1975) note that *non-risk*-adjusted performance fee plans are beset with problems. Apparently, this was also observed by the Securities and Exchange Commission, who stated in a letter of transmittal to the Institutional Investor Study: "When an adviser is compensated on the basis of total return or return relative to an index having a lower volatility than the portfolio itself, an

---

[148]   This article provides one of the most comprehensive surveys in academic principal-agent literature and current practice in the mutual fund and hedge fund industry.[148]

[149]   This article leverages the original text extensively to keep the original content intact.

[150]   Muralidhar (1999) argues that the traditional CAPM is incorrect because it does not account for principal-agent relationships and is a statement of capital markets and asset pricing when all participants are principals. As a result, any measures derived from the traditional CAPM are incorrect when applied to agents. Instead, a more general CAPM needs to be derived, based on principal-agent relationships, of which the traditional CAPM is a specialized case. The risk-adjusted measure proposed later in the article would be consistent with the more general CAPM.

incentive is created for the manager to assume greater risk. Thus, when incentive fees are present,...(it) appears desirable to eliminate as fully as possible the realization of compensation by investment managers based in part on risk borne by portfolio beneficiaries." [151]

Modigliani and Pogue (1975) point out a possible solution to the problem in the same study: "To accomplish this end the Commission intends to give serious and prompt consideration to requiring that incentive fees be based only on volatility adjusted investment returns. Incentive compensation would thus be permitted only on that portion of total investment return in excess of what general market movements affecting securities displaying equivalent volatility would produce on an unmanaged basis. Technical methods for basing incentive fees on such risk or volatility adjusted returns were adopted for analytic purposes by the Study. Although the techniques employed are of relatively recent origin, it appears that measures of risk-adjusted investment "performance" such as employed in the Study are feasible. Their use, as well as other methods for accomplishing this end that may be developed, can provide appropriate and unbiased methods of calculating managerial compensation that would discourage the assumption of excessive risk in managed portfolios, permit superior advisers to obtain additional compensation and permit the profitable operation of smaller economic units not having access to large and efficient sales organizations." [152] Modigliani and Modigliani (1997) achieve this objective, as explained later in this chapter.

"The Commission, via the 1970 Act essentially has the authority to require risk-adjusted measures for incentive fee plans. The Commission now has authority under the Investment Advisers Act of 1940 as amended by the Investment Company Amendments Act of 1970 to determine an appropriate index or other measure of investment performance for incentive compensation purposes that reflects the degree of volatility displayed by managed portfolios". [153]

The Modigliani and Pogue (1975) approach examines both proposals analytically and with the aid of simulation. They argue that CAPM relates the expected return on a portfolio to its systematic risk, as measured by beta (β_p). That is,

[151]   "Adoption of Rule 205-1 Under the Investment Advisers Act of 1940 Defining 'Investment Performance' of an Investment Company and 'Investment Record' of an Appropriate Index of Securities Prices," Investment Advisers Act of 1940, Release Number 327, U.S. Securities and Exchange Commission, Washington, D.C., August 8, 1972.

[152]   "Adoption of Rule 205-2 Under the Investment Advisers Act of 1940, As Amended, Defining the Specific Period Over Which the Asset Value of the Company or Fund Under Management is Averaged," Investment Advisers Act of 1940, Release No. 347, U.S. Securities and Exchange Commission, Washington D.C., November 10, 1972.

[153]   "Factors to be Considered in Connection with Investment Company Advisory Contracts Containing Incentive Fee Arrangements," Investment Advisers Act of 1940, Release Number 315, U.S. Securities and Exchange Commission, Washington, D.C., April 6, 1972.

$$E[r(P)] = r(F) + \beta_p * (E[r(M) - r(F)]), \tag{7.1}$$

where $E[r(P)]$, $E[r(M)]$, and $r(F)$ are the expected returns on the portfolio, market index, and riskless bond, respectively. Thus, the realized return during the period can be expressed as:

$$r(P) = r(F) + \beta_p * (r(M) - r(F)) + \bar{e}_p, \tag{7.2}$$

where $\bar{e}_p$ is the residual (unsystematic) element of the portfolio return which, under the CAPM hypothesis, has a zero expected return. Realized values of $\bar{e}p$ different from zero are evidence of superior ($\bar{e}_p > 0$) or inferior ($\bar{e}_p < 0$) investment performance.

Assume that the amount of the performance fee paid to the adviser is directly proportional to the return differential between the fund and the standard, $r(S)$, then the fee paid, FEE_p, is given by:

$$FEE_p = \delta(r(P) - r(S)), \tag{7.3}$$

where δ is the constant of proportionality between the return differential and fee dollars or, in the terminology of Schliemann and Stanzel (2008), the participation rate.

Consider first the non-risk adjusted Plan 1. The comparison standard is simply the market return, I. Substituting for $r(P)$ from equation (7.2) and $r(S)$ into equation (7.3):

$$FEE_p = \delta \{(\hat{a}_p - 1)(r(M) - r(F))\} + \bar{e}_p. \tag{7.4}$$

Thus, the performance fee depends on the fund's beta and market risk premium $r(M) - r(F)$, as well as the CAPM performance measure β_p. The expected fee is given by:

$$E[FEE_p] = \delta \{(\beta_p - 1)E[(r(M) - r(F))]\}. \tag{7.5}$$

If the expected market risk premium is assumed positive, the expected fee is an increasing function of β_p. For "neutral" performance relative to the CAPM standard (i.e., $\bar{e}_p = 0$), the expected fee is positive for funds with β_p greater than 1, and negative for funds with betas less than 1. Thus, Plan 1 has a built-in bias in favor of higher risk funds.

The equation shows that the fee variation in Plan 1 has two components: a market term resulting from bias in the performance measure, and a residual term resulting from incomplete portfolio diversification. The market component increases for beta differentials on either side of $\beta_p = 1$. The CAPM, however, gives no indication of how the residual component will vary with β_p, if at all.

The return standard ($r(S)$), in Plan 2, is equal to the mixture of market index and risk-free rate with the same beta as the fund. Thus, $r(S) = r(F) + \beta_p*(r(M) - r(F))$. Substitution for $r(P)$ and $r(S)$ in equation (7.3) gives the expression for *FEE*:

$$FEE_p = \delta\bar{e}_p. \tag{7.6}$$

Therefore, the expected fee can be restated as:

$$E(FEE_p) = 0. \tag{7.7}$$

Thus, under CAPM assumptions, the expected performance fee for all beta values is zero. Thus, non-zero values of $\bar{e}_p$ will be consistently rewarded or penalized for the complete range of fund betas.

In summary, Modigliani and Pogue (1975) conclude that CAPM predicts Plan 1 performance fees will be biased in favor of higher risk funds. Their model also predicts that the market-line performance standard used in Plan 2 will eliminate the bias and reduce the fee variability over time, particularly for the lowest beta funds. However, they did not arrive at a conclusion as to how best to adjust for risks in measuring performance. Using the measures of risk-adjusted performance developed earlier in Chapter 3, a more innovative approach to investment compensation is provided below. Moreover, Chapter 2 shows how CAPM is flawed; hence, new risk- and skill-adjusted investment compensation schemes are needed to delegate authority to agents.

SKILL- AND RISK-ADJUSTED PERFORMANCE AND COMPENSATION

Litterman et al (2002) argue that managers should be required to take relatively constant risk, as this enables the investor to measure their risk-adjusted performance (and their risk-taking ability). Research (Muralidhar 2004) has demonstrated how this approach may be counter-productive, as it sometimes creates substandard performance, with the manager (agent) being pushed to take risk even when they have information to do otherwise. In other words, it is not propitious to set up damaging instructions for managers when more appropriate risk-adjusted performance measures can be used which, in addition, can help to discern the manager's skill while not compensating them for blindly increasing volatility (or using leverage) or taking beta bets. Moreover, such investment activities need not be paid for, as they can be conducted free of cost by the asset owner.

The main emphasis is on investments with clearly identified benchmarks and funded mandates (more exotic mandates are discussed later in the chapter). Seigel (2003) provides a detailed, helpful overview of benchmarks that can be applied to the typical investor in different asset classes. The skill measure in Appendix 2.1 differs from the typical measure of skill indicated by Grinold (1989), Cornell (2008), and also in Raymond (2008). Raymond (2008) would use just the first term of the proposed skill measure, namely, $\sqrt{H}\left[IR(1)\right]$. However, it is important to note that, while the Information Ratio (IR) is important, the confidence in skill measure also examines the correlation between the benchmark and the portfolio, and differences in volatility of the two. It is obvious that the IR, while important for the confidence in skill analysis, does not provide a ranking identical to that based on confidence in skill.

RISK-ADJUSTED PERFORMANCE REPEATED

Chapter 3 showed how M^2 and M^3 are better risk-adjusted performance measures than the Sharpe ratio and IR. It is clear the M^2 adjustment makes the comparison in terms of basis points of outperformance by ensuring that all portfolios have the same variance as the benchmark. Yet, the late Prof. Modigliani did not connect this piece of groundbreaking work on risk-adjusted performance (estimated in terms of performance) into a fee schedule: now FEE_p can be stated as a proportion of the risk-adjusted excess relative to the benchmark:

$$FEE_p = \delta[r(RAP) - r(B)]. \qquad (7.8)$$

It should be noted that this approach of risk-adjusted compensation assumes volatility is the measure of risk, and hence does not compensate managers for naïvely leveraging the portfolio. If the investor desires the same leverage, it can be created with relatively low cost to the principal. The informed reader will see similarities in these conclusions with Prof. Modigliani's innovative work on optimal capital structure (an enlightened investor can leverage/deleverage their holding to reverse the de/leverage in a company).

The only major shortcoming is that two funds, normalized for benchmark volatility, can have different correlations with the benchmark, and hence different tracking errors. It may be concluded, therefore, that M^2 is the best applicable risk-adjusted performance measure for principals, but not appropriate in a principal-agent situation. Investors would prefer, all else being equal, funds with lower tracking error (and hence greater predictability in returns). Hence, these rankings may provide investors with incorrect information on the relative risk-adjusted performance of funds.[154] Equally important, Muralidhar (2001) shows that the M^2 measure does not rank funds identically to those based on confidence in skill, as there is no adjustment for correlations.

---

[154]   In addition, when benchmark returns are negative (e.g., in currency mandates), the M^2 measure incorrectly favors underperforming funds with high volatility over funds with low volatility. This quirk of the method generally assumes that benchmarks have positive returns.

Compensation based on M^3

Chapter 3 shows why M^3 is probably the best measure for risk-adjusting the performance of external managers who report to a principal with a limited risk budget (or confidence that the manager is skillful). For convenience, the M^3 equation is repeated here:

$$r(CAP\text{-}1) = a*r(1) + (1\text{-}a\text{-}b)*r(F) + b*r(B), \tag{7.9}$$

where the coefficients of each portfolio represent the optimal weight of that specific portfolio to ensure complete risk adjustment, shown as:

$$a = +\sqrt{\frac{\sigma_B^2(1-\rho_{T,B}^2)}{\sigma_1^2(1-\rho_{1,B}^2)}} = \frac{\sigma_B}{\sigma_1}\sqrt{\frac{(1-\rho_{T,B}^2)}{(1-\rho_{1,B}^2)}}, \tag{7.10}$$

$$b = \rho_{T,B} - a*\frac{\sigma_1}{\sigma_B}\rho_{1,B} = \rho_{T,B} - \rho_{1,B}\sqrt{\frac{(1-\rho_{T,B}^2)}{(1-\rho_{1,B}^2)}}. \tag{7.11}$$

An example of these approaches is provided in Table 7.2, with a target tracking error of 3 percent. For the assumption on the benchmark and risk-free rate mentioned below, the target correlation is 0.93, indicating that this 5-star rated Morningstar fund was taking substantial volatility (leverage) and correlation risk.

TABLE 7.2 Risk adjustment assuming a 3 percent tracking error

Fund	Return (%)	Standard Deviation (%)	Correlation to the Benchmark	D	Tracking Error (%)	r(RAP) (%)	R(CAP) (%)
Risk Free	5.5	0	0	N/A	N/A	N/A	N/A
Benchmark	17.09	13.27	1.0	1.0	0.00	17.09	17.09
Active Fund	33.24	27.57	0.71	0.48	20.45	18.85	18.43

Interestingly, under the M^2 method, this 5-star fund would have an allocation of only 48 percent, with 52 percent used to de-lever the fund (since volatility is double that of the benchmark); and under the M^3 method, it would have an allocation of only 15 percent to the fund, a 10 percent allocation to the risk-free rate (implying the fund had increased leverage, demonstrated by the high standard deviation), and a 75 percent allocation to the benchmark (implying that most of the risk-adjusted return emerged from beta bets). The implication for risk-adjusted performance compensation, and the futility of Morningstar-type ratings, is apparent.

The advantage in the M^3 measure is that it deletes the leverage and beta component from performance for a given risk budget, making it attractive for a risk-adjusted performance fee, as the investor need not pay managers for activities they can achieve independently, at minimal cost. In other words, the appropriate risk-adjusted performance fee in the investment industry should be:

$$FEE_p = \delta[r(CAP) - r(B)], \tag{7.12}$$

where $r(CAP)$ is defined for a given benchmark, tracking error budget, and pre-specified risk-free rate. Muralidhar (2001) also shows that the M^3 performance measure is the only measure among raw performance, IR, Sharpe ratio, and M^2 that ranks external managers identically to rankings based on confidence in skill. The intuition is that it is the only measure that explicitly adjusts for differences in volatility and the degree of correlation between the investment manager portfolio and the benchmark.

THE SHARAD MEASURE

All the performance measures discussed above have a common short-coming: they assume identical evaluation time periods across various external managers. This is rarely the case, as investment managers have varied inception dates for their products. Muralidhar (2002) combines the M^3 equation with the confidence in skill equation to create a new performance measure – SHARAD (Skill, History and Risk-ADjusted performance) – allowing for a comparison of managers, regardless of the length of their track record. This measure is highlighted in the next section. Raymond (2008) makes a similar sort of adjustment where the fees paid for skill are merely a function of time, which could be incorrect if the more appropriate skill measure demonstrated above is used. Figure 7.4 shows how confidence in skill is influenced by additional history.

Practical Implications of Risk-Adjusted Compensation

It is assumed that managers should be paid a low, fixed fee, and the appropriate risk-adjusted performance fee in the industry should be as in equation (7.12); but in reality, the fee structure in the industry is asymmetric:

$$FEE_p = max\{\delta[r(CAP) - r(B)], 0\}, \tag{7.13}$$

where $r(CAP)$ is defined for a given benchmark, tracking error budget, and pre-specified risk-free rate. Raymond (2008) makes the practical recommendation that the fixed fee should be proportional to the risk budget. A key aspect of this discussion is that it is impractical to generalize, due to the risk adjustment, that compensation would be lower than in Plan 1 of Modigliani and Pogue (1975). Muralidhar (2000) demonstrates that, in some cases where $r(CAP) > r(P)$ for an investment manager, then under risk-adjusted compensation, effective risk management is better compensated than if compensation is based purely on performance. This may give the creative investor the option of deciding, *ex-ante,* what performance fee they are willing to pay their managers (and the manager's willingness to negotiate such agreements may testify to their true skill).

The analysis assumes a simple situation where payment is made at the end of the entire period in a lump sum, and the investor (principal) implicitly makes decisions on leverage and beta management of the portfolio. In effect, M^3 assumes that enlightened investors conduct their own leverage and beta management overlay independent of their external managers. If such an overlay is not conducted, then, in effect, setting up risk-adjusted performance compensation could lead to problems, as the investor would have to pay the manager potentially more than they actually generated on a risk-adjusted basis.

In addition, in practice, managers are paid on a quarterly basis and not at the end of a single period. Typically, these payments are also made subject to high-water marks so that the manager is not paid twice for the same performance. In effect, to ensure this concept is applied on a quarterly basis, the payment to a manager would be based on a daily analysis during the entire quarter, and the calculation would be net of all previous fees (including flat fees), and after accounting for high-water marks.[155]

Until now, it was assumed that a single investor would compensate a single manager vis-à-vis a simple benchmark (e.g., S&P 500). However, apparently the same approach could be used by a Board to evaluate an investment staff, as $r(P)$ is now the performance of the entire portfolio across multiple assets and managers, and $r(B)$ is the return of the entire benchmark for the fund (50 percent S&P 500, 50 percent Bond Index).[156] The advantage of this approach is that the Board can utilize the same approach to risk-adjusted compensation of the investment staff which they use to compensate external managers, interweaving a potential alignment of interests at all levels of the fund. In this portfolio application of risk-adjusted compensation, $r(F)$ is still the risk-free rate, but here again a fixed risk-free rate is assumed over the entire horizon when, in reality, the risk-free rate is stochastic. Therefore, the investor and manager have to agree on how the risk-free rate is measured over a multi-period time frame. In addition, though it appears the correlation

---

[155]   If compensation is adjusted according to confidence in the managers' skill, the performance fee would have to be some fraction of $r(SHARAD)$. This assumes a unique utility function with regard to preference for risk-adjusted return and confidence in skill, an area for future research.

[156]   The same can be applied to liability benchmarks.

between the portfolio and the benchmark is a static variable that can be easily estimated, in reality the correlation is dynamic and varies over time as new observations are added.

A current feature of the diatribe against Wall Street is that many traders made exorbitant profits in the initial years of a trade, but eventually left the respective institutions with worthless assets. The compensation of the Lehman Brothers' CEO is a classic case of compensating a company that is now bankrupt! The above analysis indicates that there is low confidence in skill for an investment with only a year of performance data; hence compensation should be adjusted for this low confidence. The SHARAD measure probably needs to be adjusted to hone it into a time- and risk-adjusted tool for compensation, but the underlying principle offers the framework for an appropriate compensation scheme. In other words, *the loose ends may be secured if risk-adjusted performance fees are not completely paid at the end of every quarter, but are rather held in reserve in a separate fund/account to be paid on the basis of growing confidence in the manager's skill, as additional information on confidence in skill is accumulated through the length of the mandate.*

Application to unusual investment opportunities

At the beginning of this chapter, it was assumed that mandates were fully funded and measured relative to clearly articulated benchmarks (which represented the investment opportunity pursued by the investor and manager). The consequences of restrictions on funding or clearly articulated (and measured) benchmarks have less impact. In many cases, endowments and foundations invested in opaque, illiquid instruments, which could complicate the application of the risk-adjusted compensation method discussed here.

Overlays and Benchmarks with Negative Returns

Many clients implement overlays by using derivatives to capture alpha from currency, tactical asset allocation, and SMART rebalancing. Typically, overlays are largely unfunded (as some cash may be required for margin for futures or settlement of forwards, but these are trivial relative to the notional size for typical unlevered programs), and are often measured relative to a zero return benchmark or what is deemed as a pure alpha mandate. In such a case, the benchmark is zero returns with zero volatility, and the risk-adjusted compensation measure reverts to a standard compensation measure or a fraction of the cash generated from the mandate. In some overlays, such as currency hedging mandates, the benchmark is a portfolio of notional currency forwards, but here the problem is that the benchmark may provide a negative return over long periods of time and, in such a case, both M^2 and M^3, if not adjusted, could produce an incorrect result.[157] The reason negative benchmark returns for funded assets are ignored is that a sensible investor would much rather keep their money in cash rather than invest in an asset with negative returns (unless it was an unusual source of diversification).

It has been argued that, while a simple index may not exist for currencies, inefficiencies in currency markets allow for the creation of naïve alpha (or exotic beta) whereby simple rules generate alpha. Examples of proposals that served as naïve alpha benchmarks include: favor momentum (buy the currency that went up); buy the currency with the higher interest rate (the carry trade); buy the currency with the flatter yield curve (a potential PPP trade); and sell short-dated options.[158] It may be suggested that these "exotic betas" or "naïve rules" be the basic benchmark over which performance fees are paid.

CHARACTERISTIC-BASED INDICES

The recent profusion of indices, modeled on market-based factors instead of capitalization, takes advantage of certain inefficiencies and has crept into portfolios. These indices may be regarded as a simple active strategy, and hence the performance of this index should be compared to a standard capitalization weighted benchmark, and the provider of such indices should be paid risk-adjusted compensation. This may lead the providers of such indices to manage risk more actively than would have been possible with the static rules. Investors in such funds would do well to understand the benefit of dynamic management of risk.

HEDGE FUNDS AND FUND-OF-FUNDS

Hedge funds have been the leading target for people wishing to rein in manager fees that have a high fixed fee component (typically 2 percent) and a 20 percent share of returns (typically without reference to any benchmark or risk norm). Hedge funds are not intrinsically an asset class, but rather a cluster of investment strategies with limited constraints with the freedom to leverage, and with negligible relationship to a benchmark (Seigel 2003). Here, it is incumbent on the investor to identify the optimal and relevant benchmark for every strategy, and some banks have created indices that attempt to mimic the performance of certain hedge fund styles such as long-short equity. Clearly, the traditional benchmarks of LIBOR + 5 percent (or T-Bills + 5 percent) are not effective in allowing for risk-adjusted compensation, as the

---

[157]   To understand this comment, compare a portfolio with negative returns to a benchmark which also has negative returns but with a different volatility. Now leverage and deleverage à la M^2 leads to unusual results.

[158]   See Strange (1998), Muralidhar and Neelakandan (2002), and Arikawa and Muralidhar (2007).

volatility underlying the interest rate component may not be suited to the creation of an effective benchmark. Two possible solutions are: (i) to use a "naïve" passive benchmark such as those created by banks; and/or (ii) to utilize the asset class benchmark from where this allocation has been carved out, as this is the opportunity cost of making this decision. (Note: If the claims about the lack of correlation of these assets to typical beta investments are true, the investment staff will benefit from the Board holding them to a similar risk-adjusted compensation, as they would have diversified the performance of the overall fund.)

In a further twist to the complexities, the fund-of-funds binds many hedge funds together and charges a flat fee and a performance fee in addition to the hedge fund fees. This product has the benefit of access to funds that the average investor cannot access,[159] portfolio construction, and portfolio allocation. As far as is discernible, clients are not provided with adequate attribution of the sources of excess return generated by the fund-of-funds provider – i.e., whether the returns are from strategic allocation, style allocation, manager selection, or manager allocation.[160] However, once an appropriate benchmark is established for a fund-of-funds (by using, say, a passive investible index), the same attribution technique can be applied, and the fund-of-funds should be paid risk-adjusted compensation only if it has managed to clearly lower volatility while increasing returns, without adversely impacting the correlation to a passive index.

ILLIQUID ASSETS – PRIVATE EQUITY AND REAL ESTATE

Though this technique is useful for compensating real estate managers operating in the liquid space, it must be noted the prevalence of high flat fees and performance fees is in the private equity, illiquid real estate area. The drawback with these assets is that either they are not valued frequently, rendering the risk calculations dubious at best, or clients use vintage year indices fraught with the same problems. This aspect is set aside for future research.

SUMMARY

This chapter set out to throw new light on the subject of risk budgeting, showing that smart investors who are concerned about the skill of managers cannot simply allocate a tracking error risk budget without specific direction to the manager on how they would like that risk to be created. This chapter also highlighted a new compensation structure for agents who are overseen by principals, regardless of

---

[159] This is a dubious claim if a large fraction of the entire industry claims that access is their key selling point.
[160] Muralidhar (2005c).

whether they are investment staff reporting to Boards, or investment managers directed by investment staff. The proposal was to create a norm by which performance fees were adjusted for risk taken (relative to some clearly specified benchmark), ensuring that investment managers are not compensated for leverage and beta decisions which the principal can achieve relatively costlessly. Using the M^3 measure of risk-adjusted performance shows how appropriate incentives can be created for investment managers to deliver satisfactory risk-adjusted returns for investors. The same technique can also be used by investment Boards who delegate investment responsibilities to investment staff via a multi-asset benchmark.

Since this risk-adjusted performance measure aligns investment outcomes accurately with skill-based rankings, investors can be confident they are not paying for luck. This new approach, with some refining over time, is meant to revolutionize the current patterns of compensation for investment professionals and coordinate objectives with investment actions. As the late Prof. Franco Modigliani and Leah Modigliani commented in 1997, "Yes – you can eat Risk-adjusted Performance!"

8

SMART Manager Allocation for Improved Solvency

In Michigan, it is illegal to tie a crocodile to a fire hydrant. [161]

"All I said was that the trades were stupid and dumb, and they took that and blew it all out of proportion". Ron Davis [162]

BACKGROUND

Why is alpha from security selection required? If the client can improve solvency by means of SMART LDI and SMART Rebalancing, isn't that enough? It is apparent from the analysis thus far that a reasonably well-selected SAA (with a high correlation to the ILP), combined with SMART LDI and SMART Rebalancing, ensures solvency even for partially underfunded pension funds.

There are simple answers to these questions – if investors have sufficient faith in their ability to hedge the liability index and rebalance the portfolio effectively, the case for active alpha from security selection is weakened, especially given the operational headaches (custody, transition, monitoring, etc.) and costs that accompany the search for alpha. However, if the success ratio is adequate and the investor is confident of the potential of adding alpha from security/manager selection (as there may be regulatory, market, or index-based inefficiencies[163]), then this layer of alpha may be a means of diversifying further, with the aim of outperforming the liability benchmark. Sourcing excess returns from liability, beta, and alpha decisions is not mutually exclusive. Specifically, in the current market environment, manager alpha gains significance where naïve hedging of liabilities may raise the correlation but does nothing to bridge the return differential between the liability and the LDI hedge.

---

[161] Hyman (1992).
[162] Petras (2001), page 58, citing Ron Davis, Minnesota Twins pitcher, commenting on press reports mis-quoting his criticism of team managers' trading top players.
[163] See Muralidhar (2001), Chapter 12.

Crocodiles tied to hydrants...sounds strange? In a similar vein, managers hired by investors and then tied to specific benchmarks and portfolio structures can go against the laws of effective portfolio management. One would expect that overseeing external asset managers would not have been impacted dramatically by market changes, but this is not the case. Considerable discontent spread among CIOs in 2008 when many "alpha" managers did not deliver excess returns relative to their benchmarks, and many so-called alpha managers were accused of delivering only beta. Instead of arguing whether managers deliver alpha or beta, or whether portable alpha programs are the way forward or should be trashed, we offer a much more proactive approach to external manager programs. Previous research points out that the success of CIOs and even fund-of-funds (FoFs) lies less in manager selection and more in the three tenets of successful real estate investments: Allocation, Allocation, Allocation[164] (Muralidhar 2005c and Muralidhar and Muralidhar 2005).

Three key allocation decisions in managing FoFs are to: (i) strategically allocate to various hedge fund styles; (ii) tactically allocate across types of hedge funds; and (iii) dynamically allocate to individual managers. In the end, manager selection, on which FoFs spend most of their time, will end up being a mug's game, as there is very little that is proprietary in manager selection. At the same time, getting these three allocation decisions right may need a fair amount of proprietary knowledge, resulting in returns for which clients should be glad to pay additional fees. The same norms are applicable to CIOs of pension funds and dynamic allocation to external managers.

Active versus passive management has been a subject of common debate (Muralidhar 2001, Chapter 12) and, more recently, the focus has been on separating alpha from beta (Callin 2008; Brown 2009[165]); but, again, since the customary measures of performance have been very naïve (e.g., emphasizing outperformance relative to a benchmark without appropriate adjustment for risk or Information Ratio), pension funds globally have registered poor performance. Those focused on multi-manager portfolios, including Muralidhar (2001, Chapters 11 and 12) and Brown (2009), discuss multi-manager portfolios for a given risk budget or a comparison of active managers to passive benchmarks *over a static window and, regrettably, on static allocations to managers*. Further, the problem is compounded by active managers including beta bets in their portfolios and, since performance measures do not separate the two, when beta declines – as it did in 2008 – manager performance slows down as well. The most glaring example of this poor performance was in the "hedge fund" space, where managers were supposed to outperform cash, but dipped over 15 percent on average instead, indicating a serious tilt to a long beta position.

[164] Muralidhar (2005a).
[165] Brown (2009).

Even the FoFs, supposedly designed to help investors tap into the network and institutional knowledge of investment professionals, for a heavy fee, could not provide protection to the end investor. In short, had investors or FoFs applied better risk-adjusted performance measures (and managed portfolios on that basis), combined with dynamic manager allocations, they might have saved themselves from marked underperformance and sizable fees.[166]

Muralidhar (2001) acknowledges that a case could be made for dynamic manager allocation, and Muralidhar and Tsumagari (1999) proposed a proactive approach for currency managers. The latter ran a paper program, but unfortunately never implemented this approach.[167] Recent advances in capabilities of managers, better transparency of positions, and even academic research (Avramov and Wermers 2006) point us in a new direction.[168] This chapter makes the additional leap in innovative approaches to suggest (i) a multi-manager selection process that maximizes fund level alpha generation for a given risk budget; (ii) disregarding the marketing pitches of "Separating Alpha from Beta"; and (iii) ensuring that dynamic allocation to managers is effective from an ALM perspective. It also briefly covers currency programs as an easy alpha source, since few investors globally have availed of this source of alpha (and the results derived herein apply to other overlay programs advocated for pension funds).

TRADITIONAL APPROACH

The industry has evolved over time from portfolios where manager allocations were determined by the SAA to totally separate alpha and beta decisions.

Alpha Linked to Beta

As mandates to managers mimicked the SAA, alpha or excess returns were based on the SAA. In other words, if 30 percent of the fund was allocated to Domestic Equity, then 30 percent was allocated to managers in this bucket, and there was an attempt to extract alpha from these mandates without regard to whether this asset class was the most attractive for the purpose (or whether dynamic allocation made sense[169]). Moreover, detailed analyses were conducted on the issue of whether or not external managers in these asset classes outperformed benchmarks, as this was the basis for choosing between active versus passive management in any asset class (Muralidhar 2001, Chapter 12). In such analyses, typically, asset

---

[166] In the case of hedge funds, many FoFs had to give up liquidity (i.e., shut down programs with manager) and allow managers to install gates.
[167] Muralidhar and Tsumagari (1999).
[168] Avramov and Wermers (2006).
[169] See Muralidhar (2001), Chapter 12 – The Greater Fool Theory of Asset Management.

classes with imperfect benchmarks, or investment opportunities impacted by strange regulatory inconsistencies, showed the greatest scope for static alpha – e.g., Small Cap Equities in the United States and emerging markets. Asset classes, such as international equities, benefitted from a one-time historic bet on the weight of Japan in the benchmark and, once this was corrected, it appeared that international equity managers did not actually generate alpha on a static basis.

Separating Alpha from Beta

Since innovative pension managers recognized the inefficiency of the foregoing approach, as it tied the proverbial crocodile to the fire hydrant, "Portable Alpha" came into being, with the earliest usage attributed to Jack Coates at Weyerhauser and Marvin Damsma at BP America.[170] Under this regime, managers were hired to generate alpha from the most attractive asset classes/opportunities, and beta was created through the use of futures. As Brown (2009) categorizes these opportunities, "Portable Alpha is an organizational structure designed to allow one the luxury of fishing only in those select ponds with the most and easiest fish to catch." One may dispute the claim of "most" and "easiest to catch", notwithstanding the major explosion in the use of these strategies by hedge fund FoFs in 2005-2007. Books were written on how clients could port fixed income alpha onto S&P 500-type benchmarks (Callin 2008), but such claims have to be read with reservation, as they were espoused by employees at asset management companies pitching products instead of information and education. However, the most durable portable alpha is one that advocates identifying portfolios of excess returns (independent of the benchmark or asset class classification) and utilizing creative instruments to introduce them into portfolios.

The two major issues in these portable alpha mandates are: (i) who manages the beta, and (ii) who manages the dynamic allocation to the so-called portable alpha managers.[171] With regard to the first, marketing presentations of managers invariably show positive long-term return of the beta asset (see also Callin 2008; and Brown 2009), and portable alpha as another positive add-on. Clients did not realize that, by delegating (in many cases) the rolling of futures contracts to managers to create beta, pension funds took an implicit bet that beta would always be positive – clearly disproved in the global slowdown of 2008. Rolling futures contracts to create beta was an implicit bet on the market, poorly managed, thereby hurting pension fund performance; more important, it led to cash margin calls, putting pension funds under stress when the alpha disappeared.

---

[170]   See Cavallo (2007).
[171]   Muralidhar (2005c).

Hiring Managers Based on Information Ratios

Chapter 3 demonstrated that Modigliani and Modigliani (1997), in a seminal, though sadly under-utilized approach, revealed the industry's huge mistake in evaluating managers based on outperformance relative to a benchmark (or even adjusting for risk by using the popular Information Ratio). In short, they showed how a manager can easily game a benchmark purely by borrowing money and investing in the benchmark asset. Such an operation only increases the portfolio's volatility and outperforms the benchmark (thereby leading to a positive information ratio) without any skill or effort. This follows because analyses did not appropriately adjust for the differences in volatility before comparing returns.

Multi-manager Portfolios – Naïve Optimization

Moreover, nobody hires just one manager, which raises the challenge of how best to hire and manage a multi-manager portfolio. Most previous commentators, including Waring and Castille (1998), argued that CIOs should hire multiple managers in a portfolio on the basis of a naïve optimization of manager alphas, assuming that maximization of information ratios is the key objective.

Regrettably, all these approaches are still purely static and myopic, as they do not address the CIO's portfolio needs in targeting the primary goal of ensuring adequate solvency with minimal risk for the pension fund.

INNOVATIVE APPROACH – THE ALPHA ENGINE

In the more eclectic version of managing portfolios, investment strategies are chosen for their multiple properties in enhancing returns while simultaneously improving risk management. As a result, strategies using derivatives are also highlighted.

CURRENCY AS A SOURCE OF PORTABLE ALPHA

Currency overlays, which have been markedly underutilized or obviously misunderstood, are a valuable source of alpha, as (i) the currency market is dominated by non-profit players, providing the perfect backdrop for active management; (ii) it is one of the most liquid markets in the world and trades around the clock; (iii) investment in currency overlays does not require cash upfront – as it is traded using derivatives – and if these programs are successful, they generate valuable cash for investors; (iv) even simple rules result in profits; hence, the average investor need not hire an active manager; [172] (v) there are well-established industry track

---

[172]   See Strange (1998) and Muralidhar (2003).

records, and a majority of managers have generated alpha uncorrelated to traditional and non-traditional investment opportunities; and (vi) one can easily attribute outperformance of benchmarks to skill with minimal data.[173] In an odd twist, the DnB argued that a Dutch pension plan applying a dynamic currency hedge ratio vis-à-vis foreign investments (or a Dynamic Beta hedge) effectively increased overall risk and thereby needed larger buffers – a decision that proved fatally incorrect when Dutch pension plans incurred meaningful cash flows to settle passive hedges during the 2008 collapse of the Euro against the U.S. dollar and Japanese yen. In a whimsical way, neglecting to exploit currency alpha is tantamount to handing over a pension fund's balance sheet to the market to exploit!

MULTIMANAGER PORTFOLIOS BASED ON M³

Muralidhar (2001, Chapter 11) enhanced the manager selection process to show how CIOs could allocate assets on a static basis across all active managers, the leveraging asset (cash), and beta (regardless of whether it is a single asset or a portfolio composite). In short, the equations for calculating measures of risk-adjusted performance in Chapter 3 can be utilized to find optimal allocations to manager, cash, and beta.

Consider $r(CAP)$ for a portfolio of managers (K), each of whom is allocated w_i, where $r(CAP)$ is the M³ risk-adjusted portfolio return. Utilizing equations (3.1), we obtain:

$$r(CAP\text{-}K) = a*r(K) + (1-a-b)*r(F) + b*r(B), \tag{8.1}$$

where F is the risk-free rate, B is the benchmark, and $r(K) = \Sigma_i w_i * r_i$.[174] The investors want to select a, b, and w_i such that:

$$\Sigma_{CAP-K}^2 = \Sigma_B^2 \tag{8.2}$$

and

$$TE(CAP\text{-}K) = TE(target). \tag{8.3}$$

The solution for a and b, as described in Appendix 3.2 with modification for a portfolio of managers, is:

$$a = +\sqrt{\frac{\Sigma_B^2(1-\rho_{T,B}^2)}{\Sigma_K^2(1-\rho_{K,B}^2)}} \ , \tag{8.4}$$

[173]   See Strange (1998), Baldridge, Meath and Myers (2000), Muralidhar (1999), and Muralidhar (2003).
[174]   Here the terms "benchmark" and "market portfolio" are used interchangeably.

$$b = \rho_{T,B} - \rho_{K,B} \sqrt{\frac{(1-\rho_{T,B}^2)}{(1-\rho_{K,B}^2)}} \qquad (8.5)$$

and w_i is extracted from the solution to these equations. Muralidhar (2001) highlights a few key points from this approach, the most critical being that it approximated maximized risk-adjusted returns (as opposed to the maximizing Information Ratios, where both cash and beta assets were permitted) and had the highest confidence that performance was skill-based.

DYNAMIC ALPHA AND BETA MANAGEMENT OR MANAGING MANAGERS

A major area for value-added by pension fund investment decisions that is largely untapped is the value from managing manager allocations on a systematic, dynamic basis. The previous analysis for optimizing manager allocations, beta, and leverage points to a static approach, but Chapter 4 has shown that a strong case can be made for dynamic manager allocation decisions (especially since it relies on an analysis of relative return differences). If anything, it is apparent that manager hiring and their allocations are extremely "artful" decisions. Brown (2009) states, "Alpha's availability is never constant. It is in a continual state of flux – either growing or shrinking. Its status is evolutionary, or in the case of 2008, it was revolutionary."[175] However, Brown (2009) suggests changing managers in preference to dynamic allocations when he states, "Replace a manager when his forward-looking alpha opportunity becomes smaller or disappears. Replace a manager when another manager comes along who has a more attractive forward-looking alpha opportunity."

In assuming static manager selection, Swensen (2005) makes the same mistake as most investors. In reviewing the evidence, Swensen (2005) notes, "In a well-executed study, Robert Arnott, Andrew Berkin, and Jia Ye examine mutual-fund returns over the two decades ending in 1998. The results…show that during the twenty years covered by analysis the average mutual fund underperformed the market (as measured by the Vanguard 500 Index Fund) by 2.1 percent per year…The Arnott team's work provides a *prima facie* case for avoiding active mutual-fund management."[176] One is reminded of Marion Barry's comment, "Outside of killings, [Washington] has one of the lowest crime rates in the country."[177] It must be assumed that the mutual funds under survey must have outperformed their index at some point in their performance cycle, as one cannot accept that any fund could survive

---

[175]   Page 5.
[176]   Page 213.
[177]   Petras and Petras (2001), page 35.

20 years without a single period of outperformance. *A dedicated investor needs to find these positive periods, analyze why the **manager's** investment process led to such outperformance, and ensure that they allocate to the manager whenever the same factors are in play.* This is where SMART rules can be applied to manager allocations.

Swensen (2005) goes further, noting how daunting the task of selecting good managers is, namely, "Only 22 percent of funds in the twenty year sample manage to produce returns that exceed the Vanguard 500 Index Fund result. Even more discouraging for active management may be the slim 1.4 percent per annum advantage garnered by the winners. The overwhelming majority (79 percent) of mutual funds lose ground to the market with losers losing by a greater margin (-2.6 percent per annum) than the margin (1.4 percent per annum) by which the winners win."[178] Admittedly, this advice is provided in the context of retail investors, though the result is open to question, as smart retail advisors can easily be provided a valuable service by focusing not on the averages but rather on individual managers and when they perform.

Avramov and Wermers (2006) show that it is possible for investors to outperform their benchmarks by allocating assets across managers who individually may not beat their benchmarks. This can be achieved by being smart about when and how much is allocated to a manager (key aspects of a rule), depending on an analysis of market conditions and an evaluation of which manager is likely to benefit from the current environment (or a better understanding of why these managers are not highly correlated with each other or the benchmark). Howell (2004) presents a similar approach to tactical manager allocation, in the context of hedge funds and FoFs. In short, Muralidhar's analysis (2001, Chapter 12) is incorrect because, from Avramov's and Wermers's (2006) study it is apparent that, even accepting that managers underperform a benchmark over a long span, if they had a period when they beat the benchmark and the investor had conducted adequate due diligence, they would have allocated the assets away from the passive benchmark to this manager over the relevant period (and, at an extreme, even shorted the benchmark). The unsatisfactory analysis of manager alpha on a static basis (and hence unproductive recommendations for passive versus active management) is reminiscent of the absurdity of Arnott's (2009) argument for stocks versus bonds.

The process for making such decisions is identical to the process highlighted for beta, namely, a pension fund can use SMARTs, as shown in Chapter 4 (Figure 4.3 provides an explicit rule). If anything, the problem is more acute with hedge fund FoFs where allocations are not managed because these funds (i) have not focused on such approaches; and (ii) have used hedge fund manager lock-ups and other

---

[178]   Page 214.

liquidity options they forfeited as an excuse. Howell (2004) shows how this process can be conducted in the hedge fund space with very few factors, making the 2008 experience with FoFs very frustrating. Such omission has cost investors a heavy price (Muralidhar 2009b), as no attribution is made of these actions in FOF rankings, and sticky allocations detract from performance when a style is out of favor (Muralidhar 2005b).

CASE STUDY USING CURRENCY MANAGERS

Given the earlier comments on the potential of currency alpha, this section provides a brief case study, using a multi-manager currency portfolio where an investment bank provided data of a series of managers on their platform. The benefit in conducting such an analysis on currency managers is that since these programs are run as overlays, allocations can be shifted with minimal notice, cost, and market impact.

A hypothetical multi-manager program was created, assuming a static allocation of 12.5 percent of the total notional value to each of the eight managers (Figure 8.1). Neither the name nor the investment style of any of the managers was provided, but only the daily performance data was recorded from October 2002 to December 2005.

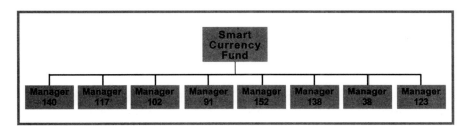

Figure 8.1. SMART currency fund structure.

Tables 8.1a and 8.1b provide the managers' basic performance and risk statistics, along with the correlations among the various managers. In short, each manager performed reasonably well (some better than others) and, on a static basis over the period 2002-2007, the static fund had a higher return-risk ratio than the best manager, with a drawdown comparable to that of the best manager. This can be partially explained by the relatively low correlations among the managers but, as pointed out earlier, the low correlations (highlighted) also offer the creative investor the potential for developing a dynamic SMART Currency fund. Here the moot question is: which factors can explain return differentials that can be exploited across managers?

TABLE 8.1a. Currency managers – key performance and risk statistics

Name	Annualized Return	Annualized Standard Deviation	Annualized Return-Risk Ratio	Maximum Drawdown
Portfolio Decision				
Smart Currency Fund	5.64%	3.85%	1.46	-4.76%
Manager 140	8.40%	8.50%	0.99	-12.35%
Manager 117	0.95%	5.66%	0.17	-8.83%
Manager 102	6.98%	15.44%	0.45	-17.34%
Manager 91	4.40%	4.43%	0.99	-7.81%
Manager 152	8.73%	8.53%	1.02	-12.08%
Manager 138	7.95%	8.16%	0.97	-11.03%
Manager 38	1.82%	3.31%	0.55	-3.87%
Manager 123	3.60%	9.93%	0.36	-17.88%

TABLE 8.1b Correlations among currency managers (2002 – 2005)

	140	117	102	91	152	138	38	123
140	1.00	0.06	0.05	-0.03	0.47	0.38	-0.06	0.09
117		1.00	0.06	0.01	0.07	0.09	-0.07	-0.03
102			1.00	0.01	0.06	0.04	0.10	0.15
91				1.00	-0.05	0.02	0.01	0.09
152					1.00	0.31	-0.031	0.10
138						1.00	-0.01	0.06
38							1.00	0.19
123								1.00

TABLE 8.2. shows the results of a simple factor analysis conducted by utilizing factors that are reasonable for currency managers. The interpretation of this table is quite straightforward and, as described in Chapter 4 (Figure 4.3), a SMART allocation decision can be made between Managers 102 and 117, using the EUR Implied Volatility data; namely, when the EUR implied volatility is low, allocate to Manager 102 and away from Manager 117. Similarly, every box in the table can be used to develop SMART rules across the various factors. For many manager pairs, several factors do not provide any information – a common feature in such analyses.

TABLE 8.2. Factor analysis: Using factors to explain return differentials

Factors/Manager Pairs	117-140*	91-140	91-152	91-102	102-117	91-138	117-123	38-91	38-152	38-146
EUR Option Implied Volatility					-		+			
JPY Option Implied Volatility	+	+				+				
EMBI Risk Aversion Parameter		+	+							
Default Premium			-	-		-		+		
CBOE VIX									+	
Gold Spot										-
US 10 yr to 1 mon Yield Slope					+					
JPY 10 yr to 1 mon Yield Slope		+								
CBOE Put/Call Ratio							-			
EU/USD Spot										+

The factor analysis is converted into a strategy composed of many such rules, and the sample performance is reported in Table 8.3. A static 12.5 percent allocation to all the managers would have generated 7.02 percent annualized returns, whereas the SMART strategy would have added 1.07 percent additional returns (assuming that the shifts could be made free of cost at month-end). The strategy was not optimized in any way, i.e., no attempt was made to choose rules that lowered absolute volatility and drawdown, but the excess statistics demonstrate that it is worth implementing the program.

TABLE 8.3 In-sample (2002-2005) performance of SMART manager allocation strategy

Total	Annualized Return	Annualized Standard Deviation	Annualized Return-Risk Ratio	Maximum Drawdown	Confidence In Skill	Success Ratio
Bmk	7.02%	4.12%	1.70	-3.30%	N/A	N/A
Strategy	8.09%	4.69%	1.73	-4.03%	N/A	N/A
Excess	1.07%	0.87%	1.24	-0.95%	98.53%	61.54%

Running this strategy out-of-sample from February 2006 to January 2007 achieves remarkable results: while the managers registered poor performance caused by the global decline in volatility (as most currency managers are inherently long volatility, as shown in Muralidhar and Neelakandan (2002)), the SMART strategy performed well, adding 1.65 percent excess returns. This performance came with 42 percent annual turnover across managers a 5 percent shift in allocation for each manager relative to the initial 12.5 percent allocation. The success ratio of 75 percent indicates the strength of this approach.

TABLE 8.4 Out-of-sample (2006-2007) performance of SMART manager allocation strategy

Performance Summary							
Trailing Period							
	Total	Annualized Return	Annualized Standard Deviation	Annualized Return-Risk Ratio	Maximum Drawdown	Confidence In Skill	Success Ratio
1 Year	Bmk	2.18%	3.72%	0.59	-2.71%	N/A	N/A
	Strategy	3.83%	3.88%	0.99	-2.13%	N/A	N/A
	Excess	1.65%	0.50%	3.30	-0.20%	99.95%	75.00%

To summarize, this simple example demonstrates the flaws in the typical portable alpha and optimal manager allocation recommendations, as static allocations are a bet on manager performance with wide scope for improvement. All it takes is a little effort to examine why correlations across managers/assets are what they are, and then to develop a factor-based analysis to formulate SMART rules.

THE NEXT LEVEL – HELPING TO IMPROVE SOLVENCY

To show the SMART approach applies globally, a Japanese pension fund case study shows how SMART asset and manager allocation across traditional asset classes and managers – without the use of exotic investments or alternatives - leads to improved solvency just through the dynamism (Figure 8.2). This case study is deliberately kept simple to underscore how a minor change in the process of managing pension funds – by implementing intelligent dynamic decisions– can lead to solvency gains.

The SAA for this hypothetical Japanese fund, which was set by the consultant, was 40 percent Domestic Fixed Income, 30 percent Domestic Equity, 10 percent Foreign Fixed Income, 17 percent Foreign Equity, and 3 percent Cash. As described in Arikawa et al (2005), the liabilities were replicated, using liquid Japanese financial instruments. This section examines how the fund would have performed relative to liabilities for the following operations: (i) Static SAA; (ii) Range rebalancing, assuming 5 percent ranges around each asset class – typical for most Japanese pension funds; (iii) Simple Beta – developing SMART approaches, but with the goal of generating the highest Information Ratio from rebalancing decisions; (iv) SMART Rebalancing to improve solvency; and (v) adding SMART Alpha. The goal is to show that applying traditional asset-only approaches (Simple Beta) could leave pension funds short of ensuring optimal solvency. This simulation was set up in 2005; hence, all results post 2005 are out-of-sample (see Arikawa et al 2005).

The annualized liability return (using the technique in Chapter 3) was 2.19 percent over the June 2003-February 2009 period. The static SAA would have generated 1.28 percent annualized against the benchmark (i.e., a decline in surplus of -0.91 percent annualized). Active managers added 0.34 percent annualized over this period for a total underperformance of -0.57 percent.

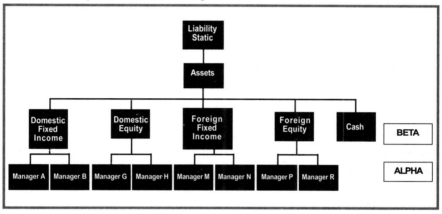

Figure 8.2. A typical Japanese pension fund – managing alpha and beta to improve solvency.

The range rebalancing option common in Japan perpetuates annualized underperformance of the total asset portfolio relative to liabilities, with an annualized deficit of -0.19 percent. SMART market-factor based rules to rebalance across the four primary assets, *with the goal of generating the highest Information Ratio*, would have generated a deficit of -0.18 percent annualized (as the Simple Beta strategy adds 0.39 percent annualized), as shown in Table 8.5. The Simple Beta strategy was implemented by applying nine rules, and was optimized to ensure the highest Information Ratio, using the in-sample data.

SMART Rebalancing (Beta) went an additional step and chose only those rules that had the appropriate correlation to the liabilities. As shown in Arikawa et al (2005), SMART Beta management selected only the four rules that had a negative correlation between the excess returns and the SAA. This approach would have had a lower Information Ratio of only 0.88 (in comparison to the Simple Beta strategy with an Information Ratio of 1.3). Under the SMART Beta, the rules and their weights were not optimized; but, clearly, just implementing naïve beta strategies or pure

TAA strategies is very different from running an Intelligent Beta Strategy relative to liabilities.

TABLE 8.5 SMART alpha and beta strategy improves solvency (June 2003-Feb 2009)

Portfolio Analysis	Return	Risk (Volatility)	Correlation with Liability	Volatality of Surplus	Max Drawdown of Volatility
	(%)	(%)		(%)	(%)
Liability Portfolio	2.19	0.09	N/A	N/A	N/A
Static SAA (with Static Manager Alpha)	1.62	8.62	-0.01	8.62	-34.27
Range Rebalancing	1.99	8.57	-0.01	8.57	-33.38
Simple Rebalancing	2.00	9.18	0	9.18	-35.51
SMART Beta	2.40	9.29	0.01	9.29	-35.02
SMART Alpha and Beta	2.45	9.29	0.01	9.29	-34.93

To implement a SMART Alpha process, Arikawa et al (2005) formulated simple manager allocation rules, based on the two foreign equity managers who had been hired by the Japanese pension fund (Managers P and R), using the momentum of the MSCI Kokusai index and market fundamentals. This simple marginal allocation tilt (which could easily be effected by using cash flows that are required to manage a pension fund) could have generated an annualized 29 bps of additional value within the international equity segment and, in turn, 5 bps at the total fund level. This very simple example, within a single asset class, was highlighted to make the case, and what is shown is that solvency is assured while gradually improving the drawdown. One can easily see the impact of adding value from a *systematic rules-based approach to managing all manager allocations in all asset classes.*

In this case study (especially since it is out-of-sample), solvency is achieved through SMART Alpha and Beta Management, and the correlation with liabilities is improved marginally, but at the cost of higher volatility of the surplus and drawdown. The only additional conclusion is that SMART Beta is not the same as the best TAA strategy or the strategy with the highest Information Ratio. As the potential to add more value from additional SMART decisions across other managers is obvious, it is not pursued further.

SUMMARY

This chapter presents a new design for pension fund management. It allows pension fund managers to be smart about managing assets relative to liabilities while, at the same time, allowing them to access alpha flexibly, manage managers dynamically for true alpha, and improve solvency. Developing rules to track market movements and their impact on all beta and manager decisions creates a systematic process that generates consistent recommendations which are not influenced by emotion (though leaving scope for applying informed judgment in implementing these rule recommendations).

This chapter shows how optimal risk-adjusted and skill-adjusted performance measures need to be used to extract the contributions of leverage and beta from manager performance. These performance measures are effective because they can advise pension funds on optimal structuring decisions across cash, beta, and multiple managers and, moreover, remain consistent with evaluations of skill. Moving to such an approach also lends itself to dynamic manager allocation. In other words, the goal is to help pension funds meet their ALM obligations through a SMART LDI process, and the lessons of 2008 confirm that SMART Dynamic Management is the way forward.

9

Off-Target Date Funds[179]

There is the joke about a crack marksman who visits a village only to find that every wall is pockmarked with bull's-eyes – with the centers perfectly shot out. He walked into a local pub and asked the bartender who the marksman was. The bartender pointed to a scruffy-looking country bumpkin at the end of the bar. The marksman walked up to the bumpkin and promised him a substantial amount of money if he could tell him how he became such a good shot. The bumpkin took the money and told him the answer was simple – he shot first and then painted the bull's-eye around the shot!

BACKGROUND

The same could be said about target date funds that have pervaded the United States, which by some estimates have reached $185 billion in assets under management.[180] These instruments were sold to individual investors as a panacea for their retirement problems, and 2008 revealed the shortcomings of these products. As a result, the DoL scheduled a series of hearings in June 2009 to review these products. For example, the 2010 target date fund fell, on average, 24.6 percent (i.e., average across all providers according to Morningstar), which means the investors hoping to retire in the next few years lost over a quarter of their principal – hardly what one would expect for products marketed as, " **Simplicity:** Pick one fund – your decision's done; **Confidence:** Each fund is professionally managed and diversified; **Convenience:** Each fund is automatically adjusted over time."[181] The question is: what is truly meant by "your decision's done"? What constitutes professional management? What is the value of "automatic adjustment?"

---

[179] This chapter would have never been written if not for the incredible amount of time taken and education provided by Karin Brodbeck, Roger Paschke, Charlie Ruffel, and Matt Smith.

[180] *Institutional Investor,* March 2009, page 34.

[181] Manager X – Retirement Date Funds Summary, March 2009. We will keep this manager's name confidential as this article is not about the practice of a single manager but rather of the industry as a whole – this manager being just one of the larger players.

According to *Institutional Investor* (2009), T. Rowe Price's 2010 product returned -26.7 percent in 2008 (and it is not clear if the negative performance is before or after accounting for fees). The manager of T. Rowe Price's retirement products is quoted as saying, "2008 is one year out of many," – small consolation for the 60-year olds who invested in their fund and paid reasonably high fees for the privilege. Our guess is that other managers are equally culpable in not managing the risks inherent in such products.

The problems in the DC industry are more acute, as noted in Swensen (2005): "Serious problems result from forcing individuals to accept responsibility for retirement saving, beginning with lack of full participation in defined-contribution plans. According to a 2001 Federal Reserve Survey of Consumer Finances, more than one of four eligible 401(k) plan candidates chose not to participate. Of these employees that do participate, less than 10 percent made the maximum contribution. When participants change jobs, a distressingly high percentage cash out their accumulated retirement plan assets. Without setting aside the seed corn to begin the asset accumulation process, employees face a bleak retirement harvest."[182]

This chapter reviews the current TDF offerings and highlights them in reasonably generic terms. In doing so, it focuses on the many aspects of the design that are poor (or expensive) and risky, and asks whether these risks were adequately disclosed to investors. TDFs were created to serve a specific need – of those who participated in DC schemes, most were not financially savvy and hence made poor investment decisions. For example, many contributors who held company stock ran the risk of losing their savings when the companies went bankrupt. During the technology bubble, many investors in risky technology funds wiped out their pension accumulation. Others invested in stable value funds which did not provide adequate wealth at retirement. TDFs were supposed to be an improvement on these several insecure offerings – helping with the rebalancing to portfolios with less equity as one approached retirement.

This discussion is embellished with an analysis of the impact of the 2008 market downturn on savings and investment behavior. The implication is that products have to be improved, and some suggestions are given for plan sponsors to help participants. The chapter also offers a simple solution to reducing costs by as much as 0.5 percent per year – this is a straight line improvement to investment returns. It then discusses fees and how fees might be lowered, and even how the fee structures should be re-designed to ensure proper alignment of interest, given that investors get dismayed to discover 30 years from now that they had been sold a poor product and that their fees cannot be recaptured if the fund provider was either lucky (if they outperform the benchmark) or lacking in skill (if they underperform). The

---

[182]   Page 22.

discussion then turns to how these funds might be appropriately benchmarked, specifically on a risk- and skill-adjusted basis, and how plan sponsors should attribute performance to the various decisions being made by the providers (not always clear to the end participant) to see if they are getting their money's worth. Sadly, the easiest way to benchmark these funds is on a current performance basis, so an approach that can be applied to give some measure of expected wealth is briefly featured.

At the outset, one must acknowledge that there is no clear academic theory on how individual investors should save and invest to achieve retirement goals (as the problem is too complex); hence, commentators have argued for socializing risks in country pension schemes or replicating DB-like profiles in product offerings through guaranteed real return products (Modigliani and Muralidhar 2004). Interestingly, Ghilarducci (2008) would provide support to the recommendations of Modigliani and Muralidhar (2004), even though she does not acknowledge the prior work on the topic. Therefore, while this chapter is aggressive in its critique of TDFs, the intent is to raise the bar, as mistakes in DC plans end up impacting individuals who are the least capable of bearing such risks.

THE TYPICAL TARGET DATE FUND

"We on this side of the House are not such fools as we look." Unknown House member.[183]

The Basic Structure

For a given "target date" typically restricted to years ending in 0 or 5, the standard fund can be characterized by a starting allocation to a high level asset allocation (stocks, bonds, and cash), a glide path (or a predetermined rate of reallocation between equity and fixed income/cash), and a desired allocation at the retirement date. The fund seeks, through these three parameters, to achieve an average allocation that is also pre-specified. Typically, the assumed retirement age is 65.

"Each fund's asset mix becomes more conservative – both prior to and after retirement – as time elapses. This reflects the need for reduced investment risks as retirement approaches and the need for lower volatility of a portfolio, which may be a primary source of income after retiring. Once a fund reaches its most conservative planned allocation, approximately 30 years after its stated retirement year, its allocation to stocks will remain fixed at approximately 20 percent of assets. The remainder will be invested in fixed-income securities."

---

[183]   Petras and Petras (2001), quoting a House member overheard retorting to taunts.

"The allocations reflected in the glide path are also referred to as "neutral" allocations because they do not reflect tactical decisions made by Manager X to overweight or underweight a particular asset class based on its market outlook."[184]

WHAT THE INVESTOR IS AND IS NOT DELEGATING TO THE FUND MANAGER

A series of risks that these target date fund products engender are summarized in Table 9.1 to indicate how lop-sided the balance is between the participant who bears the risk and the entity to whom the authority to make decisions has been

Characteristic of affiliate		Expected retirement wealth affiliate	
Current age	25	Balance at retirement	2284673
Retirement age	65		
Current Salary	50000	End Career Salary	240051
Initial account Balance	0		
		Average career salary	121740
Contribution rate	10.00%		
		Expected replacement rate on final salary	71.94%
Return assumptions (during career)		Expected replacement rate on average salary	141.85%
Expected Salary increase (nominal)	4.00%		
Expected return on contributions (nominal)	8.00	**Assumptions after retirement**	
Assumptions after retirement			
		Life expectancy	20
Life expectancy	20		
		Expected return (nominal rate)	8.00%
Expected return (nominal rate)	8.00%		
Expected benefit inflation	3.00%	Expected benefit inflation	3.00%
Calculation of contribution rate given a certain replacement rate target			
INPUT		**OUTPUT**	
Target Replacement Rate		**Contribution rate that will reach this target**	
Target replacement rate	100.00%	Contribution rate if targeting final Salary	13.90%
		Contribution rate if targeting average salary	7.05%

Figure 9.1. The pension, contribution, and investment trade-off calculator.

delegated. By virtue of making a single selection of a target date fund, the participant opts for many risks, and this section is intended to highlight such risks to plan sponsors so that they pressure the providers to improve the design of these products.

Objectives: To some degree, the investor is delegating this key decision to the fund manager, as the investor objective is never clearly examined. Muralidhar (2001) has shown how the optimal allocation (static and dynamic) for DB funds depends on target wealth/replacement rates, initial wealth, and risk tolerance (not to mention time). It is also clear from their discussion that the process of making investment decisions in DC plans is identical to that in DB plans, except that DB plans have a longer time horizon and a greater ability to bear risk (because of pooling). The plan sponsor bears some responsibility in helping participants articulate objectives and

---

[184] Manager X Retirement Funds, Prospectus, October 1, 2008.

ensure that correct products are available to satisfy the objectives. The process requires inputs such as: (i) current wealth and desired income at retirement; (ii) target retirement age and expected life post-retirement; (iii) assumptions about investments and inflation, resulting in the following output: (a) how much to save going forward; and (b) what return to target. An example of how this analysis should be conducted is provided in Asad et al (1997), and the template for this retirement trade-off calculator is shown in Figure 9.1.

Table 9.1: The lop-sided nature of risks borne by participants

Decision	Risk Borne By	Delegated to
Objectives at retirement	Participant	Provider is leading Participant to wrong objective with bad products. Plan sponsor needs to bridge the gap.
Asset allocation over time (formal glide path)	Participant	Provider, with no recourse if participant's true objective (comfortable pension) is not met.
Rebalancing around glide path	Participant	Provider, with no recourse(e.g., refunding fee) if this action detracts value.
Detailed sub-asset allocation	Participant	Provider again, with no recourse to fees paid if such selection is poor.
Choice of funds and fees	Participant	Plan Sponsor can choose among different vendors.
Choice of benchmark passive indices	Participant	Plan Sponsor, but not really clear if they can exercise much discretion, given the service provider's goal to provide products in bulk.
Risk management	Participant	Provider, who again is absolved of all responsibility, as only an asset allocation is agreed to and not a target pension or retirement wealth
Currency risk	Participant	Provider, who often will not manage such risks because they got the participant to agree to this implicitly.

In Figure 9.1, a 25-year old with a starting salary of $50,000 hopes to retire at 65. If they contribute annually 10 percent of current salary (with nominal salary growth of 4 percent), live 20 years post-retirement, and earn 8 percent returns (with 3 percent inflation), they can receive 72 percent of final salary or 142 percent of average salary, through retirement till death. Alternatively, as the bottom part of Figure 9.1

shows, targeting 100 percent replacement leads to specific recommendations on contributions.

There is nothing in the fund selection process that comes close to highlighting this trade-off between pensions, contributions, and investment returns. Asking individuals to select funds based on a retirement date or some arbitrary measure of risk tolerance is fraught with problems, as the link between funds and objectives is weak. The investor makes the fiduciary decision on objectives (which can be implied from the choice of fund, as shown in Muralidhar 2001) but, in effect, is being poorly served and advised by the fund manager and the plan sponsor. Interestingly, Gardner and Fan (2008) discuss in detail the need for providing a comfortable pension, but then fall into the same trap as other providers in their desire to create a "simple, transparent, and consistent" product.

Detailed Sub-Asset Allocation: Each fund seeks to achieve its objective by investing in a set of underlying mutual funds which represent various asset classes and sectors. In other words, once a fund commits to holding a 50-50 Stock-Bond mix, how that 50 percent is allocated to international and domestic stocks or value versus growth stock, etc. is a decision delegated to the fund manager, and often the time of allocation of these assets is also delegated to the fund manager, as timing is not pre-specified. Once again, product providers are allowed to take a bet on timing and allocation that must be captured in subsequent attribution.

Choice of Funds and Fees: Many providers include only funds that are a part of their fund family, whereas others represent open architecture and include outside manager funds as well. For example, choosing only funds from within a fund family assumes that no other outside fund, on an after-fees and cost basis, is effective. Moreover, some products use strictly passive funds, whereas others opt for more expensive, active funds. The value of the choice of even passive funds (as there is a choice between replicating a benchmark through futures, passive funds, or ETFs – each with resulting implications for performance and cost) will be examined in detail.[185] Recently, firms like Charles Schwab have begun to feel the pressure on fees, but even after their so-called reductions, the fees are in the range of 0.6-0.76 percent. Later, the chapter demonstrates that these fees are exorbitantly high for a simple TDF.[186]

Choice of Benchmark Passive Indices: Closely linked to the above decision is the passive index to which the assets are benchmarked in each asset class. This has implications for cost-effective replication and also potentially the impact/value of active management. This decision is also delegated to the fund manager by the

---

[185] Average DC fund fees = 0.72 percent - *http://www.plansponsor.com/pi_type11/ ?RECORD_ID=45978&page=2*

[186] *http://www.pionline.com/apps/pbcs.dll/article?AID=/20090421/REG 904219997&nocache=1*

investor, because of the lack of knowledge or appropriate advice in respect of the impact of this decision. Chapter 3 has shown how pension funds can benefit from selecting futures-based benchmarks; a similar exercise will be suggested later in this chapter.

Reallocation Process: Each fund is managed to a specific retirement year (target date) that is typically included in its name (e.g. TDF 2040), and the investor is responsible for choosing this date. Over time, the allocation to asset classes and funds will change according to a predetermined "glide path" (the glide path is the reallocation of asset classes over time). Moreover, two TDFs with the same time to maturity have the same allocation to equity and fixed income. While managers proclaim that this is in the interests of consistency, one could argue that this is not in keeping with SMART VN Rebalancing, as a fund with a 45-year history (with five years remaining) of great performance has greater solvency and risk-bearing capacity than another fund with the same time to maturity but with poor performance. While the glide path is usually prescribed, the prospectus for the average fund gives latitude to the fund manager around the target (e.g., +/-5 percent around the glide path), how this range is utilized within the sub-asset classes, and also the timing of these shifts, and hence investors delegate this too to the fund manager. In the section on attribution, the chapter addresses how the industry should measure and manage such discretion.

The prospectus is typically coy with regard to the fact that the fund manager does not deny that they are taking a tactical view on the market in designing a glide path, but only that it is devoid of a market view. It will be shown that the tactical decision based on age may be a lot more insidious than one that is based on market views, as it is effectively being set up as the investor's decision, thereby absolving the fund manager of the fiduciary responsibility thereafter (something most individuals would shirk from doing if the facts were presented this way).

Risk management: The fund's objective and who is responsible for managing risks is not clear, as shown in Table 9.1. The fund does not guarantee any retirement income (or target annuity as a percentage of salary – called the replacement rate). Again, the language of the typical prospectus, vetted by lawyers no less, states that the process of reallocation is intended to satisfy "the need for reduced investment risks as retirement approaches and the need for lower volatility of a portfolio."[187] However, if bonds perform very poorly close to retirement and are extremely volatile, then the investor has no recourse as their glide path has the investor's earlier approval. In effect, risk management is now largely the responsibility of the investor, who is making decisions about markets, often 20-30 years in advance,

---

[187]   Manager X prospectus. The prospectus is chock-full of language on investment risks – currency risk, duration risk, etc, but are silent about not achieving the investor's goal.

with little knowledge or ability to gauge the risks involved. The claim that this portfolio is conservative is linked to the need for income in retirement without regard to the impact on the value of the principal.

Again, the language in the prospectus in advising investors on how to make investment decisions is noteworthy. "Consider your estimated retirement date and risk tolerance. These funds' investment programs assume a retirement age of 65. It is expected that the investor will choose a fund whose stated date is closest to the date the investor turns 65. Choosing a fund targeting an earlier date represents a more conservative choice; targeting a fund with a later date represents a more aggressive choice."[188] One can easily show that these statements are plain wrong.

Currency risk: Many funds invest in foreign assets and highlight the impact of currency risks. However, Muralidhar (2001) has shown that the choice of a long-term benchmark for currency carries with it an implicit bet on the U. S. dollar. For example, an unhedged (fully hedged) benchmark for international assets, which is then passively replicated, takes an implicit view that the U.S. dollar will be weak (strong). Unless active currency management is employed in the international equity fund – a rare occurrence, and even rarer would be the finding that these managers are professional currency managers –, the investor is taking an unmanaged currency bet.

THE SURVEY SAYS

There is a famous game show in the United States called "Family Feud," where two clans compete against each other in answering questions relating to a survey conducted on the general public. Before announcing the results, the host usually leads off with the line, "...and the survey says..." before revealing the answers from the survey, and the clan members realize the accuracy or inaccuracy of their guess. In a similar vein, a recent survey of the general population provided results on their understanding of TDFs: sadly, the survey paints a dismal picture of the participants' understanding of these products. One would expect that if Table 9.1 were shown to participants, plan sponsors, and DoL representatives, the reaction would be more fear than willingness to participate in these products. The article is taken verbatim from Plan Sponsor magazine's website to ensure completeness.

"Promises They Can't Keep: Misconceptions about Target-date Funds

A recent survey from Envestnet Asset Management revealed individuals have trouble understanding target-date funds.

Only 16 percent of survey respondents said they had heard of target-date funds prior to the survey, and 63 percent of those incorrectly described them.

After reading a composite description of target-date funds, respondents said the funds offered the following promises:

---

[188]   Ibid.

- Nearly 62 percent of respondents thought they would be able to retire on the fund's target date;
- 62 percent said they could spend less time tracking their progress toward retirement goals;
- Almost half (48.6 percent) said they could stop worrying about investment and savings decisions and leave everything up to a professional;
- Roughly 38 percent of respondents believe the funds will produce a guaranteed return;
- More than one-third (35.5 percent) of respondents believe their money will grow faster in target-date funds than in other investments; and
- Almost 30 percent believe they can save less money with the funds and still meet their retirement goals.

Respondents also had little sense of the risks of investing in target-date funds:

- 41 percent think there is little or no risk of losing money in a one-year period, and 57 percent believe it is unlikely that they can lose money in any 10-year period;
- One-fifth of respondents believe it is less likely they could lose money in target-date funds than in money market funds, while 50 percent believe the odds were equal;
- 28 percent thought they were less likely to lose money in target-date funds than in equity mutual funds, while 52 percent thought the odds were the same; and
- 38 percent of respondents thought the risk levels in funds with the same target date would be very similar.

When asked to choose from a list of seven potential target-date portfolios, the majority of respondents selected the most aggressive fund, based on expected returns over a 10-year period. Only 8 percent of [the] respondents said [that] selecting a retirement savings rate was the most important retirement planning decision they could make.

Envestnet surveyed 251 individuals aged 25-70 employed now or in the past year."[189]

THE NUMBERS – SOMETHING HAS GOT TO GIVE

To explain the general implications for the risks borne by DC participants, the attached example highlights the key actions that a year like 2008 would imply to ensure a reasonable retirement. For most young participants, these plans may provide the entire retirement income (given the uncertainties of global Social Security programs).[190]

---

[189] *www.PLANSPONSOR.com.* May 5, 2009

[190] See Modigliani and Muralidhar (2004).

The case study reviews three identical individuals at different stages of their lifetime – the first, a 25-year old employee who has just joined the workforce with a $50,000 per year salary. To keep the analysis similar, the case study also highlights the same individual, assuming that she/he had commenced employment in 1988 and is currently 45 years old; the third is an individual on the cusp of retirement, who joined the workforce in 1968 (and is currently 65 years old). The model with its required inputs and outputs as shown in Figure 9.1 is used in the analysis. The assumptions for the general economic environment, demographics, and asset markets are provided in Table 9.2. For simplicity, inflation is assumed to be a static 3 percent every year, and real salary growth is assumed to be 1 percent annually; the participant is expected to live for 20 years post-retirement and contribute 10 percent of the current salary (with no caps – again for simplicity) into a pension plan.

The base assumption is that assets earn a guaranteed 8 percent for every year except 2008, when they earn -20 percent. Asad-Syed, Muralidhar, and van der Wouden (1998) provide a simple model to help participants establish the linkages among the variables – for a target replacement, for the given parameters, there is a unique contribution and vice versa (Figure 9.1). In other words, if one sets their mind on a target replacement rate, and experiences a bad year of performance, contributions must increase and/or the rate of return on future investments must increase.

Aon (2008) demonstrates that a reasonable replacement rate for an average cohort is approximately 70-78 percent of the final salary. As post-retirement costs,

Table 9.2. Assumptions for the case study

Return in 2008	-20 percent
Annual Fees	0.75 percent
Starting Income Standard Contribution	50,000 10 percent
Return on Assets Prior to and After 2008	8 percent
Annual Salary Growth	4 percent
Annual Inflation Working Life	3 percent 40 years
Post-Retirement Life	20 years

including taxes, are lower, individuals need to target a much lower post-retirement income. Table 9.3 provides the results and shows what would happen in a perfect world. If the various parameters are fixed, then in a perfect world with no stochasticity of variables, the participant would receive approximately 72 percent of the final salary (or 142 percent of the average salary). Conversely, should the participant choose to receive a 100 percent replacement rate in every year of retirement, then at an 8 percent annualized return, they must contribute approximately 7 percent for a pension that is based on the average salary and 13.9 percent for a pension that is based on the final salary.

Table 9.3: A Perfect World – The link among replacement rates, contribution rates, and rates of return

Scenarios	Replacement Rate	Balance at Retirement	Contribution at 8% for 100% Replacement	Contribution at 7.25% for 100% Replacement
Perfect Life - Average	141.85%	2,284,673	7.05%	8.87%
Perfect Life - Final	71.94%	2.284,673	13.90%	17.50%

The last column in Table 9.3 demonstrates one of the more insidious aspects of the current TDFs – namely, the impact of fees. By all accounts, the fee of the average product is approximately 0.75 percent annualized. This is high for the services provided, and fees can and should be dramatically reduced; but the key point is that the application of fees reduces the net return which, in turn, **raises the required contribution by 1.82 percent a year** (if the client seeks a 100 percent replacement on the average salary) **and by 3.6 percent a year for a participant focused on the final salary.** This simple table demonstrates the dramatic impact of fees – however small – on saving behavior, but the advice is not being provided to participants.[191] This is particularly relevant because in 2008 many companies dropped or dramatically lowered their 401(K) match in the United States – simply put, they implicitly told participants to lower their retirement expectations, especially given the damaging impact of asset performance in 2008.

To highlight the impact of a year like 2008 on retirement planning, Table 9.4 demonstrates how it affects participants in various cohorts – from a new entrant, to a mid-career employee, and a person on the cusp of retirement. For simplicity, assume that all TDFs earned -20 percent in 2008. As many fund providers have not changed their long-term expected return forecasts, continue to assume that the glide path ensures an 8 percent (or 7.25 percent after fees) annualized return. This means that fixed income returns must increase over time (as these portfolios tilt more into fixed income), a situation that is probably at odds with the current level of rates and the potential impact of inflation. For the new entrant, a big shock like the 2008 bleak performance requires higher contributions, i.e., contributions that are only slightly higher than the original target contribution – but if a company match has been

---

[191] I thank Roger Paschke of the Hearst Corporation for motivating this discussion. In his quest to design the best system for his participants, he continues to focus on advising staff on how to save, and the next table is in response to my discussions with him.

withdrawn, then the participant needs to step up to the plate to make up the difference (and this will hinder consumption at a macro level which does not augur well for the future return on equity).

Table 9.4: Impact of 2008 and fees on different cohorts with different retirement objectives

Age in 2007	Wealth at end 2007	Wealth at end 2008	Contribution at 8%	Contribution at 7.25%
25 Year Old-100% Average	5,400	4,320	7.10%	9.03%
25 Year Old-100% Final			14.18%	17.90%
45 Year Old-100% Average	344,383	275,507	15.01%	16.92%
45 Year Old-100% Final			28.72%	31.42%
64 Year Old-100% Average	2,115,438	1,692,350	N/A	N.A
64 Year Old-100% Final				

The problems really begin to show in the case of the 45-year old employee, as the negative return was earned on a pool of assets that was reasonably substantial (i.e., **the -20 percent returns was not applied just to the contribution for 2008, but to the entire savings until that date**). In simpler terms, given the reduced time to make up shortfalls as one ages, the 2008 performance requires that a 45-year old participant double their contribution to remain hopeful of achieving the original target replacement rate. **With the 65-year old, the number is not reported. The required contribution is in excess of 400 percent, as the depletion of wealth is devastating**!

So, to the T. Rowe Price manager who said that 2008 was just one year out of many, we say: Tell it to the 65- year old, and even to the 45 -year old who now has to save double. However, a smart plan sponsor's expectations from this same manager should be on the lines of: "'maybe the **bulk of the fees need to be deferred and paid only if the target return is achieved.**"

SIMPLE FIXES AND SUGGESTIONS FOR IMPROVEMENTS

"Honest businessmen should be protected from the unscrupulous consumer."
Lester Maddox[192]

The industry's current approach to the problems of the 2008 downturn border on the inefficient. Rather than fixing what is broken, the entire focus is on (i) whether to include outside managers or not, or add passive managers to lower fees; (ii) add illiquid, high fee asset classes such as private

---

[192]   Petras and Petras (2001), page 31, quoting Lester Maddox, then governor of Georgia, on why Georgia should not create a consumer protection agency.

equity and hedge funds; (iii) find a way to incorporate the managers in the DB plan to lower manager costs; (iv) meddle with the glide path; and (v) add new asset classes (TIPs, emerging markets) to "increase diversification." There is apparently some attempt to start to guarantee annuities as the focus shifts from asset allocation to retirement income, but this is far from the norm.[193] Since, unfortunately, none of these measures achieves any lasting benefit, a few alternatives are suggested below. In addition, this chapter makes a minor contribution to the serious attempt to benchmark and rate these funds, and attribute performance to various decisions.

Providers Must State a Target Return (or Replacement Rate)

At a minimum, plan sponsors should require TDF providers to state a long-term return on their various products. While there is no guarantee that these will be achieved, at the least the participant will know where they stand and can engage in thoughtful retirement planning, using the model in Figure 9.1 and a version of the analysis provided to support Table 9.2. In this manner, TDF products may be ranked more clearly, based on their target return, using either absolute or risk-adjusted rankings. However, plan sponsors tend to be concerned that participants who are not financially sophisticated may not be capable of making the distinction between higher returns and higher risk.[194]

Providers Must Be Explicit about what Risks Participants Bear, and Guide them on Such Risk-Taking

If providers continue to provide TDF products, the least they can do is improve their disclosures of risks being borne by participants and the ways to mitigate the risk. For example, all these TDF providers are massive investment complexes – with complete teams of well-trained staff who can provide advice (for free) on how the funds are likely to perform in the coming year, given their outlook on stocks versus bonds. With such information, a smart participant can at the least switch from the fund they are in to another that reflects the best thinking of the fund complex. In effect, **getting out of a fund that is likely to underperform is risk management**. Stepping out of a few land mines will allow a high probability that retirement objectives are achieved without substantial additional sacrifices.

---

[193] *http://www.pionline.com/apps/pbcs.dll/article?AID=/20090421/REG/ 904219997&nocache=1.*
[194] I thank Roger Paschke for this clarification.

Create Exposure to Assets through Futures and Dramatically Lower Costs

If the key to achieving long-term retirement objectives, at least with the blind rubber stamp of the Department of Labor's QDIA, is to focus on asset allocation, then maybe the various fund providers should give participants a break and use futures to create a broadly diversified portfolio of assets that are liquid, transparent, readily traded at low cost, have limited credit risk, etc. Today, for the average U.S. client, the following exposures can be readily created: U.S. Large Cap, U.S. Small Cap, MSCI EAFE, MSCI Emerging (low liquidity today, but if $10 billion moved to this market, liquidity would improve dramatically), U.S. Government Bonds, Foreign Government Bonds, Currency, and even Commodities. One would expect that utilizing futures to create asset class exposure can **save participants as much as 0.5 percent annually relative to industry average costs**. Therefore, this can also be considered to be the benchmark to measure all TDFs, as discussed later, as this is the most liquid, transparent, lowest cost portfolio.

Apply SMART Rebalancing to the Various Funds

Since the fund managers are taking a host of bets, almost as a matter of practice, it seems like the most valuable bet would be to implement a SMART Rebalancing program. In this fashion, the link to an artificially chosen and DoL rubber-stamped dynamic asset allocation can be easily mitigated. So if it turns out that older cohorts are largely being pushed into fixed income – but with current yields and the likelihood of further debt being issued by the government to bail out an economy in trouble or any rise in inflation – the general consensus is that fixed income will perform worse than, say, cash or equities. In such a case, then fund managers (and even the DoL) should implement some version of SMART Rebalancing to protect the naïve participant.

Ensure Clear Attribution of Performance

As shown in Chapter 1, the same principles of attribution can be applied to TDFs as they are operating in much the same way as pension funds, and have only three sources of excess return over the futures-based benchmark; namely, (i) manager value added (by mandate); (ii) choosing benchmarks different from the futures-based benchmarks; and (iii) dynamic allocation to various decisions versus a static allocation. Figure 9.2 is a repeat of the same chart shown in Chapter 1.

Cut Fees and Defer Them till Sufficient Time Has Passed

Once fund managers use futures contracts to create asset class exposure and drop the basic fee, then plan sponsors should go the additional step of righting another wrong – **namely, not paying managers upfront for performance that is not guaranteed for many years into the future**. Fund managers should get a basic fee of a few basis points to set up the structure of the funds, but the balance of the fee should be paid out only when they can credibly show that they have outperformed the static, naïve benchmark on a risk- and skill-adjusted basis.[195] Setting up the right incentive scheme is critical to ensuring that fund managers do not go on a massive asset-gathering run, but rather focus on delivering the objectives that the participants need. This will be covered in more detail in future research, as a number of operational issues need to be clarified.[196]

Dallas Retirement Fund
Evaluation Period: 01/01/2000–08/18/2010

Aggregated Performance	Year to Date	Total Period
Excess Annualized Return	0.83%	2.42%
Tracking Error	1.18%	1.98%
Information Ratio	0.7	1.23
M2 Excess Return	0.78%	2.57%
Maximum Excess Drawdown	4.00%	-6.70%
Ratio of Excess Good Risk to Bad Risk	0.68	1.24
Benchmark Annualized Return	4.37%	7.80%
Portfolio Annualized Return	5.20%	10.22%
Confidence in Skill	74.82%	100%
Success Ratio	38.46%	55.97%

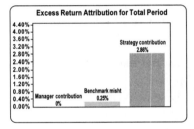

Figure 9.2. Analyzing TDF performance – risk-adjusted and clearly attributed.

BENCHMARKING, RISK-ADJUSTING, AND RATING FUNDS

This is a topic for a complete book on its own, given the diversity in starting allocations, glide paths, choice of benchmarks, etc. Gardner and Sirohi (2007) present a simple but very effective measure of performance which they term the Target Date Performance Measure (TDPM). They propose a measure as follows:

$$TDPM = W_F / W_B * 100 \qquad\qquad (9.1)$$

---

[195] We will pursue this in separate research, but in a nutshell, this would require calibrating all target date funds to a fund that is run (a) with a static allocation which, at the current average expected return of all vendors, achieves, say, an 8 percent expected return; and (b) assumes that all assets are created using futures – so the benchmark indices are also chosen. The glide path is a tactical bet as is the choice of managers other than the most liquid option. Now, every fund can be measured against this live fund on an after-fee basis, and risk adjustment could be done using either the M-square or the M-cube (will require a target risk budget). Also, the manager will be paid only the balance of the fee once the confidence in skill exceeds some threshold, such as 75 percent. All of this has been covered in Chapters 2, 3, and 7.

[196] I thank Karin Brodbeck for this comment.

where W_F is the wealth generated at the target date by holding a target date fund from inception to target date; W_B is the wealth generated at the target date by holding the benchmark fund from inception to target date; and 100 is used for normalization. The attractive feature of the TDPM is that all funds can be measured on wealth rather than returns; and all funds in a family can be compared. The problem is that as there is no risk- and skill-adjustment, one needs to develop norms along the lines of adjusting for the fact that the fund manager can increase the fund's volatility, or the fact that one fund having a higher TDPM than another in the short term may be more a matter of luck than of skill.

SUMMARY

Target funds have ballooned to approximately \$185 billion, yet the fact that performance tumbled dramatically in 2008 has proved unquestionably disastrous. A cursory examination of these funds is sufficient to realize that they have been poorly designed, ineffectively marketed, and not explained to the participants. The marketing material is designed to prevent lawsuits, but does not let the average participant in a 401(K) plan realize what investment decisions they are making, as opposed to delegating to the fund providers, and that too for high fees. The chapter debunked the appeal of these products by highlighting the poor design, suggested benchmarks for these funds that allow for risk-adjusted performance (across all target dates and fund families), and discussed more appropriate fee structures, given the length of mandate and the high likelihood that these products will not fulfill investors' expectations. This analysis will probably lead to a totally new regulation of these funds and hopefully have them removed from a list of Qualified Default Investment options allowed by the DoL unless the United States wants to bail out yet another industry for poorly designed regulation.

10

Conclusion

"And what is more, I agree with everything I have just said." Piet Koornhoff[197]

The year 2008 was a watershed for the investment management industry, as volatile markets exposed the flaws in the theory and the practice of pension fund management. Solvency declined dramatically, globally, as the asset-liability mismatch was exposed (as was the irrelevance of bad LDI); hedge funds did not deliver on the promise of generating alpha (for very high fees); rebalancing policies detracted value because they anchored themselves to a declining portfolio; liquidity dried up; and equity became the only asset to sell, causing further problems. However, warning signs were everywhere, and many analysts had shouted "Wolf!" only to be ignored. The year 2010 has presented similar challenges as volatility has buffeted portfolios. Ultimately, good investing is about knowing What To Do, When To Do It, How Much To Do, and Why. The easiest way to incorporate this good process is by developing Rules to help guide asset, currency, and manager allocation decisions based on pertinent economic and financial factors. Using the SMART approach removes emotion from the decision and ensures that overburdened and under-resourced CIOs focus on the key decisions that impact returns and risk. With such a robust process, CIOs need not pay ridiculously high costs to purchase tail risk hedges pitched by asset managers.

The primary source of the problem is financial theory and its standard bearer – the CAPM. Academics who have never managed pension funds ignored the most dominant class of institutional investors – those who delegated decisions to others – and the impact of the behavior of pension funds on markets. First, these investors worry about relative risk and relative performance, which impacts the choice of investment strategy and the manager hired. Second, the whole focus on optimal portfolios (à la Markowitz) assumes certain asset correlations, masking the bet that investors make on markets, and the economic factors that drive these bets. Finally, the CAPM-type results focused on static solutions to portfolio problems, ignoring the time dimension (the inter-temporal CAPM of Merton notwithstanding) in making decisions.

[197] Petras and Petras (2001), page 3, attributed to Piet Koornhoff, South African cabinet minister, ambassador to the United States.

As a result, CIOs had to deal with four major shortcomings: (i) the fixation of the investment management industry on **static prescriptions to manage assets in dynamic markets**, especially for long-term SAAs and naïve rebalancing; (ii) asset managers who offered naïve "magic bullet" solutions to sell products rather than solve pension fund problems – most evident in LDI, tail-risk hedges, and multi-manager programs (which, again, are static solutions); (iii) performance measures/ fees that did not adjust for risks or skill, and hence served the asset manager more than the pension plan – most evident in hedge funds, but quickly followed by mainstream asset managers; and (iv) benchmarks recommended to pension funds that are difficult to replicate in the futures market, making it hard for CIOs to be nimble in managing a fund (without taking "fake" tracking error), especially as markets zigged and zagged. The value attached to dynamic decision-making was miniscule, with many analysts deriding "market timing", without realizing that every bet in a portfolio, starting with the SAA, is market timing!

Mistakes are sure to be repeated if we do not learn from them, and while there has been considerable introspection on expected return and volatility assumptions, relatively little attention has been paid to the correlation statistic. Ignoring the fact that correlations across two assets or managers may be dynamic, investors must focus on a much simpler problem, namely, understanding the implied bet in choosing a correlation value in setting an SAA or manager structure. A low correlation between stocks and bonds is caused by the fact that they respond differently to economic growth, interest rates, oil, etc. The same is true for every other correlation statistic between two assets or two managers. Therefore, in setting an SAA or in selecting a portfolio of managers and assuming specific correlations (and expected returns), pension funds are making a bet on these economic relationships, *and one must exploit them in the implementation and management of a portfolio.*

Static policies for dynamic markets are undoubtedly flawed and have to be changed with the support of appropriate liquid, transparent, and low-cost, futures-based benchmarks; implicit bets (especially in the static SAA, rebalancing and liability and currency hedges) need to be made explicit and managed dynamically; naïve performance measures have to be improved to properly adjust for risk and highlight skill or lack thereof; and the CAPM needs to be revamped dramatically. Investors must understand how various market factors influence assets or managers and then develop a set of rules so that as the factors evolve over time, the optimal portfolio evolves simultaneously. For example, as the price of oil rises, the optimal portfolio may be 59 percent stocks, 41 percent bonds (versus a 60/40 SAA), and the optimal liability hedge may be less than 100 percent. This is termed "View-based" rebalancing. Similarly, as solvency declines, a "View-Neutral" dynamic LDI would reallocate the optimal SAA to be overweight in a liability replicating fixed income allocation.

As Woody Brock states, the future is about optimal strategies rather than optimal portfolios. Effective CIOs will establish optimal portfolios for specific states of the world and then dynamically adjust their portfolios as the market moves from one state to the next. Developing rules to track market movements, and their impact on all liability, beta, and manager decisions, creates a systematic process that generates consistent recommendations, which are not easily influenced by emotion (though clearly leaving scope for intelligent, qualitative judgment in the implementation of these recommendations).

SMART (Systematic Management of Assets using a Rules-based Technique) management of assets and liabilities leads to improved solvency and a lowering of ALM risks. SMART is about good process – namely, only measured and monitored risks can be managed ("M-cube of investing"). Rules that make explicit the underlying factor relationships alert CIOs to make key decisions to appropriately position the portfolio for better solvency (and not just a return over an investment benchmark). Good risk-adjusted performance measures ensure that the managers they hire generate, and are compensated for, risk- and skill-adjusted performance. Therefore, this book is also a call to arms to change manager compensation so that the bulk of the fees can be deferred until skill is established.

To summarize, pension funds should incorporate three levels of dynamism in managing the assets and liability to improve solvency: (i) Dynamic LDI; (ii) View-Neutral Solvency-Based Beta Adjustment; and (iii) View-based (or market-factor based) SMART Beta and Alpha Management. Explicit factor analysis and exposition of these rules lend themselves to transparency and good governance, whereas optimized portfolios are derived from black boxes where the investor is not sure whether the decision is driven by the return, correlation, or volatility assumption. This book presents a new design for pension fund management that allows CIOs to be smart about managing assets relative to liabilities and, at the same time, allows them to access alpha flexibly, manage managers dynamically for true alpha, and improve solvency.

It is our hope that as markets start to rally, investors do not forget the lessons learned from the volatility of 2008-2010, and *do not* follow Mark Twain's advice when he stated, "Never put off until tomorrow what you can do the day after tomorrow."[198]

[198] *http://www.quotationspage.com/quote/416.html*

REFERENCES

Admati, A. R. and P. Pfleiderer, (1997). Does It All Add Up? Benchmarks and the Compensation of Active Portfolio Manager, *The Journal of Business*, 70(3): 323-50. The University of Chicago, IL.

Ambarish, R. and L. Siegel. (1996). Time is the Essence. *Risk*, August, 9(8).

Aon. (2008). *Replacement Ratio Study™, A Measurement Tool For Retirement Planning*. Aon Consulting, Chicago.

Aon. (2009). *Aon Consulting Business Leaders Survey*. Aon Consulting, UK. *http://insight.aon.com/?elqPURLPage=4234*

Arikawa, M. (2004). *Innovations in Pension Fund Management*, Japanese translation, Nikkei Shinbun, Tokyo.

Arikawa, M. and A. Muralidhar. (2007). Hedging Currency Risk in International Investments and Trade. *Center for Advanced Research Foundation Working Paper,* CARF-0-90, University of Tokyo, Japan.

Arikawa, M., A. Muralidhar, and S. Muralidhar. (2006). The Case for View Based Dynamic ALM for Japanese Pension Funds: A New Approach to Liability Driven Investing. *Center for Advanced Research in Finance Working Paper,* CARF F-89, University of Tokyo.

Arnott, R. (2002). Risk Budgeting and Portable Alpha, *Journal of Investing*, Summer, 11(2): 15-22.

Arnott, R. (2005). Performance Fees: The Good, the Bad, and the (Occasionally) Ugly, *Financial Analysts Journal*, July/August, 61(4): 10-13.

Arnott, R. 2009. Bonds: Why Bother? *Journal of Indexes,* May/June 2009 - *http://www.indexuniverse.com/publications/journalofindexes/articles/149-may-june-2009/5710-bonds-why-bother.html*

Asad-Syed, K. and A. Muralidhar. (1998). An Asset Liability Approach to Value-at-Risk. *Investment Management Department Working Paper Series 98-023*, The World Bank, 1998.

Asad-Syed, K., A. Muralidhar, and R. van der Wouden. (1998), Determining Replacement Rates and Contribution Rates for Savings. In *Rethinking Pension Reform,* Cambridge University Press: London, UK.

Avramov, D. and R. Wermers .(2006). Investing in Mutual Funds when Returns are Predictable, *Journal of Financial Economics,* 81: 339-77.

Baldridge, J., B. Meath, and H. Myers .(2000). Capturing Alpha through Active Currency Overlay. *Frank Russell Research Commentary*, May 2000.

Barrett, T (2006). Beta Management: An Integrated, Transparent, Rules-based Framework, Executive Director and Chief Investment Officer, San Bernardino County Employees' Retirement Association, presentation at Institutional Investor - Hedge Fund Conference, October 23, Chicago, USA.

Baz, J., F. Breedon, V. Naik, and J. Peress. (1999). Optimal Currency Portfolios: Trading on the Forward Bias. *Lehman Brothers Analytical Research Series*, October.

Berkelaar, A. B., A. Kobor, and M. Tsumagari. (2006). The Sense and Nonsense of Risk Budgeting, *Financial Analysts Journal*, 62: 63-75.

Black, F. and R. Litterman. (1992). Global Portfolio Optimization, *Financial Analysts Journal*, September/October, 48(5): 28-43.

Black, F. and R. Litterman. (1991). Asset Allocation: Combining Investor Views with Market Equilibrium, *Journal of Fixed Income*, September: 7-18.

Blitz, D. C. and A. Hottinga. (2001). Tracking Error Allocation, *The Journal of Portfolio Management*, 27: 19-25.

Boender, G.C.E. (1997). A Hybrid Simulation/Optimization Scenario Model for Asset/ Liability Management. *Report 9513/A Econometric Institute*, Erasmus University, Rotterdam. *20th Anniversary special issue of European Journal of Operational Research*.

Boender, G.C.E. (1998). Optimal Rebalancing for Defined Benefit Pension Plans, ORTEC *Mimeo,* Rotterdam, NL.

Boender, G.C.E. and F. Heemskerk. (1995). A Static Scenario Optimization Model for Asset/Liability Management of Defined Benefit Plans. *Report 9512/A Econometric Institute*, Erasmus University, Rotterdam.

Boender, G.C.E., H. Hoek, C.L. Dert, and F. Heemskerk. (2007). A Scenario Approach of ALM. In *Handbook of Asset Liability Management,* pp. 830-59. S.A. Zenios & W. Ziemba (eds.). North Holland: Elsevier.

Boender, G.C.E., B. Oldenkamp, and M. Vos. (1997). Solvency Insurance with Optioned Portfolios: an Empirical Investigation. *Proceedings of the 7th International AFIR Colloquium*, Australia.

Boender, G.C.E., P.C. van Aalst, and F. Heemskerk. (1998). Modeling and Management of Assets and Liabilities of Pension Plans in the Netherlands. *World Wide Asset and Liability Modeling*, pp. 561-80. W.T. Ziemba and J.M. Mulvey (eds.), Cambridge University Press.

Bogle, J. (2009). Strengthening Worker Retirement Security, *Statement of John C. Bogle, founder and former chief executive of The Vanguard Group, before the*

Committee on Education and Labor, US House of Representatives, Washington, DC, February 24, 2009.

Brennan, M. (1993). Agency and Asset Pricing. *Anderson Graduate School of Management Working Paper*, Los Angeles, May.

Brock, H. W. (2005). The Three Principal Ideas – A Socratic Dialog, *SED's New Asset Allocation Logic* – Chapter IV, Strategic Economic Decisions, Hawaii.

Brown, R. (2009). Birth, Death, Rebirth of Portable Alpha, *Working Paper*, www.pionline.com

Callin, S. (2008). *Portable Alpha Theory and Practice*. Wiley Finance: New York.

Campbell, J. Y. and R. J. Shiller. (1998a). The Dividend–Price Ratio and Expectations of Future Dividends and Discount Factors, *Review of Financial Studies*, 1:195–228.

Campbell, J. and R. Shiller. (1998b). Valuation Ratios and the Long-run Stock Market Outlook, *The Journal of Portfolio Management*, Winter: 11-26.

Cavallo, A. (2007). The Origins of Portable Alpha, *Man Investments Research Papers* - https://www.maninvestments.com/multimedia/pdf/library/origins_portable_alpha.pdf

Chow, G. and M. Kritzman (2001). Risk Budgets, *The Journal of Portfolio Management*, Winter: 56-61.

Collie, B. and J. Gannon. (2009). Liability Responsive Asset Allocation, *Frank Russell Viewpoint,* April 2009, Tacoma, WA.

Cornell, B. (2009). Luck, Skill, and Investment Performance, *The Journal of Portfolio Management,* Winter, 35(2): 131-34.

Cornell, B. and R. Roll. (2005). A Delegated-agent Asset-pricing Model. *Financial Analysts Journal*, 61: 57-69.

Das, S. and R. Sundaram. (1998). On the Regulation of Fee Structures in Mutual Funds. In *Quantitative Analysis in Financial Markets,* Vol. III. Courant Institute of Mathematical Sciences.

Davanzo, L. and S. Nesbitt. (1987). Performance fees for investment management, *Financial Analysts Journal,* January/February, 43(1): 14-20.

Dert, C. L. (1995). Asset Liability Management for Pension Funds. Ph.D. thesis, Erasmus University, Rotterdam.

Dert, C.L. (1996). A Dynamic Model for Asset-Liability Management for Defined Benefit Pension Funds. Research Memorandum VU Amsterdam 1996, 53.

Dowd, K. (2000). Adjusting for Risk: An Improved Sharpe Ratio, *International Review of Economics and Finance*, 9: 209-22.

Fernholz, R. (2005). Stock Market Diversity, *INTECH Working Paper*, Princeton, NJ.

Figelman, I. (2004). Optimal Active Risk Budgeting Model, *The Journal of Portfolio Management*, Summer: 22-35.

Gardner, G. and Y. Fan. (2008). Russell's Approach to Target Date Funds: Building a Simple and Powerful Solution to Retirement Saving, *Russell Research,* January 2008, Tacoma, WA.

Gardner, G. and A. Sirohi. (2007). The Russell Target Date Performance Measure: Description of Methodology, *Russell Investments Working Paper,* Tacoma, WA.

Ghilarducci, T. (2008). *When I'm Sixty-Four: The Plot Against Pensions and the Plan to Save Them.* Princeton University Press: Princeton, NJ.

Graham, J.R. and C.R. Harvey, (1997). Grading the Performance of Market Timing Newsletters, *Financial Analysts Journal,* 53(6): 54-66.

Grinold, R. C. (1989). The Fundamental Law of Active Management, *The Journal of Portfolio Management*, Spring: 30-37.

Grinold, R.C., and R. N. Kahn. (1999). *Active Portfolio Management: A Quantitative Approach for Producing Superior Returns and Controlling Risk.* McGraw-Hill: NY.

Hammond, D. (1997). Establishing Performance-Related Termination Thresholds for Investment Management. In *Pension Fund Investment Management*, F. Fabozzi (ed.) Frank Fabozzi Associates: New Hope, PA.

Hight, G. (2009). Just When we Needed Asset Allocation, it Failed us, *Pensions and Investments White Papers, www.pionline.com.*

Hodgson, T. (2006). Making AA More Dynamic, *Investments and Pensions Europe,* February 2006, pp. 25.

Howell, T. (2004). What's My Style? - A Tactical Guide to Choosing Hedge Fund Styles, *AIMA Journal*, April: 18-19.

Investments and Pensions Europe – online version (February 16, 2009), *http://www.ipe.com/news/Trade_bodies_warn_against_hard_hitting_measures__30830.php.*

Jacobsen, B. and S. Bouman, (2001). The Halloween Indicator, 'Sell in May and Go Away': Another Puzzle, *http://papers.ssrn.com/sol3/papers.cfm?abstract_id=76248*

Jorion, P. (2003). Portfolio Optimization with Tracking Error Constraints, *Financial Analysts Journal*, September, 59: 70-82.

Krishnamurthi S., A. Muralidhar, and R.J. P. van der Wouden. (1998a). Pension Investment Decisions. *Investment Management Department Working Paper Series 98-001*, The World Bank.

Krishnamurthi S., A. Muralidhar, and R.J. P. van der Wouden. (1998b). An Asset Liability Analysis of Retirement Plans. *Investment Management Department Working Paper Series 98-004*, The World Bank.

Kritzman, M. (1987). Incentive Fees: Some Problems and Some Solutions, *Financial Analysts Journal*, January-February: 27-38.

Lee, W. (2000). *Theory and Methodology of Tactical Asset Allocation*. Wiley Finance: New York.

Lee, W. and D. Lam. (2001). Implementing Optimal Risk Budgeting *The Journal of Portfolio Management*, Fall: 56-60.

Leland, H. and M. Rubenstein. (1988). The Evolution of Portfolio Insurance. In *Dynamic Hedging: A Guide to Portfolio Insurance*, Don Luskin, (ed.). John Wiley and Sons.

Lim, P. (2008). How to Rebalance While Walking on Eggs, *New York Times*, August 9 (Business Section).

Lim, P. (2009). How to Rebalance Without Diving Into Stocks, *New York Times*, February 28 (Business Section).

Litterman, R. et al. (2003). Developing an Optimal Active Risk Budget. *Modern Investment Management: An Equilibrium Approach*, John Wiley and Sons: New York.

Litterman, R., J. Longerstaey, J. Rosengarten, and K. Winkelmann. (2001). The Green Zone... assessing the Quality of Returns, *The Journal of Performance Measurement,* Spring: 5(3).

Logue, D.E. and J. S. Rader (1997). *Managing Pension Plans: A Comprehensive Guide to Improving Plan Performance (Financial Management Association Survey and Synthesis Series)*. Harvard Business School Press: Cambridge, Mass.

Margrabe, W. (1976). Alternative Investment Performance Fee Arrangements and Implications for SEC Regulatory Policy: Comment, *The Bell Journal of Economics*, Autumn, 7(2): 716-18.

Markowitz, H. (1959). *Portfolio Selection.* John Wiley and Sons: New York.

Merton, R. C. (1973). An Intertemporal Capital Asset Pricing Model. *Econometrica*, Econometric Society, September, 41(5): 867-87.

MetLife US Pension Risk Behavior Index[SM]. (2009). MetLife Corporation, January 2009. NY.- *http://www.whymetlife.com/downloadsMetLife_US_PensionRiskBehaviorIndex.pdf*

Modigliani, F. and L. Modigliani. (1997). Risk-adjusted Performance, *The Journal of Portfolio Management,* 23(2):45-54.

Modigliani, F. and A. Muralidhar. (2004). *Rethinking Pension Reform.* Cambridge University Press: London, UK.

Modigliani, F. and G.A. Pogue. (1975). Alternative Investment Performance Fee Arrangements and Implications for SEC Regulatory Policy, *Rand Journal of Economics,* Spring, 6(1): 127-60.

Montier, J. (2010). I Want to Break Free, or, Strategic Asset Allocation is not Static Asset Allocation, Grantham Mayo van Otterloo Perspectives, May 2010.

Mulvey, J. (1988). A Surplus Optimization Perspective, *Investment Management Review,* 3: 31-39.

Mulvey, J. (1994). An Asset-Liability Investment System, *Interfaces,* May-June, 24(3): 22-33.

Muralidhar, A. (1999a). Death of the CAPM. *Unpublished Working Paper.*

Muralidhar, A. (1999b). Currency Overlay Performance: Luck or Skill? *Investments and Pensions – Europe,* September.

Muralidhar, A. (2000). Risk-adjusted Performance – The Correlation Correction, *Financial Analysts Journal,* 56(5): 63-71.

Muralidhar, A. (2001a). *Innovations in Pension Fund Management.* Stanford University Press: Palo Alto, CA.

Muralidhar, A. (2001b). An Explanation to the Discount/Premium Puzzle in Currency Markets. *JP Morgan Investment Management Investment Insight,* May.

Muralidhar, A. (2002). Skill, History, and Risk-Adjusted Performance, *Journal of Performance Measurement.* Fall.

Muralidhar, A. (2003). Where Overlay Comes In. In *Currency Management: Overlay and Alpha Trading.* Jessica James (ed.). Risk Books: London.

Muralidhar, A. (2004). When the Green Zone can Land you in the Red Zone, *Journal of Performance Measurement,* Summer: 8 (4).

Muralidhar, A. (2005a). Uncovering the Treasure Within, *Investments and Pensions – Europe,* January.

Muralidhar, A. (2005b). Dynamic Alpha and Beta, *Investments and Pensions – Europe,* November.

Muralidhar, A. (2005c). Attributing Performance in Fund of Funds. *Hedgeweek*, January 31, London, UK. *http://www.hedgeweek.com/articles/pdf_page.jsp?content_id=9424*

Muralidhar. A. (2009a.) Linking Managers' Rewards to their Risks, *Professional Investor*, Spring: 46-48. *www.cfauk.org*.

Muralidhar, A. (2009b). Miserable Hedge Fund FEEling AlphaEngine Global Investment Solutions, LLC, *Working Paper*.

Muralidhar, A. (2009c). The Error in Tracking Error Budgeting, *Unpublished Working Paper*.

Muralidhar, A. and H. Neelakandan. (2002). Options to Enhance Currency Overlay Programs, *Investments and Pensions – Europe*, February.

Muralidhar, A. and Khin Mala U. (1997). Establishing a Peer Comparator Universe for an Institutional Investor, *Journal of Pension Plan Investing*, Spring: 1(4).

Muralidhar, A. and S. Muralidhar. (2005). Three Keys to Success in Fund-of-Funds *AIMA Journal*, Winter.

Muralidhar, A. and S. Muralidhar. (2009). The Case for SMART Rebalancing In *QFinance: The Ultimate Resource*, pp. 297-300. Bloomsbury Publishing: London.

Muralidhar A. and M. Tsumagari. (1998). Derivative Strategies for Pension Plans. *Investment Management Department, Working Paper P98-008*, The World Bank.

Muralidhar, A. and M. Tsumagari. (1999). A Matter of Style. *Futures and OTC World*, Issue 336, April.

Muralidhar, A. and R. J. P van der Wouden. (1999). Saving Pension Funds Some Money and Future Headaches *Working Paper*, *www.mcubeit.com*

Muralidhar, A. and J. W. Stuijvberg. (2005). Devising an Investable Liability Index, *Investments and Pensions – Europe*, October: 46-47.

Muralidhar, S. (2007). A New Paradigm For Rebalancing. *The Monitor*, March/April 22(2): 1-5.

O'Higgins, M. (1999). *Beating the Dow with Bonds*. Harper Collins Publishers

Peskin, M. (1997). Asset Allocation and Funding Policy for Corporate-Sponsored Defined-Benefit Pension Plans. *The Journal of Portfolio Management*, Winter: 66-73.

Petras, R. and K. Petras. (2001). *The 776 Stupidest Things Ever Said*. Broadway Books: New York.

Rahl, L. (2000). *Risk Budgeting: A New Investment Approach*. Risk Books: London.

Raymond, D. (2008). Paying (Only) for Skill (Alpha)—A Practical Approach, *CFA Institute Conference Proceedings Quarterly*, June, 25(2): 51-59.

Roll, R. (1992). A Mean/Variance Analysis of Tracking Error, *The Journal of Portfolio Management,* Summer, 18(4): 13-23.

Schliemann, M. and M. Stanzel. (2008). Performance based Compensation Contracts in the Asset Management Industry, *Journal of Performance Measurement*, Spring: 61-78.

SEI. (2009). *Rebalancing Reset: A New Approach in a New World of Institutional Investing*, SEI Institutional Perspectives, March 10, Oaks, PA.

Seigel, L. (2003). Benchmarks and Investment Management. *The Research Foundation of AIMR*, CFA Institute, Charlottesville, NC.

Sherer, B. and D. Martin. (2005). *Introduction to Modern Portfolio Optimization*, Springer-Verlaag.

Sharpe, W. (1994). The Sharpe Ratio. *The Journal of Portfolio Management,* 20(1): 49-59.

Sharpe, W. (2002). Budgeting and Monitoring Pension Fund Risk, *Financial Analysts Journal*, September/October: 74-86.

Sharpe, W. (2009). Adaptive Asset Allocation Policies. *Standford University Working Paper,* Palo Alto, CA.

Solnik, B. H. (1974). An Equilibrium Model of the International Capital Market *Journal of Economic Theory*, August, 8(4): 500-524.

Sortino, F. A. and R. van der Meer. (1991). Downside Risk, *The Journal of Portfolio Management*, 27-31.

Strange, B. (1988). Currency Overlay Managers Show Consistency, *Pensions and Investments*, June 15.

Sullivan, R. (2010). Risk Parity: a Triumph of Hope over Economics, *Pensions and Investments,* June 28.

Swensen, D. (2005). *Unconventional Success: A Fundamental Approach to Personal Investment.* New York: Free Press.

Swensen, D. (2007). Managing Your Portfolio Frequent Rebalancing Helps Maintain Allocation Targets. *Wealth Management Exchange. http://www.wealthmanagementexchange.com/articles/14/1/Managing-Your-Portfolio-Frequent-Rebalancing-Helps-Maintain-Allocation-Targets-/Page1.html*

Swensen, D. (2009). *Pioneering Portfolio Management.* (Revised edition). New York: Free Press.

Vos, M. (1997). The Use of Optioned Portfolios in Asset Liability Management for Pension Plans (in Dutch). Master's thesis, Erasmus University, Rotterdam.

Waring, B. and C. Castille. (1998). A Framework for Optimal Manager Structure, *Barclays Global Insight,* 1 (2).

Waring, B., C. Castille, C. Whitney, and J. Pirone. (2000). Optimizing Manager Structure and Budgeting Manager Risk, *Journal of Portfolio Management,* Spring: 90-114.

Winkelmann, K. and R. Howard. (2001). Developing an Optimal Active Risk Budget *Goldman Sachs Investment Manager Research,* July.

Watts, R. (2006). In Defence of Liability Driven Investment, *Global Pensions,* September: 44.

Woodbury, D. and W. Neal. (1999). Fund Advisor Compensation: An Application of Agency Theory, *Proceedings of the Academy of Accounting and Financial Studies,* 4(1): 48-58, Myrtle Beach.

Zwanenburg, M. W. (1998). The Added Value of Exotic Optioned Portfolios in Asset Liability Management (in Dutch). Master's thesis, Erasmus University, Rotterdam.

WEBLINKS

CHAPTER 1

"DnB's own pension plan must submit recovery plan," *www.ipe.com*, March 25, 2009.

February 16, 2009). *http://www.ipe.com/news/*
Trade_bodies_warn_against_hard_hitting_measures_30830.php

http://www.pionline.com/apps/pbcs.dll/article?AID=/20090318/DAILYREG/903189974

http://www.ipe.com/news/
PME_mulls_pensions_cut_in_2010_31010.php?type=news&id=31010

CHAPTER 2

http://www.cs.cmu.edu/~ralf/quotes.html

CHAPTER 4

http://www.pionline.com/apps/pbcs.dll/article?AID=/20090515/DAILYREG/905159994/1034/PIDailyUpdate.

http://www.wealthmanagementexchange.com/articles/14/1/Managing-Your-Portfolio-Frequent-Rebalancing-Helps-Maintain-Allocation-Targets-/Page1.html

CHAPTER 5

http://www.pbgc.gov/media/pension-legislation/content/page15921.html

CHAPTER 6

http://insight.aon.com/?elqPURLPage=4234

http://papers.ssrn.com/sol3/papers.cfm?abstract_id=76248

GLOSSARY[199]

AAPF: ABN AMRO Pension Fund

Alpha: Relates (in this book) to returns in excess of the benchmark (not adjusted for risk or beta).

ALM: Asset-liability management is the practice of managing risk that arises due to mismatches between the assets and liabilities.

AUM: Assets under management

Bp: Basis point. A unit that is equal to 1/100th of one percent, and used to denote the change in a financial instrument. The basis point is commonly used for calculating changes in equity indexes and the yield of a fixed-income security.

Beta: Describes how the expected return of a stock or portfolio is correlated to the return of the financial market as a whole. An asset with a beta of 0 means that its price is not at all correlated with the market; that asset is independent. A positive beta means that the asset generally follows the market. A negative beta shows that the asset inversely follows the market; the asset generally decreases in value if the market goes up and vice versa (as is common with precious metals). In addition, in this book beta refers to decisions relative to the benchmark

CalPERS: California Public Employees' Retirement System

CAPM: Capital asset pricing model. A model that describes the relationship between risk and expected return and is used in the pricing of risky securities.

CAPs: Risk-adjusted portfolio, adjusted for differences in correlation, created through the M-cube adjustment.

CIO: Chief investment officer

CRAPM: Capital relative asset pricing model. A model that describes the relationship between risk and expected return and is used in the pricing of risky securities based on a relative analysis of markets.

DB: Defined benefit. An employer-sponsored retirement plan where employee benefits are based on a formula using factors such as salary history and duration of employment.

---

[199] This section has leveraged Wikipedia and Investopedia extensively.

DC: Defined contribution. A defined contribution in which a certain amount or percentage of money is set aside each year by a company for the benefit of the employee. There are restrictions as to when and how you can withdraw these funds without penalties.

DnB: Dutch Central Bank

DoL: U.S. Department of Labor

ETF: Exchange traded fund

FAJ: *Financial Analysts Journal*

FoF: Fund-of-funds. A fund-of-funds is a collective investment scheme that uses an investment strategy of holding a portfolio of other investment funds rather than investing directly in securities.

Funded Status: Ratio of assets to liabilities

GP: General partner

IDP: Investment Decision Process is a method of expressing the hierarchical structure of decisions in a portfolio. This concept was developed by the Shell Netherlands pension plan.

IR: Information Ratio is a measure of risk-adjusted performance

IRA: An Individual Retirement Arrangement is a retirement plan account that provides some tax advantage for retirement savings in the United States.

IRS: United States Internal Revenue Service

KISS: Keep it SMART and simple

LDI: Liability-driven investing. A form of portfolio management in which the main goal is to gain sufficient assets to meet all liabilities, both current and future. This form of investing is most prominent with defined-benefit pension plans, whose liabilities can often reach into the billions of dollars for the largest of plans.

LP: Limited partner

Maximum drawdown: Defined as the largest drop from a peak to a bottom in a certain time period.

M² or M-square: Risk-adjusted performance measure developed by Franco and Leah Modigliani that normalizes for differences in volatility.

M³ or M-cube: Risk-adjusted performance measure developed by Arun Muralidhar that normalizes for differences in volatility and tracking error.

PBGC: Pension Benefit Guarantee Corporation – entity in the United States that provides insurance against sponsors of DB plans going bankrupt.

PME: Bedrijfstakpensioenfonds Metalektro in the Netherlands

PPA: United States Pension Protection Act (2006) that governs DB and DC pension plans and contains many new provisions to enhance the security of participants' pensions.

QDIA: Qualified Default Investment Alternative. The Pension Protection Act of 2006 provides a safe harbor for plan fiduciaries investing participant assets in certain types of default investment alternatives in the absence of participant investment direction.

RAP: Risk-adjusted portfolio created through the M-square adjustment.

RFP: A Request for proposal is an invitation for suppliers, often through a bidding process, to submit a proposal on a specific service.

SAA: Strategic asset allocations. At the inception of the portfolio, a "base policy mix" is established based on expected returns. Because the value of the portfolio can change given market conditions, the portfolio constantly needs to be re-adjusted to meet the policy.

SHARAD: Skill, history, and risk-adjusted performance developed by Arun Muralidhar that normalizes for volatility, tracking error, and length of performance history.

SMART: Systematic management of assets using a rules-based technique

SMART VB: SMART View-based

SMART VN: SMART View-Neutral

SS: Social Security

Success ratio: Percentage of days/months that the performance was greater than the benchmark

SWF: Sovereign Wealth Fund

TDF: Target date fund. Target date funds invest in a mix of stocks and fixed-income securities, and the percentage of these assets classes switches to more conservative investments as a fund approaches its target date. The switch in allocation is known as a "glide path."

TDPM: Gardner and Sirohi (2007) present a simple but very effective measure of performance which they term the Target Date Performance Measure or TDPM.

INDEX